To Angela

You Cannot live As I Have Lived and Not End Up Like This

The thoroughly disgraceful life & times of Willie Donaldson

by Terence Blacker

EBURY
PRESS

1 3 5 7 9 10 8 6 4 2

Published in 2007 by Ebury Press, an imprint of Ebury Publishing

Ebury Publishing is a division of the Random House Group

The Random House Group Limited Reg. No. 954009

Addresses for companies within the Random House Group
can be found at www.randomhouse.co.uk

A CIP catalogue record for this book is available from the British Library

Printed and bound in Great Britain by Mackays of Chatham Plc

Typeset by seagulls.net

ISBN 9780091913861

Mixed Sources
Product group from well-managed
forests and other controlled sources
www.fsc.org Cert no. TT-COC-2139
© 1996 Forest Stewardship Council
FSC

'I don't see how you can conceive happiness without love.
Friends, money, a good job are nothing, absolutely nothing.'
1955

'Emma Jane seems determined to turn my brothel
into a home. This must be resisted.'
1975

'She's driving me mad. She's vain, deceitful, spoilt,
manipulative, feckless, unfaithful, unreliable. She isn't
even on the telephone. She's the ideal woman.'
1995

'The wicked acts are no more the
whole truth than the virtuous ones.'
2000

Contents

1

A life of sorts

For the twenty-five years that I had known him, Willie Donaldson had screened his calls. He was someone who liked to be in control, who dreaded the surprise telephone call, the unscheduled encounter on the street. There were people to avoid: enemies, creditors, over-loyal acquaintances from the past, friends who might call him at the wrong moment to chat, to fix up a lunch or – a particular dread – to invite him for a weekend in the country. From the mid-1980s, there had been a crack habit to maintain and, with it, a series of doomed, obsessive liaisons, bringing him into close contact, professional and personal, with dealers, ex-cons, users and tarts.

These were the people from whom he really wanted to hear. Very occasionally, one would ring Willie and, rather than having to hang around in the waiting-room of his answering machine until he picked up or didn't, one was straight through. On those occasions, he didn't sound himself. Normally a great telephone conversationalist, he would be hurried. His voice, usually rather welcoming, sounded disappointed. There was someone coming over, he would say breathlessly. Could we talk in the morning?

A couple of years before he died, Willie had thrown away his writer's notebooks and various items from the past, but he kept the tapes from his answering machine. One night, shortly after I had decided to write this book, I listened to them. It was a more upsetting experience than I had anticipated. Letters, notes, diaries have an inbuilt formality to them but the tapes of incoming calls, sometimes full conversations, have an unrehearsed intimacy. The voices of Willie's life crowded in, one after another: brisk PAs from TV production companies, crack partners, friends from the past, professional visitors from escort agencies, flirty Sloane Rangers, dealers, the odd publisher, his part-time agent, a gravel-voiced hood calling himself Pizza-Face Scarlatti, who might equally have been Peter Cook playing one of his regular jokes or a real gangster – the voices were from all ages, all classes. They were cheerful, amorous, exasperated, concerned, hysterical (*'It's lies – all lies!'* one woman screamed) and, sometimes, down-right scary.

For each of these people, a different Willie Donaldson existed. For some he was William, others Willie, a few Button. The occasional call from officialdom (no pick-ups there) addressed him by his first name, Charles.

An old-fashioned machine, the answerphone had a loud tone before each message and on one or two of the cassettes the distant, ghostly echo of previous conversations could be heard in the background. The precariousness and oddity of my friend's life was there and with it, the impossibility of doing justice to its full strangeness and wonderful gamey variety.

Of course, someone had been here before and he, too, had struggled with the problem. In his memoirs *From Winchester to This*, Willie wrote: 'In real life a person is an unknowable jumble of contradictory qualities. Brave and cowardly. Cruel and kind. Treacherous and loyal. Feckless and prudent. In fiction, this would be confusing … This is a mistake writers of biography make. They try to shape a life, to give it a fictional coherence. They should just tip the whole mess on to the page and say: "Here is a life of sorts. Make of it what you will".'

Willie worked over his life in his writings. While most of the facts he recorded were approximately true, they were, above all, a writer's material. He edited, distorted, added and deleted. He told his own version of the truth. Corruption, morality and the madness of fame were his great themes, and he was determined that his readers would understand that, when it came to bad behaviour, he wrote with hard-earned personal authority. 'I've done some terrible things,' he would say to friends, and we knew that it was true. The complex erotic fantasy life he lived out was real enough, and so was the narcotic fuel which propelled it, but there were other things that he was less open about – debts, dodgy dealings, rumours of blackmail. To a journalist who asked about his life around the time of his third and final bankruptcy in 1994, he simply said: 'I've been a complete cunt.'

Had he? It seemed odd that a man whose comic prose had such wild energy, whose autobiographical writings were so unsparingly clear-eyed, could have lived a life of such irredeemable self-indulgence. His words, after all, had given such pleasure, and had been important in their way. *The Henry Root Letters* were not just astonishingly funny. They heralded the dawning of a new age. Just as Peter Cook's impression of Harold Macmillan in *Beyond The Fringe* is now seen as the moment when Britain learnt to laugh at politicians, so Henry Root's vision of contemporary Britain, where senior policemen, minor TV stars, Mrs Thatcher and Esther Rantzen all essentially belonged to the same world, one dominated by publicists, image, soundbites, was the first indication that the age of celebrity was upon us.

Willie had an extraordinary sensitivity to social trends: fifteen or so years after Root, he created another comic monster in his character Liz Reed, whose TV production company Heartfelt Productions was a leading player in the increasingly competitive compassion market. A few years later, it would be no particular surprise to see some of Liz's wilder projects – *Disabled Gladiators*, perhaps, or *Who Put Heroin in My Kiddies' Sweets?* – reported in the TV listings.

But for all the mad verve of Willie's overtly funny books, it was when he was writing about himself (past and present, lovers, friends and enemies, his various acts of financial, sexual and narcotic misbehaviour, matters of conscience and guilt) that he was at his best and most interesting as a writer. Few, if any, of the flashier writers about sexual obsession or drug dependence have, for all their overwrought prose, caught them with the chilling force of Willie's lacerating autobiographical novel *Is This Allowed?* Many boastfully modest memoirs have been written about the Sixties, but Willie's account in *From Winchester to This* of how the past bears on the present – and the other way round – is more surprising and moving than almost all of them.

3

Willie Donaldson was a comic moralist. He was generous to friends, younger writers and strangers who wrote to him. He was wonderful company. There was a natural, if unconventional, kindness to him. Yet, distorting the past and the present for the sake of a joke, he chose to portray himself as a reckless decadent, a corrupter of innocence, a moral bankrupt, a chancer, a squanderer of money, privilege and luck. That is the version of Willie that has lived on.

'There's a rather odd rumour going about that Willie Donaldson has been found dead.'

I was at my desk at home in Norfolk when the call from Jamie Fergusson, obituary editor of the *Independent*, reached me.

Jamie had been contacted by someone on the *Guardian*. A junior reporter on the paper had been the source, via her father who knew a caretaker in Fulham.

I rang around. None of our mutual friends knew anything. Eventually I called Cherry Donaldson who, although she and Willie had separated in 1987, was still officially the tenant of his flat and knew the practical, usually shambolic details of his life. She too had heard nothing.

I rang the local police station, where the duty officer suggested I called the coroner's office. It was closed. I tried the police again. The duty officer, a woman with the bored, whiny voice of someone announcing trains on a very hot day, was disapproving of my persistence. She suggested that I rang the coroner's office during working hours.

'But, you see, none of his friends know about this,' I said, trying to be reasonable.

'I'm sure that the coroner will be able to help you in the morning, sir.'

'I'd prefer not to wait until the morning.'

'At the end of the day, this is just a rumour, sir. What we're talking here is rumour control.'

'There's his wife,' I said, trying another tack. 'She's very upset.'

'Wife, sir? Wouldn't she know already?'

4

'They didn't live together.'

The woman police officer considered the full oddness of what I was telling her.

'You don't think that ringing up his wife was a little bit insensitive, sir?'

I hung up. Willie could have turned this into a wonderful story, self-important and thick members of the constabulary being something of a speciality of his.

Cherry spoke to the police. They rang her back to confirm that a seventy-year-old man had been found dead at the address she had given. It was true. Willie was dead.

The estate of Charles William Donaldson was not left in good order. Two days after his death, Cherry and Charlie Donaldson, his forty-five-year-old son from his first marriage, entered the flat where almost thirty years previously they had all lived.

The place was in a grim and squalid state. A film of fat, the residue of thousands of fry-ups, covered the kitchen. In Willie's sitting-room and in the 'literary room' where he worked, credit card statements, unanswered letters from friends and magazine photographs of his last great love Rachel Garley were pushed into folders containing the various drafts of the work that had preoccupied him while he was with Rachel, *Canetti et Moi* (by Rachel Garley). His computer was logged on to a lesbian porn site.

In the last few years of his life, Willie had discovered the joy of credit cards and, by the time of his death, had run up debts of more than £18,000. Other small or significant acts of ducking and diving involving tax and VAT pushed his potential, posthumous indebtedness towards £25,000.

Cherry Donaldson, his heir from a will drawn up in 1987, consulted a lawyer who advised her to distance herself from the dangerous shambles of his estate by renouncing probate.

A side effect of this decision is that he has no literary executor to supervise his published work: a publisher wishing to reissue *The Henry Root Letters* or a producer interested in filming *Is This Allowed?* has, at the moment of writing, no one to talk to.

Willie's estate, which currently consists of debts, is in legal limbo.

On the obituary pages, Willie was given a fitting send-off. The *Daily Telegraph* is said to have a house rule that only heads of state and popes are given a full page but Willie broke the rules in death as in life; its very funny obituary was headlined 'WILLIAM DONALDSON, Wykehamist pimp, crack fiend and adulterer who created Henry Root and *Beyond The Fringe*'. In the *Guardian*, Christopher Hawtree wrote that 'Donaldson lived by the seat of his pants – which were often cast aside, for his abundant good humour, the ultimate aphrodisiac, brought him more than a dalliance with the actor Sarah Miles and the singer Carly Simon.'

In *The Times*, he was 'a womanising satirist and novelist who squandered several fortunes on wild living' while, in the *Independent*, Willie's friend and former co-writer Simon Carr provided a more nuanced and personal account. 'In the absence of a reliable biography we can only piece together the life of William Donaldson,' Simon wrote. 'His gifts for fiction, his personal fortifications and his theatrical ambitions both in and out of the theatre obscure much of the autobiographical data.'

This sense that Willie had somehow given us all the slip, providing a false alternative narrative of his life, would not go away. I re-read *From Winchester to This* and, strangely, the book that had disappointed me when I had read it on its publication in 1998 – its clever-dick evasions seemed calculated to irritate any reader who just wanted to be told the story – now struck me as an astonishing and moving piece of work. But, behind the brilliant wit, deft writing, the expressions of shame and regret, there was, I was beginning to think, a subtle process of deception, perhaps self-deception, going on. Willie had presented his life as one of tragi-comic decline: huge wealth leading to humiliating poverty, love to perversion, champagne on a Sunningdale lawn to a crack den in Ladbroke Grove, friendship to betrayal. His writing, as he described it, was an irresponsible skitter across the surface of contemporary life, involving jokes and facetiousness and wasting the time of serious people.

It was this version which was faithfully reproduced in the obituaries, and it was wrong. Here was a man whose untrustworthiness in all things had become legendary, and yet he had been trusted to tell the essential truth about himself.

I wanted to find out what happened to Willie Donaldson: a man who had known, worked with, employed, and gone to bed with some of the most remarkable people of his generation but who would only present his memories of them through a fairground mirror of jokes; who appeared to have a reckless confidence yet was riddled with self-loathing; who confessed all and revealed nothing; who was so extraordinarily funny and yet so sad.

The English upper middle-class has over the past century thrown up its share of characters – insiders who choose to live on the outside, charming shysters who move from one dodgy enterprise to the next, squanderers of money and love, footlers and fools who have eventually paid the price for a life of self-indulgence. Willie was all of those things, according to his version and that of his enemies, but the caricatures were not enough in his case. I began to wonder whether this apparent decline, this loss year by year of cash, reputation and a slim chance of happiness, was not something else – a sort of perverse triumph, a liberation from the past and its expectations.

There was something else. When anyone dies, unless he is very old, those that loved them are likely to be left with a sense of unfinished business – conversations, disagreements and plans are left uncompleted. With Willie, this sense was particularly acute for it was his habit to compartmentalise his life. There are areas and incidents to which he would refer only glancingly, or disguise in the form of a joke, or simply dismiss.

Listening half-guiltily to those tapes, I realised that for me there would be more to writing his biography than merely trying to put together the details of an extraordinary story of triumph and decline that he never quite managed to tell himself.

We are brought up to believe in a certain model of friendship: solid, reliable, the gift of someone who will stand by you and offer support and sympathy through the bad times as well as the good. In my experience, Willie Donaldson was none of those things. He actually prided himself on his lack of moral fibre. Trying to explain this to me once, he told me that, if I were in hospital, dying, and called him to my bedside for a final farewell, and then moments later he had received another call from a service flat where Francesca Annis (a fantasy figure at the time) told him she was waiting for him, he would have no choice. It had to be Francesca.

His was never exactly a shoulder to cry on. I turned to him at the end of my marriage and we had an awkward and pointless conversation. It was as if I were asking advice about a crisis in some distant land whose language and customs he had never learnt.

Friendship is slipperier than one might think. Even if I were not writing about him, there would be no day on which thoughts of Willie would not have drifted into my mind. Over a year after his death, I miss our conversations on the telephone, our lunches. His perspective on the world – a trashy story in the tabloids, a bit of politics, some writerly humiliation that one of us had suffered, scandalous gossip of friends in trouble or misbehaving – was always interesting, unusual and funny. The opinions that most of us hold tend to bear the faint fingerprints of others: a column read, an interview watched. His were always predictably unpredictable and entirely his own.

Willie was a good, sharp reader; it was his hard-earned approval that many of us wanted above all when we wrote. He was generous in his opinions, curious. Unlike most writers when they are on the ropes (and somehow, even when he was in the bestseller lists or waltzing around Europe with a TV crew, he conveyed the impression that a knockout punch was never far away), he admired openly and without jealousy the work of younger, hotter, better-paid rivals. 'Breathtaking,' he would say about something he had read. 'I don't know why we all don't just give up.'

Now I knew there was more than just a question of discovering what happened to him in his life. I wanted to track down my friend.

Few people get a good send-off at a crematorium. The process is too grimly industrial, with funeral parties stacked up like aeroplanes over Heathrow, to allow the individuality and uniqueness of a life to come through. The groups of murmuring, dark-suited mourners, waiting their turn with their hearse, their coffin, their loved one, their memories and sadness, look remarkably similar. At the final fire, one life is pretty much like another.

There is usually an odd sense of awkwardness on these occasions and Willie's funeral, a private event at Mortlake crematorium in south-west London, was odder than most. The compartments were represented – family, a couple of wives, a Page Three girl, school friends, some TV types, a few writers – but few knew anybody outside their own little group. The small chapel was not full.

Willie's sister Jane had arranged the service, opting sensibly for the safe C-of-E form although Willie was a resolute non-believer. But then, as the vicar, a Cambridge contemporary, reminded us, which of us *really* know what the other believes? I was pretty sure most of those present had a good idea of what Willie believed and said so in a brief address, at the end of which I read a passage about Willie's Winchester days from *Is This Allowed?* There was more laughter in the crematorium than is entirely seemly at a funeral.

As, at the end of the service, the coffin trundled off towards the flames, Charlie Donaldson, in the front row, asked his step-mother Cherry Donaldson if the body would be burnt now. She said it probably would be.

'That's a bit heavy,' Charlie murmured. 'I think I would have preferred a burial.'

'Bit late for that now,' said Cherry.

And as the coffin of Willie Donaldson disappeared, a bark of laughter, in a voice that was uncannily like his, echoed through the crematorium.

Charles.

2
Family Fantasy

'I'm in a mood at the moment to blame my parents for almost everything,' Willie wrote in 1990, as he began to work on his memoirs. 'The moderate hash I've made of things is undoubtedly their fault.'

Haunted increasingly by memories of his childhood – the memoirs were originally to be entitled *From Sunningdale to This* – Willie would conjure up in his later writing a picture of dysfunctional privilege, complete with a distant and disappointed father and a mother who, to quote the confident words of one of Willie's obituarists, was 'snobbish and bullying'. Those who knew Willie as an adult confirmed this version. 'His problems began with his mother,' one person told me; 'he could never forgive himself for despising his father', said another. Something, I assumed, must have gone very wrong, back there in Sunningdale.

The Donaldsons were certainly rich. When Charles William Donaldson entered the world, on January 4, 1935, he was born into a solid shipping dynasty that had borne the family name since being established by William and John Donaldson in 1854. Based in Glasgow, the Donaldson Line owned a fleet of nineteen passenger and cargo ships under the control of various interlinked companies, headed by Willie's father Charles Glen, his uncle Fred and cousin Norman.

The chairman of the company, Willie's grandfather Charles (the family believed in simplicity when it came to christening their children) lived in squirearchal grandeur at Airthrey Castle, near Perth. An uncle owned the winner of the One Thousand Guineas and the Oaks. Another raced several yachts, one of which represented its country in the British-American Cup. His uncle Fred (scandalously, Willie kept this to himself) was joint master of the Lanarkshire Hunt. 'All the Donaldsons were keen on sport and the country life,' reads the official company history *The Donaldson Line: A Century of Shipping.*

In 1927, Charles Glen Donaldson had married Elizabeth Stockley, a girl who, although she also came from a smart, mercantile background, quickly decided that she had no intention of leading the life expected of her, passing chilly weekends on large estates in Scotland while the men were out shooting birds. In 1932, the Donaldsons went south to live in Sunningdale although, apart from a spell at the Admiralty during the war, Mr Donaldson continued to spend the week in Glasgow, working at the shipping line's main office and staying at the Central Hotel.

It was this great dislocation, and the difficulties it caused Mr Donaldson, which would form the basis of Willie's case against his mother but, as it turns out, there is another, more reliable testament to those early years of his childhood.

'It occurs to me that it may be interesting for you in the years to come, to have a diary of the war, or rather, a diary of what *you* were doing in the war,' Elizabeth, better known as Betty, Donaldson wrote in a leather-bound notebook in January 1940. 'I wish I had one of the last war, although there are a lot of things I was too young to bother about that I should like to know, and you two may feel the same.'

So begins an unusual and sometimes moving account of the war years, as seen from a large house beside the golf course at Sunningdale, and recorded in two notebooks, the first of which is addressed to Willies's older sister, Eleanor Jane, and the second to Charles, as Willie was then known. Betty had the clever idea of addressing the diary to the children who were also largely its subject, making it a sort of extended letter to their future selves. The pages are dominated by news of the war, mostly disastrous in the first book, which was dedicated to Eleanor Jane, interspersed with cuttings and photographs from the newspapers, bracingly patriotic poems by AP Herbert, published transcripts of speeches by Chamberlain and Churchill, and the odd account of society weddings.

Betty Donaldson (holding the flowers), officiates at the launching of
the Donaldson Line's HMS *Corinaldo II* in 1949. Mr Donaldson
is at the back of the group, third from the right.

SOCIAL CLUB   (i) Girls and Boys   Diana Fisher, Charles Donaldson

Under the direct patronage of
H.H. Princess Marie Louise
and
H.H. Princess Helena Victoria

MISS DORICE STAINER'S

DANCING MATINEE

On SATURDAY, FEBRUARY 8th, 1941
at 2.30 p.m.

In aid of
THE BRITISH RED CROSS SOCIETY and
ORDER OF ST. JOHN OF JERUSALEM
for Gifts and Comforts for the Patients of Winkfield Place Convalescent Home,
Windsor Forest

Chairman:
MISS H. K. HENRY, A.R.R.C.

Deputy Chairman:
MRS. JOHN FLEMING

Girls and Boys, 1941.

But because family life went on, there are also family photo-graphs, the programme for Miss Dorice Stainer's Dancing Matinee, Eleanor Jane's first letter home, a school report for Charles.

Betty Donaldson was a good, clear writer and her account conveys the fear and the defiance of 1939 to 1941 and the grow-ing sense of hope as the war progressed. Perhaps because she really did sense that the life they had taken for granted could come to an end at any moment, and that what she was writing might one day be a reminder of a lost civilisation, she is more candid about her feelings than perhaps one might expect from a woman of that generation and that class.

Here is Betty Donaldson on the week when war broke out.

That was a dreadful week, Darlings. A week of the most heavenly weather you can imagine, and you were enjoying yourselves so much that the contrast of what was hanging over us seemed so much worse. I said very little to you about the war because last September Charles cried, when he had seen the guns in London, and said, 'I don't want to be killed,' so I was afraid of frightening him. However we were boarding up our skylights by this time and fitting dark blinds. On August 31 we heard on the wireless instructions for the evacuation of children from London and the industrial towns. The war had suddenly come much closer. On September 1, Germany marched into Poland and Warsaw had already been bombed. Well of course after that I wasn't frightened of being at war any longer, I was afraid of *not* going to war quick enough to help Poland after all our promises. How often since then have we listened to the wireless with anxious hearts, but nothing *yet* has been quite so dreadful to me as that Sunday morning, at eleven o'clock, when I sent you out to play in the garden away from the sound of the great announcement and sat alone to hear the decision that was to change all our lives. Out of the silence came Neville Chamberlain's voice – terribly sad, but so resolute and so clear. Here is his speech...

A few hours later, German torpedoes claimed their first victims of the war, sinking a passenger liner called the *Athenia* off the coast of Ireland. It belonged to the Donaldson Line.

> I was awoken at four am by a wretched reporter ringing to up so speak to Daddy.
>
> It was an awful shock, coming so quickly, and it seemed, in the night, as if the Germans must be sinking all our ships at once, but really it was just chance that the very first one was Daddy's. As Mrs King, at the electrical shop said to me, 'it brought the war home to Sunningdale'.

In those early months, the war certainly seemed close to home. On May 24, Betty Donaldson reported that the Germans had reached Boulogne and that 'everyone predicts an early invasion'. Under pressure from friends and even from her husband to take the children away to Scotland, she wrote, 'I have a feeling that as you are English children and should not leave England in her blackest hour, so you are Sunningdale children and have no right to your home if we leave it now'.

They stayed, braving bombing raids, during one of which the neighbouring house was destroyed, and at least one false alarm.

> About eleven-thirty Mrs Cooke woke me up to tell me that Cooper had arrived to 'guard the house', as the church bells were ringing. All ringing of church bells has been stopped except to warn the people of the landing of German troops by parachute or otherwise. So you can imagine my feelings – 'they've come at last, well here we are' sort of feeling. Cooper had a gun but no ammunition, but insisted on staying outside and assuring us that no German would get into the house while he was there and I could sleep in peace. Needless to say, I didn't sleep a wink all night.

In spite of these frights and alarms, life in the Donaldson household seems to have retained an odd normality. Mr Donaldson was away much of the time at the Admiralty. Charles attended the same school as Eleanor Jane until, in September 1940, he moved to a school in Virginia Water after something of a false start.

Unfortunately you didn't like school at all, Charlie Bill, and after two days refused to go again. As Eleanor Jane was going to Guildford to have her tonsils out on September 20, and as the weather was too lovely for a little boy of four to be indoors anyway, you weren't made to go.

Meanwhile, there were birthday parties, sports clubs and rehearsals at Dorice Stainer's dancing classes at the village hall on Saturday mornings ('Charles has developed a talent for ballroom dancing'). The picture that emerges of Mrs Donaldson's growing son is one of confidence, bordering on heartiness. At his nursery school, he was moved up a class, having become too big and boisterous for the other children. His mother marvelled at the way that he, the youngest boy at dancing classes, would ask the older girls to dance. He was quick on the uptake and not above showing off – 'Is there *anything* you don't know, Charles?' his sister would ask. Like any proud mother, Betty Donaldson noted down her son's every quip and *bon mot*, including this exchange with his maternal grandfather, when Charles was six.

With Eleanor Jane, in fancy dress.

Sept. 11 We spent the day today at Guildford, where Charles found his grandfather picking off dead flowers. 'It is all I am any good at,' said Fah, 'You know it is easier to destroy than to build up – that is, Charles, it is easier to do away with flowers than to make them, like everything else.' Charles, who always likes to have the last word, as you know, answered slowly, 'Yes, except with knots – then it is easier to do than to undo them.' Am I extremely foolish or was that rather a clever thought for a child of six, on the spur of the moment?

In 1942, Mr Donaldson donned naval uniform for the first time (something he had hitherto resisted) and was part of a delegation from the Admiralty to America, his departure provoking an anguished entry in his wife's war diary ('Oh my darlings if you don't see him again you will have had the best father any children ever had'). The children were upset, too, although Charles's anxiety was alleviated by a promise that he would be paid sixpence for every week his father was away. Thirteen weeks and six shillings and sixpence later, the family was reunited.

Mr Donaldson may have been rather an aloof figure but, by the standards of the day, he was closely involved in the lives of his children, attending birthday parties, going on trips to the seaside and putting up with clever-dick remarks from his son over the breakfast table. However, almost all photographs of him then and later exude uneasiness and melancholy. Posing on the mound in the garden from where he would like to look at the golf course – his nickname at the time was 'Pooh Bear' so the hillock became 'Bear Mountain' – he looks more Eeyore than Pooh.

The truth is that Charles Glen Donaldson was an unhappy man. His problem was not, as his son would claim half a century later, that he had a snobbish bully of a wife and longed to be away from the Home Counties and back among his own folks in Scotland. He had been born into a family business for which he was temperamentally unsuited. He was a shy man, who liked playing dance tunes on the family piano and singing along to them. Betty Donaldson would say occasionally that he really should have played in a dance band. Chronically indecisive and lacking in the

Daddy, on Bear Mountain.

Mr Donaldson at home.

most basic leadership skills, he must have found the business of managing a successful shipping line, with his hunting, yachting, castle-owning family, something of a nightmare. 'It was a problem he inherited, this awful shipping line,' Willie's sister Jane says today.

Under these circumstances, the escape to Sunningdale organised by Betty Donaldson represented perhaps not a surrender to social pressure but its very opposite, an act of rebellion. A rift developed between Betty and the Donaldsons in Scotland, who never quite forgave her for taking away Charles Glen to Sunningdale, but her motives were probably not selfish or snobbish, but an attempt to save her husband from the crushing burden of family expectation.

If she failed, it was because, characteristically, Mr Donaldson tried to please both sides, staying in Scotland during the week and his family over weekends and during holidays. He drank, even early in the marriage and, although he was clearly adored by Betty and the children, he became a rather withdrawn figure at home. Julian Mitchell, Willie's best friend in his late teens, remembers that the Donaldson house had 'a palatial downstairs loo where Mr Donaldson had a cubicle for his exclusive use, as he was supposed to have picked up some lethally infectious bug in the east'.

Later, Willie would recall the occasion when his father once took him to Broadstairs to look at boats, telling him that he had always longed to sail but was unable to afford it. It was a lesson in the absurdity of financial caution, Willie wrote, that served him well throughout his life. His sister Jane has a different interpretation of their father's reluctance to buy a boat. 'Not being able to afford it was an excuse,' she says. 'He wouldn't have been forceful enough to have a boat in Chichester harbour.'

In 1943, two days before Christmas, the pressure of work at the Admiralty took its toll on Mr Donaldson and the sensitive digestive system to which his wife would occasionally refer. He suffered from a perforated duodenal ulcer and was operated upon at Windsor hospital. For him the war was over, and he spent the rest of it in Sunningdale.

It was Betty Donaldson who took up the considerable amount of slack left by her sweet but ineffectual husband, although her loyalty towards him in the diaries is unwavering, even when his political attitudes are rather less tough-minded than hers – 'Daddy is simply wonderful the way he is not even bitter about France's treachery,' she writes at one point. Her particular *bête noire* was the Americans. 'Personally, I *despise* the Americans more than the Germans,' she wrote in 1940 and, at the end of the first book, written for Eleanor Jane, she has some advice for her daughter.

> While we are on the future may I beg you not to marry an American if you can help it. They are still *talking* about 'All Aid to Britain' as they talked about all aid to Finland, Greece and Jugoslavia, but none ever arrived. I think you would get very tired of the amount of talking you would hear if you married an American.

It would not have been difficult to portray this opinionated, strong-willed, ferociously loyal woman as a hilariously formidable Home Counties matron, and that was what Willie eventually chose to do. The side of his mother that he omitted to mention was a woman who loved the theatre, and who took parties of Willie's friends to see comedians and matinees in London. A hardback exercise book, found amongst the debris of his flat, reveals another aspect of his mother which remained secret. The book contains Betty's handwritten attempts to write first one novel, then another.

Like many first attempts at fiction, they are revealing. Both contain a smug and rather stupid family, landed and titled, who live in Scotland. In both, the protagonist is a woman who struggles to suppress her impatience and rage at being trapped in a stultifying set-up, with dreary conversations, a distrust and boredom of those outside their small, privileged circle, a fraudulent snobbery ('The Forsythes liked to be as Highland as possible and forget the nearness of the Glasgow shipyard') and family dinners, at 7.30 prompt, amidst 'that atmosphere of mutual self-satisfaction into which she was only accepted as Sandy's wife, a situation more awful than if she had been excluded altogether'.

In the second, rather extraordinary story, the wife escapes from this Highland hell, but only briefly. She has fallen in love with the fiancé of her best friend and agrees to go away with him for a one-week affair on the agreement that, when it is over, he will marry her friend while she dutifully returns to her husband. All goes to plan until a friend notices that, when they return from the different destinations they had each invented, the adulterous couple have strikingly similar suntans. At that point, tantalisingly, Betty Donaldson's novel either petered out or was written up elsewhere.

A couple of years later, Betty embarked upon a new, full-length story of about twenty-five thousand words, which she typed out and kept. A *Famous Five*-type adventure set in Scotland, the story is faster-moving and the prose rather clunkier than in her diaries or her other fictional writing, but there is a reason for that. It was written with her twelve-year-old son. On its title page, the manuscript bears the words 'FAMILY FANTASY by William and Elizabeth Donaldson'.

In summer 1944, aged nine, Charles William Donaldson became a boarder at Woodcote House, the prep school, run by Mr and Mrs Paterson, where he had been a day boy for the previous two years. In her diary, Betty Donaldson reported that Charles had settled in well and had even, rather creepily, told Mr Paterson on his first night at school that he approved of the boarding school system.

That was the headmaster's version anyway. There is another story of Willie's first night – one which has entered the Donaldson mythology and was to appeal so much to his friend JP Donleavy that he wrote it up, lightly disguised, in his novel *The Beastly Beatitudes of Balthazar B.* Willie had arrived at the new school, clutching a small stuffed elephant. Inevitably, some older boys took it and tore it apart. Later, as Willie tried miserably to go to sleep, a boy called Anthony Walton, a friend from Sunningdale, emerged from the bathroom. In one hand, he held the sewing kit which each of the boys was given so that they could repair their own socks, and in the other was his elephant, repaired.

But Charles was soon progressing well in class. With long hair and pale skin, he looked, one of his school friends remembers, 'like a slightly wicked cupid'. He was good at football and was soon captain of the under-tens. Now and then Mrs Paterson would call Betty Donaldson to report on how Charles was getting on. Mrs Donaldson's diary contains several references to calls from Mrs Paterson about Charles's progress. On one occasion, a discussion took place between parent and the headmaster's wife as to whether Charles was too young and small to play in the first team (he was). Only readers who have attended a traditional English prep school will know how extraordinary and unusual this civilised behaviour was.

Neither the school nor the war seems to have slowed down the social life of Eleanor Jane and Charles. Over the Christmas holidays at the end of 1944, they went to five theatre parties, four ordinary parties and three dances.

Willie's particular enthusiasm was comedy and later, Mrs Donaldson took a group of boys and girls to *Piccadilly Hayride,* the last revue in which the great Sid Field appeared and the West End debut of Terry-Thomas. Afterwards the party was taken to the Savoy Grill. Anthony Walton, the elephant-saver from Woodcote House, remembers that 'in some peculiar way, Willie rather than his mother seemed to be in charge'.

Shortly after starting my research for this book, I met Willie's best friend from those days, Ray Salter. Not only did they attend the same prep school, but they lived near to one another and their families were close – when Ray's father died in 1951, Mr Donaldson was the only non-family member to attend the funeral.

Together Willie and Ray attended Miss Dorice Stainer's dancing classes and later, when they were both in their teens, they would travel up to London together to the theatre or to watch Svetlana Beriosova, the famous ballerina. At some point, Willie began to address Ray, who was a year his senior, as 'Uncle Ray'.

It was a bright February morning when I drove up to the Georgian rectory near Winchester where the Salters now live. The snowdrops were out, the sun was shining and three neighbours had just arrived, rackets in hand, for the weekly game of tennis. Ray had recently had a couple of cataract operations – hence his availability for an interview during tennis time – but he was a fit, good-looking man, apparently at ease with himself and his position in the world.

Decades after they had first become friends, Willie would say: 'You've been so splendid, Uncle Ray. You've done so well.' He was and he has. There is something about Ray Salter which suggests the world of straightforward, decent achievement which Willie had begun to reject, perhaps even when he was at Woodcote House. If he had followed his father into the Donaldson Line, he might have ended up in the sort of high-ceilinged, sunlit room – sailing prints on the wall, Winston Churchill on the bookshelves – where Ray and I sat that morning.

The Willie Donaldson that Ray remembers from prep school was, as one might expect, rather different from the Charles Donaldson of his mother's diaries. He was popular there, but also extremely mischievous. 'You've got to remember there was a lot of seething anger about the Victorian mores that were still living on. Young people were becoming bloody-minded and difficult and Willie picked up on that earlier than most.'

Ray was clearly no angel, either. Impressively, he stole the school's Conduct Book for 1947. The list under W. Donaldson's name suggests that he had some serious general attitude problems:

Talking at prep.
Talking in form and out of turn.
Misbehaving in prep.
Stupid behaviour in prep.
In hall examining letters.

Ragging in line-up.

Yawning loudly in class.

Ray had been more horrified than most when, years later, Willie began to write so inaccurately about his childhood in Sunningdale, but he remained in touch with him until the end of his life.

It had been a surprise, this glimpse into Willie's family life beyond what he had himself written. His own version of Mr Donaldson as a sweet, watery-eyed, charming, unsteady man trapped by his background had an essential truth to it, but the portrait of Betty Donaldson now seems to have been an extraordinarily ungrateful travesty.

She, as much as her husband, was a prisoner of class. Like the character in her novel, she had a strong sense of family duty but was not prepared to be tolerated and patronised by her husband's prim, self-consciously grand family, who were so concerned that the Donaldson way of doing things, stolid and unquestioned, should be handed down the generations, with the shipping line, from father to son.

She had taken her sweet but hopeless husband south to a place where the children were not part of some dreary dynasty, where they could go to the theatre, where there was not a grouse moor in sight, where she could be herself and write her diaries and stories, where she could encourage her daughter in her ambitions to be an actor and her son with his writing.

Willie saw it all differently. Over the years, Sunningdale had come to represent to him all the things he most disliked: respectability, dinner parties, class consciousness, lawns, agreeable hostelries with Godfrey Smith in the snug bar, conservatism, disapproval, families. 'Wouldn't you drink gin all day if you lived in Sunningdale and your snobbish wife was off playing tennis with the Pinkneys?' he asked, talking about his father in a TV documentary in 1996.

But it was Sunningdale that represented Betty Donaldson's break for freedom and, on the long journey from Airthrey Castle to a rented flat off the Fulham Road, the larger, braver step was not taken by Willie, but by his mother.

William.

3
Vaguely wicked

Betty Donaldson had always wanted Willie to go to Winchester. In 1940, when he was five, she had worriedly reported in her diary that an increase in income tax to 8/6d in the pound meant that 'it doesn't look like Winchester for Charles' but almost eight years later, in January 1948, he was there, the youngest boy to arrive that term at Chernocke House, better known as Furley's.

With a housemaster, Harry Altham, who had been a first-class cricketer and who was famous for combing prep schools for sporting talent he could recruit, Furley's seemed a good choice for Willie, who had ended up as captain of cricket at Woodcote House as well as being in the first team at football. When Altham retired to be replaced by Eric Emmet, thought to be unconventional, left-wing and a man with a particular interest in philosophy, Winchester and Willie must still have seemed like a good fit.

It is an intense, passionate experience, going to public school, and it marks a person for life. Like Willie, who would return to his Winchester days again and again in his later books and columns, his contemporaries also have vivid, but varying, memories of the place. For one Old Wykehamist, who told me he had read every issue of the school magazine since 1947, it was the finest school in the world, a place that taught you how to think, that it was like a university; for another, it was merely good at raising mediocre people above their level. The playwright Julian Mitchell, who was later to become a close friend of Willie's and who used his Winchester experiences in his play *Another Country*, describes it as an institution that had remained unchanged since the 1920s.

It was very much left to the prefects to run the school and they had the right to use any form of punishment. There were two types of beating. One was 'shavering', which was a secondary form of discipline and involved a downward stroke of the cane whereas 'beating' was more serious. I was shavered for not hanging up a senior prefect's trousers in the right way.

For his first two terms at Winchester, Willie was popular with the boys and the master. He was confident and had arrived from Woodcote House with a reputation for being bright, sporty and generally above average. But when a new intake of younger boys arrived in the autumn, his attitude quickly changed. 'He seemed to decide that the best way of dealing with competitiveness was not to compete at all,' says James Cornford, one of those new boys who was to become one of Willie's closest friends at Winchester.

The school was known for having 'shirkers' and 'hearties', and Willie developed the confidence to shirk with style. Under pressure of any kind, he would lark about. Coming in to bat in an important cricket match with the match in the balance, he would play comically extravagant shots and get himself bowled out. During another match, while fielding in the covers, he realised that, if he turned around, he could play mid-wicket in an adjoining game; he claimed that, as the unofficial twelfth man, he caught someone out. He was good at tennis but, if the result of a tennis match mattered, he would play absurd, self-parodic Drobny drop shots.

'Willie didn't really excel at anything. He was strictly uncompetitive and that stood out in a competitive world,' says Jinx Grafftey-Smith, a close friend at Furley's. 'We were all obliged in our first two years to hand in each evening a daily "Ekker Roll", which detailed the amount of exercise one had taken that day. Hearty chaps had no trouble in reaching acceptable levels, but Willie's was always a masterpiece of imagination... The seeds of his later descent to the underworld were, I believe, planted and fertilised during this time.'

Some public schoolboys are remembered down the years for popularity and achievement; others distinguish themselves with five glorious years of disruption and bloody-mindedness. Willie was neither a great hero nor a legendary rebel. 'His principal interest seemed to be to cause embarrassment without actually getting caught,' Grafftey-Smith recalls.

According to one report, it was while at Winchester that Willie first wrote spoof letters, usually in the guise of a bashful teenage girl needing the advice of Evelyn Home or one of the other agony aunties of the time. 'Another one for you, Miss Donaldson,' housemaster Eric Emmet would say, bringing in the post.

Willie underperformed in class, refused to take games seriously and was in his disruptive element on the parade ground with the school corps. Jinx Grafftey-Smith, in a letter to the *Daily Telegraph* after Willie's death, recalled one of his more successful stunts, when the school received a visit from the distinguished Old Wykehamist Lord Wavell.

> Willie's cap never fitted, and his copious blond hair never seemed to stay under it anyway. As for the rest of the apparel, it was pretty much the usual deliberate mess. As the Senior Company Commander present, it fell to me to call the School Corps to attention. So far, so good. But when I had to order our house platoon to right turn, and quick march, Willie, in the middle of the squad, turned left and started to march through the platoon causing considerable chaos. The mighty Lord Wavell ... did not apparently notice, but the Furley's platoon took several minutes to regroup and move forward in the right direction. The head of the corps ... did notice and guess who got the bollocking?

Willie would tell a similar story but with one significant change. In his version, he was thrashed for insolence. He was always modest about his talent for avoiding trouble.

His friends agree on one thing. For all his subversiveness and general attitude problems, Willie was a strong, powerful, confident person. James Cornford goes further, claiming that Willie always gave the sense that he was aware of his force of character and was holding it in. 'He was very dangerous when crossed – not at all like the flâneur he presented himself as being. He could be quite savage and a bully. You were never quite sure which way he would go.' For this, yet again, poor Betty Donaldson gets the blame. Willie was indulged by his mother, Cornford says. Winchester contemporary John Adams remembers that Willie was 'just potty' about Mrs Donaldson but adds that she was indeed 'a lovely person – the sort of person you as a teenager would be attracted to. You could go and talk to her'.

One reason why Willie may have had a blasé, semi-detached attitude to his school may have been that he was developing an interest in extra-curricular activities which would later serve him in good stead. A surprising amount of his Winchester career seems to have been spent in the West End. In addition to his visits to the theatre and the ballet during the holidays with Ray Salter, there were trips with Jinx Grafftey-Smith during term time. 'We often used to spend the "whole day holiday" (known as a Hatch Thoke) in London ... By careful planning, we could get to London in time to see at least three full-length feature films before tearing back to Waterloo in order to catch the last train, enabling us to return within the permitted hours.'

Mr and Mrs Donaldson took a notably relaxed and liberal attitude to all this. When, at the age of fifteen, Willie expressed an interest in seeing the Folies Bergères revue, which was appearing at the London Hippodrome, they not only allowed him to go but accompanied him themselves. The experience, he would later claim, changed his life.

> I was enthralled. I understood immediately that these tall silent women pacing the stage with nothing on – so different to anything one saw in Sunningdale – were the self-evidently desirable representatives of their sex, since men would pay to see them with nothing on. There was no one in Sunningdale you'd pay to see with nothing on.

After seeing the Folies Bergères at an impressionable age, he wrote, his fantasy of choice was to see women as performers, tanned and naked, prowling, silent, perfect and, above all, not real. It was to dominate his adult life, this idea of sex as a staged, observed event, 'an illicit drug to be most excitingly experienced with a silent performing woman off the premises', and it was his trip to the

Hippodrome that was the first spark of what, years later, would become an all-consuming perversion. Oddest of all perhaps is the fact that this intense, intimate teenage event took place in the presence of his parents.

Willie wrote that he had returned to Winchester with the souvenir programme and had been thrashed for immorality when it was found. None of his friends remember this incident but it spiced up the fantasy.

Homosexuality, on the other hand, was greatly encouraged, he would claim. In contrast to the horror his souvenir programme from the Hippodrome had caused, his love affair with a fellow Wykehamist, who would later have a distinguished legal career, was treated in a thoroughly relaxed way by Mr Emmet and others. 'Small wonder that in later life I set up house with civilian girls but, for pleasure, preferred ... an arrangement with a silent performing woman in a service flat, a woman for a living, as it were.'

How queer was Willie when he was at Winchester? Certainly his relationship with his fellow pupil was intense enough for them to meet up in the holidays, a startling breach of the generally accepted etiquette of public school homosexuality. Willie 'was thought to be vaguely wicked', Julian Mitchell says now, 'but then so were lots of people at Winchester'. His contemporaries at Furley's, Jinx Grafftey-Smith and James Cornford, agree: Willie was randy, they say, but his main interest had always been girls.

At the age of sixteen, he had indeed managed to meet a chorus girl, currently appearing at the London Palladium, during one of his trips to London and had asked her out to dinner. The girl, whom he called 'Mary Ellen', agreed and they met on several occasions. She was very nice, Willie told Cornford, and always ordered the cheapest thing on the menu. He was aware that she was only seeing him because she was amused by this little public schoolboy, and perhaps even felt sorry for him.

But Winchester seems to have begun to bore Willie when he was around sixteen. 'He always appeared to be searching for something. I don't think he was particularly happy,' says John Adams. 'It was almost as if he was waiting for something great to turn up.'

All the same, there is a sort of warmth in the way Willie

would recall his days at Furley's. 'And then it was Winchester,' he wrote in his memoirs *From Winchester to This*.

> 'Hearty' Hodges, who dribbled a football up to books, and 'Budge' Firth, the school chaplain, who in his sermon to the leavers reminded us that we were an elite, trained to set an example to those without our advantages of birth and education. 'Never forget,' he said, 'that you are Rolls-Royces. Less fortunate folk are merely humble Morris Minors who must take their lead from you.' Those were his actual words. It's a miracle that I've turned out as well as I have.

Willie's official achievements at Winchester can be briefly summarised. He passed his higher certificate, became a house prefect, and was in the football Second XI (typically, failing to appear for the team photograph).

His informal record, on the other hand, was impressive. He had dated a chorus girl. He had experienced a life-changing moment while watching the Folies Bergères with his parents. He had enjoyed an affair with a boy who would become a judge and had disrupted a parade being taken by Lord Wavell. He had discovered that, whatever else he might be in his life, he was never going to be a team player. His Wykehamist years had not been entirely wasted.

4
Our trouble, basically, is that we're normal

In the spring of 1953, the First Lord of the Admiralty received a call from a Mrs Elizabeth Donaldson of St Bruno's House, Sunningdale, and was told that her son would be unable to do his National Service until the autumn because he was completing the deb dance season. The First Lord agreed on the spot.

Or so Willie would later claim in what was one of his wilder stories about his formidable mother. The truth was more banal. There was a dance which he particularly wanted to attend. Mrs Donaldson rang the recruiting office and told them that he was out of contact in France and would have to join with the next intake, two weeks later than planned. At no point was the First Lord of the Admiralty involved.

There had never been much doubt that Willie would do his National Service in the navy. 'Charles says he is going to be a sailor – not on patriotic grounds I'm afraid, but because he thinks it is safer than being a soldier,' Betty Donaldson wrote in 1940, shortly after her son's fifth birthday. It also suited his style. The navy was thought to be something of a soft option, at least compared to the shouting and square-bashing of the army, and serving in a submarine, which was Willie's intention, had particular advantages. Because every man's life depended on his fellow sailors and everyone needed to play his part – being responsible for the valves in his area, for example – there tended to be an easy, relatively informal atmosphere. Officers called each other by their Christian names. Midshipmen were accorded a certain respect.

Arriving for his training on HMS *Indefatigable*, Willie was a

confident eighteen-year-old and, by the end of the rigorous introductory 'upper yardsman' course, he had made an impression.
When required, in order to prove his officer-like qualities, to give
a ten-minute talk on a non-naval subject to his fellow upper yardsmen before being able to complete the course and pass out as a
midshipman, Willie chose as his subject 'Ballet as a career for men'.

'We gasped, fearful that such an effete concept would wreck
his chances,' one of those present, John Farmer, has written. 'He
spoke fluently with urbane humour and admirably addressed our
concerns about the sexual ambiguity "thought to pervade the
profession". He duly passed out as midshipman a few weeks later.
None of us has forgotten.'

In fact, naval life was to provide another chapter in the
charmed life of the young Willie Donaldson. Joining HMS
Indefatigable for training shortly after he had arrived was Julian
Mitchell, another Wykehamist. Later, on HMS *Dolphin*, they got
to know each other better.

'The ten days have been thoroughly enjoyable,' Julian wrote
in his diary on April 1, 1954.

> If I did not suspect very strongly that he would read this, I
> should say that this was almost entirely due to Willie
> Donaldson with whom I am sharing a cabin... Willie is
> attached to *Alliance* and doesn't much care for work. His
> ambition in life is never to be more than fifty miles from
> London. He thinks that I take life, and myself, far too seriously.

Willie turned out to be serious about one thing at least.

> Willie has a devotion to ballet more intense than mine to the
> drama,' Julian wrote. 'This perhaps is because his interests
> are fewer than mine; I want to write and be a great man in
> a general way. Willie has no such foolish ambitions. He
> knows he's too old to start dancing; he is not particularly
> interested in any of the arts, except ballet.

The ten days on HMS *Dolphin* provided the foundation for one of
the great friendships of Willie's life. He was 'a thoughtful and
kindly person, unable, just as I am, to stand the attitude of our

parents towards practically anything,' Julian recorded in his diary. 'I like Willie very much; we have a common sympathy of feeling – two would-be artists in the rough world of National Service.' He had 'a great sense of humour, is shy, has much the same tastes as I, is sensitive, ambitious, unhappy at the moment. I am not that yet. Not yet. I still do not have time to be bored. Not yet.'

Unhappy Willie may have been – 'I think he is quite capable of walking into the sea and not coming back,' Julian wrote at one point – but his letters from HM Submarine *Alliance*, sent as he took part in NATO exercises Morning Mist and Bright Bonfire, docked in Gibraltar, Malta and Copenhagen, while taking leave in Paris or at the Edinburgh Festival, suggest that, over the subsequent two years of his National Service, he managed to overcome his misery and make the best of naval life. 'I do little but read and write, take no exercise, eat far too much and every day get even fatter and balder,' he wrote to Julian Mitchell.

Later, writing from Malta, Willie described the hardship of living in a gunroom peopled by 'rowdy inferiors'.

> This afternoon I was sitting quietly with some twenty toughs when I noticed a sudden hush come over the room. I glanced nervously round and observed that forty pairs of eyes were on me. I glanced swiftly at my clothing checking that my trousers were in place and fly buttons done up etc – I was reading a book. They had never seen someone read a book before. They were like natives watching a white man shave.

By this point in his life, Willie had developed a personal style that was distinctly camp ('You could easily think that he could be slightly queer,' one of his friends from Winchester recalls) and life in the armed forces had done nothing to make him more restrained. His letters to Julian Mitchell are full of fluttery phrases and slightly affected queeniness. He referred now and then to 'dear Oscar', smoked black Sobranies in a white holder, referred to his longing to be home in 'heavenly, heavenly England' and indulges himself with the occasional rather self-conscious aphorism. 'I can't stand sophistication in the young, can you?' he wrote. 'It is excusable in us, but then we're artists.'

Remarkably, this languid Cowardesque wit seems to have been quite accepted and even encouraged in HM Submarine *Alliance*. 'My captain, whom I'm beginning to love, has started making me keep a journal,' he informed Julian Mitchell. Later, shortly after taking the chief stoker to the ballet ('He doesn't seem keen. I can't think why'), he reported that 'my first lieutenant has written to the authorities at Copenhagen to say that it is imperative to meet the Danish Ballet Company, for which I love him'.

When obliged to meet other serving sailors, he found them less broad-minded – not that he seems to have worried too much.

> I have been spending the last week in a destroyer. I was not happy. If my fellow playmates loved me they concealed the fact efficiently enough. I was only spoken to twice, once when the first lieutenant told me I looked more like a Wren than a midshipman and once when a large and ridiculous gunner told me I looked like an out-of-work chorus boy. He was very startled when I told him that was exactly what I was, but that I found it easier to get work as a naval officer, a job requiring considerably less talent.

It is not only Willie's personality – subversive and skittish – that seems well-developed in these letters, but also his writing style.

> Have you ever been to Scotland Julian? It's really very inter-esting. No one can understand a word you say and they all think you're quite mad. The other day I asked a newsagent if he had a copy of *Ballet Today* and the clown collapsed with helpless mirth. I've never seen a man in such convulsions. He nearly blew his front teeth out laughing. And this is the land of my birth. I am writing a small essay about rising above one's environment.

In the same letter, he describes a group of qualifying COs as 'all very executive with prep school haircuts and bulging Prussian necks'.

Obsessed with ballet, and keen to become a dance critic, Willie acted with his usual precocious confidence and contacted Richard Buckle, the distinguished critic for the *Observer* ('I have taken to sending the Buckle long and dreary essays which he goes to endless pains to correct so its tuppence to speak to me now'), meeting him occasionally in London. Buckle, who was gay, was keen to take him to the ballet in his sailor suit but there is no record, beyond Willie's own unreliable account, as to whether 'Midshipman Clever', as Buckle liked to call him, ever obliged.

At every opportunity, he and Julian saw productions in London, Paris and Edinburgh, and heatedly debated their merits and flaws in letters. 'In the first interval Willie and I quarrelled furiously, as he accused me of liking them just because they were "the latest thing",' Julian wrote, after they had seen the Azuma Kabuki dancers. 'Willie made me very angry, so I told him to enjoy something for a change and to stop trying to rate it in his scale of things.'

There was something in this charge. 'The things that make you happy have just the reverse effect on me,' Willie wrote on July 23, 1955 during what was clearly quite a serious row about happiness, art, love and their future. 'Funnily enough, after the theatre, ballet, a piece of music, or a good film I feel so depressed that I could kill myself... But as soon as these moments of excitement are over the most terrible anticlimax sets in and humdrum reality seems unbearable. But at dances, tennis parties, night clubs and Ascot I'm as good as the next man and contented.'

This rather odd confession may explain what lay behind Willie's unhappiness during this period. The tug-of-war between an artistic and a conventional life, set against a background of the expectations of his class and family, seems to have become something of an obsession at the time and was a recurrent subject in his letters. Julian was convinced that he was going to be a writer and follow the muse come what may. Willie was considerably more confused. 'Heavenly Child,' he wrote:

> Your letter made me sad – I see you're a crazy mixed up kid. We've had all this out before but I think you're too ambitious. I'm sure success in a chosen job or profession never makes for happiness ... So you fall in love, my Julian, and become a solicitor and you'll be far more contented than if you were to write the greatest plays and poems ever. This is all very childish and

simple but I think I may be right. You see our trouble basically is that we're normal. We come from well-ordered homes. The other night I went to Anna Massey's coming out dance. There were a lot of theatre people and they were so terrible – so affected and dirty and let's face it dull.

I went with Grafftey-Smith to the last night at Covent Garden. There was a kind of party which we crashed at the Nags Head afterwards. I may sound foolish but we felt so vastly superior to everyone in the room. A stilted and useless lot of queers. Of course the tragedy, and here my whole argument breaks down, is that I still want to be a ballet critic or something of that sort. I think we're both in for very unhappy lives …

The same letter, in which he had urged Julian to become a solic-itor, contained news of a decision of his own.

I have burned my boats and told Pa I don't want to go into the family business. Thus I have thrown a lot of money down the drain but I had to do something to gain a little self-respect.

Some of the style of the later Willie Donaldson is evident in his late naval persona – the jokiness, the seriousness, the cheek, the perennial agonising of the right kind of life to lead – but there are aspects of his life and taste which are utterly unrecognisable.

Willie, the deb's delight; Willie, greeting Julian Mitchell's parents at Royal Ascot; Willie, being driven by the chauffeur from his submarine to the West End: those who knew him later might just about be able to imagine these things. It is his artistic taste which is more startling.

The musical *Kismet* was, he told Julian Mitchell, 'comfort-ably the best thing on in London'. He adored 'the wonderful sound of Gielgud or Edith Evans in a great speech'. The melodies of Rachmaninov or Tchaikovsky made him melt. He was enchanted by Joyce Grenfell and thought Montgomery Clift streets ahead of Marlon Brando.

Towering above them all was someone whose beauty, radiance

and talent obsessed Willie in his late teens, Svetlana Beriosova, the prima ballerina of Sadler's Wells.

From his early teens, when he would travel to London with Ray Salter or Jinx Grafftey-Smith to see *Swan Lake* or *Giselle*, Willie had been obsessed by the ballet. By the time of his friendship with Julian Mitchell, he was knowledgeable enough to correspond with dance critics. In his letters, he commented authoritatively on the productions he had seen. The Danish Ballet Company had lacked the style and grand manner for the classical tradition, he wrote – 'They're too friendly and I suspect enjoy dancing too much'. His ambition to write about the ballet was genuine. He had, he told Julian Mitchell, 'the three qualifications necessary to be the greatest dance critic ever –

1) I know nothing about it.
2) I'm not over-awed by it.
3) I'm not queer.

But his love of Beriosova transcended the aesthetic or the artistic. Whenever she was dancing Willie, from the age of sixteen onwards, would be there. He was 'sick with excitement watching Beriosova proudly take the stage in a great adagio'.

It was not enough. He was determined to be more than just another stage-door Johnny. He sent her presents. When she rang St Bruno's House, asked for Mr Donaldson and thanked him effusively for the diamond ring he had bought her, Willie's father was kind and tactful enough to accept her thanks gracefully, and not to mention the call to his impulsive son. Willie was only told about it after his father's death.

Willie in love was a force of nature, so near to being an out-and-out stalker that only his charm kept him out of trouble. Although his pursuit of Beriosova was not overtly seductive, indeed he might not even have recognised it as erotic, it bears striking similarities to his hot-eyed courtship of the small select group of working girls and Page Three Stunnas – his Princess, his Baby, his Beloved – who illuminated his later years.

Willie generated his own mythology and, because Beriosova died, aged sixty-seven, in 1998, it is impossible to verify where the truth ends and the stories begin. According to one friend, Willie once, in order to meet Beriosova, pretended to be a journalist from the *Daily Express*'s William Hickey column who wanted to interview her. She rumbled him during the meeting, the story went, but was amazed enough to let him get away with it. Having been identified as a humble midshipman, Willie was said to have invited her to a party on HM Submarine *Alliance* and conveyed her there in a chauffeur-driven car.

At one point, Willie would later tell his friend JP Donleavy, he followed her as she toured around Europe: 'He would attend all the productions in different countries during her European tour. The standing ovations, the curtain calls – Willie would always be there. He would know which hotel she was staying at and he would stand outside in the snow and the rain and wait there until her light went out.'

The authenticity of some of these accounts is open to some doubt. Tony Walton, Willie's old friend from Woodcote House who was later to become a leading theatrical designer and was married to Julie Andrews, knew Beriosova very well. She recalled only that on one occasion Willie had leapt into her cab to give her a bouquet of flowers.

But this obsessive admiration would continue to cast a shadow over other areas of Willie's life. Jinx Grafftey-Smith remembers, when he was an undergraduate at Oxford and Willie was at Cambridge, they had met up in London. 'I'm going to show you the girl I love,' he said, and took Jinx to Hans Crescent in Knightsbridge. They waited on the street outside. 'She'll be going somewhere soon.' When a woman emerged, they followed her until she reached her destination in the suburbs, when they returned to London. 'It was quite extraordinary,' Jinx says. 'It was a bit of a lark to me, but Willie was infatuated with her.' Beriosova lived at 3 Hans Crescent. When, shortly afterwards, Willie bought his first house, it was around the corner in Hans Street.

How were things at home? Poor, sozzled Mr Donaldson was increasingly bewildered by the progress of his camp and confident son. One day William would be showering the prima ballerina of Sadler's Wells with jewellery, the next he would be receiving highly unsuitable postcards showing Michelangelo's David in all his naked glory from Midshipman Mitchell, who was in Rome. Nor did William's declared intention to become a dance critic inspire hope of change in the future; Mr Donaldson was less than enthusiastic when it came to the ballet, complaining, when obliged to sit through a performance, that he could see the male dancers' balls. National Service seemed to have done precious little to inculcate in the boy a sense of adult responsibility. On leave at St Bruno's House, Willie had managed to set fire to a tree in the garden, obliging Mr Donaldson to scuttle unsteadily across the lawn with a soda siphon in his hand.

According to Julian Mitchell and Willie's own later writings, he had taken an intense dislike to his father but there is little sign of parent-hatred in his letters, which contain soul-searching of every other kind. When, in August 1954, Willie returned home on leave, he stayed for only two days before announcing that he was off to the Edinburgh Festival with Julian Mitchell to see Richard Buckle's famous Dhiagilev exhibition. They travelled north, by first-class sleeper, to the Central Hotel, Glasgow where they discovered that Mr Donaldson had booked and paid for their rooms. It was 'both embarrassing and pleasant', wrote Julian.

Mr Donaldson does not seem to have been the slightest bit disappointed by Willie's decision not to work in the family business. Perhaps he sensed that responsibility for the Donaldson Line would be an even more impossible burden for his son than it had been for him.

'I'm reading a most interesting book on dreams and nightmares,' Willie wrote to Julian from Rothesay in the summer of 1954. 'It's quite fascinating but a trifle worrying. I appear to be suffering from acute sex frustration. I always suspected it but I resent having it proved to me by a stranger.'

A few months later, Willie was in Gibraltar and enjoyed, with his friend Bourdillon, an adventure in Spain which he recounted in uncharacteristically breathless terms.

Willie.

Honest, Julian, it was fabulous. We were ushered in to the front room and sat in armchairs while the pros paraded for us. It was like a cattle show. Well we didn't go much on the first house so we walked out. At the next house the same thing happened. This time I picked one but Bourdillon still wasn't satisfied. So I stayed while my pros changed (we were going dancing) while M'sieur B tries elsewhere. At last he's fixed up so we go dancing with our pros. Julian, it was wonderful. M.Bou et moi were too drunk to really care. But just sober enough to see the humour of it all. At about twelve o'clock we say we want an exhibition so off we go, the pros waiting tactfully outside. It was *disgusting* and most disappointing. We were taken into a bedroom with nothing in it but a bed. After a minute two girls arrive and undress. While they were going through their sexual paces, performing every kind of sexual evolution on each other me and Bourdillon were in absolute hysterics. The whole thing was like a terrible dream and quite honestly now leaves a rather nasty taste in the mouth.

In spite of the nasty taste, Willie was 'glad I've done it and bloody pleased I didn't have to go the full smack as I'm afraid I would of of had not the pros been drunk'.

The full smack would occur a few months later, when on Good Friday 1955 he and Julian travelled to Paris for a week's stay, determined to shed themselves of their virginity.

'I cannot say that our trip has been a great success so far as our initiation into sex is concerned,' Julian recorded gloomily soon after their arrival. 'Willie and I could walk, it appears, through every capital in Europe without being picked up by a prostitute under thirty. Hours later we returned to the hotel having found neither. It could only happen to us! I must read my dirty books.'

The week remained largely sexless, apart from a visit to the Casino de Paris where a Miss Pamela, with contra-rotating tits and buttocks, put on, Julian noted, 'a most interesting display'. In the end, though, the trip's principal mission was accomplished.

One night they bought some magazines and books, Apollinaire's *The Debauched Hospodar*, the fifth volume of Frank Harris's *My Life and Loves* – 'We needed great excitement before facing our prostitutes,' wrote Julian – and then set out. They visited three nightclubs and eventually found two women.

In spite of the build-up, the planning and the dirty books – or perhaps because of them – this double loss of virginity was, in every sense, an anticlimax. Willie reported gloomily that he had not even had an orgasm while Julian was dismayed by the dullness of the whole affair. But they had no regrets about their prostitutes – 'Looking back on it, these were a valuable lesson,' Julian wrote. They returned to England, men of the world at last.

In London, Willie rang home. The chauffeur answered the telephone. 'You'd better come down at once, Master William,' he said. When he arrived at St Bruno's, Willie discovered the previous night his mother had been in a car crash on the Winchester bypass. She was dead.

The loss of Betty Donaldson, the adored focus and centre of the family, was shattering. Willie returned to the navy but would fall into long silences and sometimes seemed unable to speak. Eleanor Jane, who gave birth to her son Harry shortly after her mother's death, helped with the running of St Bruno's House.

Mr Donaldson fell apart. He never returned to work at the Donaldson Line, where he was chairman. When Eleanor Jane asked him to help with some sort of decision concerning a member of staff at St Bruno's, he shook his head wearily and said: 'You know, I really don't think I can.'

A family friend, Anthony Beerbohm, who had known the Donaldsons since the days when he attended Dorice Stainer's dancing classes with Willie and Eleanor Jane, visited St Bruno's some months after Betty Donaldson had died.

'Willie took me into this immense sitting room. The curtains were drawn. There was his father, a bottle of gin on the table before him, and a packet of fifty Players. Just a sad figure.' When they had left him, Willie just said, 'I'm sorry. That's the way he is.'

Mr Donaldson was drinking himself to death. It took about eighteen months.

What's the little man up to now?

It was a good time to be at Cambridge. There was a sense that the established order was changing, that a generation of complacent, patronising and often rather stupid men who ran things in much the same way as they had been run for most of the century was running out of time. The old way of doing things, with each class in its place, a hierarchy of acceptable careers, headed by the Foreign Office and Civil Service, a world of clubs, well-born mediocrities, Buggins's Turn, was crumbling.

While Willie was at Magdalene College, Cambridge, the cracks in the Establishment would become more visible. 'The invasion of Suez in November 1956 drove the university collectively mad, though when the Russians moved into Budapest it was to go even madder,' Willie's friend and contemporary David Leitch later wrote in his memoir *God Stand Up For Bastards*.

The new generation was finding a public voice. *Lucky Jim* was published in 1954. *Look Back in Anger*, and Kenneth Tynan's support of it, shook up the theatre in 1956. *The Outsider*, a rather odd philosophical manifesto said to have been written by Colin Wilson when he was living in a ditch on Hampstead Heath, was published in 1957.

It must have been an exciting moment to be young and intelligent. The rage against the hangover spirit of the war and a clapped-out older generation was building, but had yet to find the focus that it would, three or four years later, through satire and political activism. There was a growing interest in broadcasting and the media. National Service had enabled undergraduates

43

to become more politicised and confident in their own views than they would have been two years previously, leaving school. Cambridge and Oxford, once finishing schools for future members of the Establishment, were now on the cutting edge of social change. The first generation to emerge from grammar schools after the Beveridge Report was a new force, and the presence of bright, opinionated, angry men in duffle coats made class division the theme of the moment.

There was little room for self-doubt. 'A factor not to be underestimated was the arrogance of Cambridge undergraduates,' John Bird, Willie's exact contemporary, has written. 'We thought it was only a matter of time before we took over the world.'

But background, when you are in your early twenties, is a powerful force. Willie and his privileged contemporaries may have been in revolt against the old order but there was a limit. His friends at Cambridge were other bright public schoolboys. He arrived at the age of twenty in an Austin Seven but had soon ditched that for a flashy green sports car, a Triumph TR2. He may have mocked the ninnies who hung out at the Pitt Club, membership of which required a public school background, but he did join it, with his friend Anthony Beerbohm, whom he had known since childhood and who had just arrived at Cambridge from Stowe.

Willie, Anthony and Simon Ashton, another old friend – this time from Woodcote House – became well known around Cambridge. They were high-livers, mockers of pomposity, skittish, well-bred piss-takers on the fringe of things.

The Footlights Club, with its great luminary Jonathan Miller, who had already appeared in the West End, was entering one of its boom periods; Willie and Anthony joined, but strictly as social members. John Bird, a star of the university theatre, was directing adventurous productions of Ionesco's *The Bald Prima Donna* and NF Simpson's *A Resounding Tinkle*; Willie would always say that Bird was a hero of his but he only worked with him after they had left Cambridge, and then only as the man with the wallet. A fellow Magdalene undergraduate, Bamber Gascoigne, was said to be an academic or writing star of the future and was to write and direct a West End hit *Share My Lettuce*; Willie was a social acquaintance but no more. The Cambridge Union reflected the political and social ferment of the time, but Willie had little time for that either. 'Do you go to your Union?' he asked in a letter to Julian Mitchell, who was now at Wadham College, Oxford. 'We go to ours for laughs. The standard is considerably lower than Winchester Deb Soc. Dirty little slobs from the North who can't speak the Queen's English get up and attack the Public School System. They have all the qualifications for the job of Socialist Chancellor of the Exchequer.'

This beefy snobbism, the sort of thing which later in life would make him seethe with rage, was entirely typical of the time. A similar division was accruing at Oxford where a rift quickly developed between bright, amused, more artistically minded public schoolboys and the more angry and committed, apparently humourless, grammar school boys.

James Cornford, Willie's friend from Winchester, who was now at Cambridge, confirms that Willie, for all his social gadding about, was on the outside of things. 'He wasn't part of what I call "the packs". He wasn't involved in *Granta* or Footlights. I don't know what he did at Magdalene and he certainly was not in the academic pack.' According to Bamber Gascoigne, Willie 'was on the outside of things by virtue of lethargy rather than anything else'.

So urgent was the question of class that the magazine *Cambridge Opinion* devoted a whole issue to the subject. In a brilliant essay, a student called Winston Fletcher wrote of being lower middle class at Cambridge and of the 'Tatlered boredom' of those from public schools.

> It hurts to be snubbed but it hurts to be ignored; it hurts to be poor. When we get used to them in their funny caps and cavalry twills, we can laugh at them for their ignorance, and despise them for their annoyance. But they still have the things we want, and it takes a long time learning to laugh loud enough to drown the noise of a sports car engine.

Willie (owner of a sports car, as it happened) contributed a surprisingly limp piece on class-consciousness and the press,

arguing that the Beaverbrook papers were cynically and irrespon-
sibly stirring up class hatred with its quietly sneering coverage of
the royal family and the season. But these were voices across a
chasm. As Fletcher wrote: 'movement from one group to another
is difficult'.

The BBC was preparing a documentary on the same theme
and went up to investigate Winston Fletcher. In the end, it was
Dennis Potter at Oxford that they interviewed. Potter had
acquired a name for the ferocity of his attacks on the
Establishment – Enid Blyton was a favourite target – and had
inspired his contemporary Richard Ingrams to create a comic
figure which lives on in *Private Eye*: the pseud.

Willie would always dislike the pseud joke, sensing that the
mockery of those deemed to have ideas above their station was a
bullying and peculiarly English form of anti-intellectualism, and
was already showing signs of heading in the opposite direction.
He revered the famously forbidding and uncompromising
English don FR Leavis, and respected those like Bird, Fletcher
and Miller whose political and intellectual engagement was
genuine, grown-up. In a letter to Winston Fletcher, written in
1990, Willie confessed that he had been 'highly intimidated' by
him. 'I was a prat with a green sports car and inherited income
and thus thought I was unworthy to mix with clever chaps like
you.' At Cambridge, he once confessed in an interview, he had
been ashamed of the money that he had.

Yet his wealth was the one thing for which Willie was famous.
He was a socialite, an amusing gadfly. 'It would have been impossible to be a sentient being and at Magdalene and not to know
about Willie,' Bamber Gascoigne recalls. He was apparently
confident, easygoing and generous and, though Willie himself
was quite abstemious, early-evening drinks parties at his rooms in
Magdalene's First Court became an established, almost daily
social event during his second year.

There are the seeds of a lifelong conflict here. He respected and
longed for seriousness but never quite had the confidence to be
serious. At Cambridge, he worked hard, talked incessantly about
poetry and was to edit a literary magazine, but in the end the

advantages of wealth and the pleasure of being among those with whom he felt socially at ease proved to be too alluring to resist.

During the Easter vacation in 1956, halfway through his first year at Cambridge, he wrote to Julian Mitchell: 'I intend doing the season this year and I dare swear you will snort with derision at the news. But on the whole I think I prefer the shallow extroverts of London to those tiresome introverts of Cambridge, forever setting the world aright over a bottle of cheap gin. At least they know how to live.'

Uneasiness with money had been evident during Willie's teenage years. He confessed to Julian Mitchell that he had a problem with loose change – 'Once he breaks into a pound, the change disappears,' Mitchell noted in his diary. 'He reckons it costs him a pound every time for something that costs 2/6d.' By the time he had gone up to Cambridge, his generosity had become more conspicuous. On a jaunt to London with his friend Jinx Grafftey-Smith, he booked a suite at Claridge's where they stayed overnight. 'There was a problem with money,' Jinx says now. 'The problem was there was too much of it.'

The one consistent element in the memories of Willie's contemporaries is that Willie paid. He made no fuss about this – talking about money, the Donaldsons believed then and now, is embarrassing and vulgar. It was for most of his friends a simple matter: he could afford it and they could not.

It is possible that, if his mother had lived, she might have been strong enough to do something about this extravagance but, now that she was dead, the only person who could put his foot down to restrain Willie's extravagance was his father, and Mr Donaldson had never put his foot down to anyone about anything in his life. Alone, with Betty gone, he responded to the situation in the only way he could. He gave Willie more money.

For the first time in his life, Willie, when at Cambridge, became defined by his own wealth; it was part of his personality. The very thing which gave him confidence, also took it away. Social, larky, envied and resented, Willie's natural antipathy for part of any specific group – any 'pack' – was exacerbated by his alienating wealth. 'He didn't actually have many friends,' Anthony Beerbohm says. 'Not real friends.'

Money played its part in another developing area in Willie's life. Paid sex, in spite of his unpromising first experience of it, was becoming a compulsion. Doing the season – 'dancing with well-born, spongy girls to Tommy Kinsman's band' as he later put it – was fine for flirtation and romance, but the real thing, what he really wanted, was to be found in London, usually on Curzon Street, his favoured hunting ground at the time. There was nothing unusual in paying for sex in those days before the Pill – it might even have been the norm among men of his age and background – but for Willie this was more than just a phase. 'I knew that I was a pervert when I was twenty,' he said in an interview many years later. 'By the definition that sex was all that I thought about, that it was uncontrollable.'

He took the idea further in a diary entry, written shortly before he died. 'I made this disastrous discovery at the age of twenty-one: we can't organise happiness but we can organise unboredom. It was downhill all the way since then.'

Yet according to Richard Rhys, whose rooms were on the same staircase at Magdalene, Willie was already in full revolt against the world of their parents. Rhys was a year behind Willie and, much to his irritation, was heir to the ancient title of Lord Dynevor, a castle and two thousand acres in Wales. In 1956, he was one of the undergraduates who had headed towards Hungary as the Russian tanks advanced. Unable to get into the country, he returned after ten days, and wrote an angry letter to *The Times*. Soon afterwards, he was a speaker at mass rally of protest in the Albert Hall.

Although Willie and Richard were not particularly close as undergraduates, they were kindred spirits in their refusal to tread the path expected of them, their disinclination to fit into their own family backgrounds. Their friendship would last, often through considerably more difficult times than they experienced at Cambridge, for the next fifty years.

Willie's talent for undermining his own reputation flowered at Cambridge. As Julian Mitchell took himself and his studies more and more seriously at Oxford, Willie was to all appearances going in the other direction, playing the part of an amusing, privileged lightweight. 'He adopted this pose of being an idiot,' says Anthony Beerbohm.

In fact, the man whose lethargy is remembered all these years later was working hard. He was profoundly impressed by FR Leavis, whose glowering, unsmiling disapproval of the unserious, the playful and the pointlessly aesthetic would influence him for the rest of his life. Leavis, in Willie's eyes, was a grown-up, an *homme sérieux* who had a cold, withering contempt for the childish world of laughter, spontaneity and imagination. Since Willie's quality as a writer was built on precisely those things, Leavis's most significant contribution to his intellectual development was to give him a lifelong inferiority complex and distrust of his own talent.

Willie 'regarded Cambridge as a lunatic charade ... and the undergraduate parties as the chattering of monkeys in a zoo', Julian Mitchell wrote twelve years later in his novel *The Undiscovered Country,* which contained a factual account of his friendship with Willie, and yet he remained among the monkeys rather than gravitating towards the more intellectually respectable parts of the university.

There was, on the other hand, a close and unlikely friendship with Mervyn Stockwood, then the chaplain at Great St Mary's Church, Cambridge, and already, some years before the press would call him 'the red bishop', a significant voice of radicalism within the Church of England. A collection of sermons preached at Cambridge during the 1950s was published and caused a stir within the Anglican establishment.

It seems unlikely that Willie met Stockwood while attending St Mary's church, but the vicar was an unconventional figure – sociable, gay, outrageous, with a weakness for the company of clever public schoolboys – and had a novel way of ministering to his flock. One evening he emerged from Willie's rooms in a florid and unpriestly state, stumbled blearily into a black car parked outside the college and gave the driver his address. He was sitting, he was told politely, in a hearse.

But he knew Willie well, and the two remained close after Cambridge when Willie was bucketing around London, putting on plays and misbehaving, and Stockwood was the Bishop of Southwark. Willie later would tell jokes about almost anybody in his early life, reshaping and sometimes traducing friendships for the sake of a good story, but the Bishop, as he called him, was spared that treatment.

It was Mervyn Stockwood who woke Willie in his rooms one morning in November 1956 to tell him that Mr Donaldson had died.

'He never knew what to do with me except give me money,' Willie would say later of his father. 'When I went to Cambridge he just gave me money so that I could publish a literary magazine. He wouldn't know it but his money financed the first poems of Ted Hughes and Sylvia Plath, Dom Moraes, Indian poets and in the holidays they used to come and stay and we would drink his drink. And then he died ... I don't think I had any feelings for him at all. I didn't dislike him. It was a completely formal relationship. I don't think I knew what to call him or say to him. He was just this sweet, nice shadowy man who paid for everything.'

Mr Donaldson did indeed pay for the publication of poets and writers who would go on to be famous, but it was his son who, with Julian Mitchell, had made it happen. From the time they were in the navy together, Willie and Julian had discussed setting up a magazine which would contain articles from the front line of theatre, ballet and literature, and perhaps some politics.

Now, at Magdalene and at Wadham, they set about turning these vague plans into reality. 'We both thought the existing magazines of Oxford and Cambridge were unsatisfactory, cliquish and dull,' Julian Mitchell recalled in *The Undiscovered Country*.

We decided to start a new magazine of our own, to reveal hidden talent, to link the two universities and to get outsiders to take a sharp look at our self-enclosed worlds. We spent weeks trying to think up a name for this paragon of little magazines and after rejecting *Foetus*, *Trend*, *Bifurcation* and a hundred others, settled on *Gemini* ...We launched into the project with missionary enthusiasm.

'The long-awaited *Gemini* has at last appeared...'

It was a hugely ambitious project for two first-year students. It had been decided that *Gemini*, when it appeared, would not be the usual student rag, ill-produced and riddled with self-importance and literals. It would look, and be, a grown-up magazine of between seventy and one hundred pages, well designed and professionally edited.

With typical confidence, Willie set about approaching the great men of the day for contributions. Stephen Spender agreed to write in the first issue about undergraduate poetry. Harold Hobson, then at the *Sunday Times* and doyen of drama critics, would consider university drama in the second issue. Others were stalked with less success. Kenneth Tynan was too busy. FR Leavis was too grand ('The Doctor doesn't want to get mixed up in these things,' Willie explained to Julian).

But even before its first issue had appeared *Gemini* was creating a stir. It had a team of people behind it – Anthony Beerbohm was advertising manager, Simon Ashton his business manager. There was a London office which, in early 1957, became 6, Hans Street, Willie's new house.

James Cornford remembers that, among his friends: 'Willie's activities were treated with amused contempt. What's the little man up to now?' When the little man, who was in fact a perfectly respectable 5ft 10½in, turned out to be setting up a literary magazine, Cornford's view was that 'it was a clear example of wanting to do something interesting and having too much money. The view of my contemporaries was that he was spending all this money and didn't know what it's about.' He was chasing after well-known names but out of touch with writers of his own age.

The evidence and the list of contributors to *Gemini* hardly bears out this verdict. Sylvia Plath, a post-graduate at Cambridge, and the husband she had recently married, Ted Hughes, had work accepted, and Plath wrote to Willie in the spring of 1955 to say that *Gemini* was the best thing that had happened in Cambridge since she had been there. There were poems from C Day Lewis, Geoffrey Hill, Peter Levi, Oliver Bernard, Elizabeth Jennings and Dom Moraes. Andrew Sinclair, something of a prodigy who had already published a successful novel, approached Willie at a Footlights smoker and told him that he intended to move from *Granta* to *Gemini*. Bamber Gascoigne sent in an essay on opera. John Drummond, president of Footlights and destined to be controller of Radio Three and director of the Edinburgh Festival, contributed a piece. Poems from the young Malcolm Bradbury were to be included. 'We are stirring up immense interest and indeed consternation here,' Willie wrote to Julian as they prepared to launch the magazine. 'It won't appeal to the chichi Cambridge mentality'.

What emerges from the letters between the two editors of *Gemini* is a determination to produce a publication of weight, professional enough to escape from the sense that it was an undergraduate indulgence, committed to giving new voices a platform beside established names and not afraid of providing a student's-eye view on the issues of the day (the monarchy, homosexuality, communism, class).

Willie would rarely refer to *Gemini* in his later memoristic musings and, when he did, he would say that the magazine had been set up with Julian's brains and his money. In his autobiography, the poet Dom Moraes, who was literary editor of the magazine at Oxford – and, it is said, a frequent beneficiary of Willie's generosity – had taken a similar line. Willie's role in *Gemini* had simply been to finance it. He had been 'as much an impresario, when a Cambridge undergraduate, as he was later to be in London'.

The letters prove how wrong these versions were. If anyone was the driving force behind the magazine, chasing up contacts, arranging dates to read proofs, calculating circulation (they aimed for a thousand and probably reached around six hundred), worrying about how much contributors were paid (£5 was the going rate although Moraes had once splashed out 25 guineas on three poems by Philip O'Connor), it was Willie. 'I'm not too happy about *Gemini*,' he wrote before the first issue was published. 'I think it a great shame we can't have two numbers next term, but I suppose it can't be helped and we have more time to make the first one really good.'

Willie had been right in one sense. *Gemini* did indeed cause a stir and it didn't appeal to the chichi elements of either Cambridge or Oxford. On the other hand, the reviews on its launch in March 1957 suggest that it was taken seriously in some quarters.

'The long-awaited *Gemini* has at last appeared; seventy beautifully produced pages at a remarkably cheap price,' reported *Isis*. The prose section, notably Bernard Bergonzi's essay on Lawrence Durrell and Ronald Bryden's piece on Bloomsbury, was of a high standard but the poetry section contained a good deal of dead wood: Sylvia Plath was 'bad in a turgidly wordy way'; C Day Lewis was 'uniquely boring'.

As is traditional, the view from Cambridge was rather different. Writing in *Broadsheet*, the English don Graham Hough noted that 'it is no compliment to the quite distinguished verse in this number to surround it with critical slush'. *Gemini's* motives seemed sound enough, Hough concluded rather grandly, 'but a much stronger editorial policy is needed'.

Perhaps he was right. The playful irreverence that Willie and Julian expressed in their letters to one another was ruthlessly suppressed in *Gemini* in favour of a rather severe neutrality, perhaps another example of the creative chilling effect of Dr Leavis. 'We want to produce an interesting magazine, not to have a platform for any peculiar views of our own,' recorded a self-consciously responsible editorial in the first issue.

Several reviewers, like James Cornford's friends, were more preoccupied by the perceived wealth behind the magazine than

its content. It was 'nice to look at, and a pervading air of seren-
ity glides amongst its pages (who wouldn't be serene with
considerable financial backing and at least one seedy literary lion
[Spender, presumably] in captivity?),' sneered one reviewer.
Even a rave notice from Patrick Garland – 'Some of the most
exciting pages of poetry to have appeared in any magazine this
year' – closed with a joke about the publishers making a substan-
tial loss on each copy sold, so that the greater the sales the larger
the loss. 'I hope I am not strangling the goose that lays the
golden egg if I encourage anybody interested in the written
word to buy *Gemini*.'

By the time they were in their second year, Julian was no
longer co-editor but was literary editor. There are signs that his
studies were becoming rather more important to him than
Gemini. In his last year, having decided to go for a First (which
he achieved) he became increasingly detached from the running
of the magazine.

As time went by, the tone of Willie's letters to him becomes
rather plaintive.

> Dear Julian, now don't scream. I'm not going to ask you to
> do anything for Gemini. At least not *really*. At least I want
> you to help me over something. The thing is this. We
> thought for the last number in the summer to get five Oxford
> girls [Joke: read 'boys'. Girls had not been invented to any
> significant degree as Oxbridge undergraduates] and five
> Cambridge dittoes, to write approx 600-1,000 words each
> on what they think of Oxford/Cambridge after three years.
> Soonish if possible, as they should be in by March 10
> approx. Get people who will take it seriously. I'll give them
> the form. I even thought you might have time to do one
> yourself? Yes?

In his last year, Willie suggested to Julian Mitchell that he was
going to turn *Gemini* into a limited company of which he would
be managing director. There would be an editor for Cambridge,
Oxford and any other universities which wished to be involved.
Business managers from each university would be appointed. On

the controlling board, with Willie, would be Julian and their mutual friend Chris Levenson.

The idea was too ambitious to work and, before he graduated, Willie passed on the control to a first-year undergraduate David Howell, who would one day serve in Mrs Thatcher's cabinet. Even after he had gone down from Cambridge with a 2.1 degree, Willie remained on the management board but was becoming involved in new excitements, professional and personal. The last issue of *Gemini* was published in the summer of 1959, by which time Willie Donaldson was a theatrical producer, a man-about-town, and married.

6
Willie Donaldson as employee: a brief chapter

'Have you got a job for when you're going to be a grown-up? I have. I'm going to be a literary agent with Michael Hastings. Can I be yours?'

Willie's question to Julian Mitchell, posed during their second year at university, was only half a joke. They were both becoming aware that they would soon need to be making some kind of decision about future employment.

Then as now, career options for the independent-minded arts graduate began with the media and ended with the arts. Although he had written a review for the *Spectator*, and had had his essay on 'Class Consciousness and The Press' published in *Cambridge Opinion*, Willie did not, unlike Julian Mitchell, seriously consider earning a living as a writer. Instead, he set out to be an arts middle-man.

In their final year at university, there was serious talk of Willie, Julian and Graeme Macdonald, art editor of *Gemini* and later to be head of drama at the BBC, setting up a new publishing house. With typical confidence, Willie went to the top, setting up a meeting with the eminent publisher Rupert Hart-Davis and asking his advice. Although Hart-Davis had been 'bliss and sexy', Willie reported later to Julian, he had said they would need at least £70,000 to set up a publishing house. Suddenly the idea became rather less attractive.

As university life drew to a close, Willie lowered his sights, going for an interview with the publisher Methuen, while assuring Julian Mitchell that he wouldn't accept a job from them even if they offered one – 'Horrid people, you know, and horrid books'. He was not offered the job.

Another, even less likely, opportunity occurred in the spring of 1958. The advertising business, in an attempt to improve its image, which at the time was comparable to that of estate agents today, had mounted a sustained charm offensive in Oxford and Cambridge with a view to recruiting smart undergraduates.

Among those trawling the universities for talent was the firm of Mather & Crowther. Three hundred students applied for the two vacancies for trainee copywriters. To reach the shortlist they were required, among other tests, to draw up a promotional tourist brochure for a town of their choice. Willie, betraying a certain lack of seriousness, chose Sunningdale as his tourist venue, and then enlisted the help of Graeme Macdonald, who by then was working at J Walter Thompson. He reached the short-list, was interviewed by a panel of five from Mather & Crowther, and, with one other Cambridge student, landed the job.

His fellow would-be copywriter turned out to be none other than Winston Fletcher, who had written so eloquently in *Cambridge Opinion* about the pain of being working class at Cambridge.

Each of the two new recruits was given a mentor when they arrived for work on their first Monday morning. Their training, they were told, would involve moving from department to department, learning the practicalities of how the advertising industry worked at a ground-floor level. Eventually, after a few months, there might possibly be an opportunity to do some copywriting.

A sensible, nuts-and-bolts approach was never likely to appeal to clever young arts graduates, whose three years at Cambridge had convinced them that the world was theirs for the taking. Winston Fletcher was so depressed after his first morning that he and his mentor adjourned to a pub and got drunk. He survived six weeks at Mather & Crowther before walking out from the job, but not from the industry. He was eventually to become a highly successful advertiser and author.

Willie's career was briefer. After his first morning, he went home and was never seen on the premises again. Apart from a couple of momentary lapses into part-time employment – a tutor in 1967, a gossip columnist for the *Mail on Sunday* in 1982 – it was his only experience of being a salaried employee.

When, years later, Winston Fletcher wrote in his *Campaign* magazine column about the false start in advertising that he had shared with Willie Donaldson, he sent the cutting to his former colleague. Reading about it all again, Willie wrote in a letter to Fletcher, had caused him 'uncontrollable blubbing'.

7
A funny husband

Willie liked to be in love. Later in life, his yearning for romance took some peculiar turns but now, in his early twenties, he was more conventionally generous with his affections. Letters to Julian Mitchell would often end with a list of his passions of the moment. 'I love Sonia, Isabelle (French girl), Svetlana, Doretta, you and Dr Leavis,' he writes in one.

There is one name which occurs more often than others. 'Blissful Sonia is coming up for a dance so perhaps life is not so bad.' 'Sensational Sonia was here for the weekend.' 'I'm more in love with Songey than ever and this depresses me. It's *so* undignified.' 'I remain fixedly in love. The great thing about Songey is that she's a one-man girl and I'm a one-girl man and every Saturday the four of us go dancing. Ho! Ho! Ho! Good?'

Songey was Sonia Avory, three years younger than Willie, a debutante, a brilliant tennis player whose father had played at Wimbledon, and famous beauty. Tony Walton, another of her great admirers from the period, recalls her as looking like Ava Gardner. 'She was absolutely dazzling and very sexy, a wonderful girl – one of the dazzling memories of my youth.'

They had met at a party just before Willie went to Cambridge, and Willie fell for her. She was the one. He was, almost from the first, keen to get married and eventually to have children. He courted her in the way he knew best, coming to stay with her parents, bringing bracelets and rings. A cousin of Sonia's said that she had never seen a man so in love. Mr and Mrs Avory approved of him. Within a year, they were engaged.

Background, beauty, wealth, love: Willie Donaldson and Sonia Avory must have been a golden couple, but their engagement was not without controversy. Sonia's cousin, Oxford undergraduate Anthony Page, who had known Willie at Winchester, was sufficiently concerned about his reputation for sexual loucheness to call a family meeting to discuss the situation. Songey was not to be moved.

There was another, greater crisis. Early in 1958, about six months before they were due to get married, Sonia was involved in a serious car crash. Briefly her life was in danger but she survived with a broken leg, a punctured lung, a fractured jaw and serious cuts to the face.

This catastrophic event seems to have shaken, if not shattered, the romantic dreaming state in which both of them had been living. Willie's quandary was openly discussed among his friends. Songey, scarred and lame at the time, was no longer the enchantress of the party circuit. The chasm in interest and intellect between her and Willie had become cruelly apparent. He realised that he should not be marrying her, but to cancel on the grounds that she was the victim of a car crash would have been caddish and unkind.

On the night before the marriage, Willie went out to dinner with Julian Mitchell. When they returned to the flat, Willie revealed that, in preparation for married life, he had bought a large packet of high-quality contraceptives. He retired to his bedroom to practise.

Willie and Sonia were married at Holy Trinity, Brompton on July 17, 1958. The best man was Julian Mitchell.

I was told that Sonia wouldn't talk to me. She was known to be living in Colchester but had not been seen in recent years by any of the people I had spoken to.

When I telephoned, Sonia was wary, but then so, I had found, were many of the people whose memories of Willie were painful. Eventually she agreed to see me.

It was a strange meeting that we had in her small terraced house in a side street in Colchester. It was teatime but there was no tea there, nor sugar or milk. Sonia gave me a cup of black instant coffee with the biscuits I had brought.

Marrying Songey, July 17, 1958.

The room where we sat was furnished minimally: a small TV in the corner, a table, a couple of sofas, a single picture on the wall. There was a teddy bear sitting on a seat in the corner of the room and another smaller purple teddy hung, rather strangely, on the wall. Bespectacled and with her grey hair cut in a short no-nonsense style, she had the intensity about her of someone who has little time for small talk.

'I'm the quiet one,' she told me. 'I've never really wanted to say anything about people. I always prefer to keep quiet.'

When she did talk about the past, it was a sad and surprising story that she told. She, like Willie, had known before they were married that they were making a mistake but had not had the nerve to cancel the wedding.

'He was a good man, a good character. But he wanted to be on his own a lot. He was a Capricorn. I think he was too clever, too brilliant. He had to deal with this great gift which he couldn't cope with. He was a little too intellectual for us. We felt a little sad for him.'

Far from being an uncritical part of the debutante set, as Willie had always implied in his writing, Sonia shared his disdain for that world – indeed, it was part of what made him attractive to her. From an early stage in their relationship she had known that he was more troubled and unhappy than he let on to others. He had adored his mother and her death had been one of the great blows of his life. He was clearly unable to deal with life's practicalities. 'He had so much handed to him on a plate but he made a terrible muddle of things. He just couldn't control money. He spent it like water. He would never ever be worried by money.'

The circle of friends among whom Willie and Sonia moved before they were married had portrayed her to me as a beautiful, well-born innocent who was out of her depth in her fiancé's milieu. Now, as she talked about her marriage, it seemed to me that she understood better than most what was going on. 'I'll tell you how I think it was,' she said at one point. 'It was unlike real life. It was a play life and was very precarious. He didn't live in the real world.'

Everything was going to be marvellous when they got married, Sonia told me. 'But of course it wasn't.'

It is difficult to imagine a couple less well suited to married life. The division in his mind between desire and domesticity, which Willie dates from this period, meant that the woman whom he had admired, courted, loved and married would have, once she descended from her pedestal, an uncertain role in his life.

Famously incapable of cooking anything, she was not a natural hostess and yet had discovered, when she moved into the house at 6 Hans Street, that, when something needed to be done, it was she who was expected to take charge.

In 1960, the Donaldsons had a son, who was given the family name of Charles, but by that stage the marriage had become chilly. 'Willie would lapse into his funny little ways,' said Sonia. 'He didn't seem to smile a lot. There was a Walter Mitty side to his character and he could be quite nasty.' He became so gloomy that she nicknamed him 'Doomwatch'.

Willie seems to have recognised this change in himself. Less than a year after his wedding, he was writing to Julian Mitchell to decline an invitation to a party. 'It is the same night as a Hurlingham pre-Wimbledon tennis cocktail party and you know what my wife is for that sort of thing.' In the same letter, he apologised for being rude and impossible the last time they met. 'I was going through a difficult stage. Change of life.'

The marriage was not a close one. Willie would tell Sonia that the problem was that he loved her too much, respected her too deeply, which was probably true in its way. 'He seemed frightened of me.'

Those who were part of his social and theatrical set would be invited to parties at Hans Street. Today, most of them recall the size of the sitting-room, but not the presence of his wife. She was there, though. Stars of the moment – Susan Hampshire, Cleo Laine, JP Donleavy, Susannah York – would appear in her sitting room, her husband's guests. Once an actress turned to her and asked if she wanted a drink. 'Did I want a drink? *It was my flat!*'

Sonia found these occasions increasingly difficult. 'Willie gave me this terrible inferiority complex. When you're surrounded by the beautiful actresses, you don't have the confidence.'

Eventually it became clear that Willie's contact with these beautiful actresses was sometimes more than professional or social. There were affairs, walkouts. 'There I was, alone with a dear little boy to cope with, and a funny husband. It wasn't a normal life,' Sonia says with a nice touch of understatement.

At some point Sonia must have had enough. She hired a private detective. The full, rich variety of Willie's infidelities quickly became apparent. Willie and Sonia were divorced on June 17, 1965. Willie would not see Charlie for another ten years.

She had told me a lot, Sonia. At some point in our conversation we had moved to a pub and then later, back to her home. We talked about her life, which has not been easy, and about Charlie Donaldson. The words 'frightened' and 'afraid' emerged quite often in our conversation but it seemed to me that she had been brave in talking about her great love affair with Willie and the less than great marriage that followed.

'It wasn't a normal marriage,' she told me as I was leaving. 'There was something lacking. It was as if we were together to hold parties. I just wanted someone who was dull and strong, but I got Willie.'

8

The angriest reaction from an audience she ever had

Within months of coming down from Cambridge, Willie was a theatrical impresario. It must have seemed the perfect job for him. Unlike advertising, it did not involve mentors, bosses or training. In contrast to publishing, it provided immediate contact with young actresses. It set him at the buzzing heart of London social life. He had always been interested in the stage. All it required was confidence, a strong nerve and a lot of money, and Willie had plenty of each of those.

When Mr Donaldon had died in 1957, he left £343,000 to be divided between Willie and his sister Eleanor Jane, and the family house, St Bruno's. Once the property had been sold, he was worth the equivalent of around £3 million now. He set about putting it to good use.

It had not been difficult to become an impresario. The eminent producer Jack Waller – *No, No, Nanette* was one of his – had died in 1957. His general manager Bert Leywood, a rotund and amiable former comedian, was looking for a buyer. He was the first of many to be grateful when a young man called William Donaldson took an interest in the firm.

Although Jack Waller Ltd had considerably fewer hidden debts than some of the theatrical and model agencies Willie would later acquire, it had no assets and the business was not exactly thriving. Willie, with an enthusiasm and energy that is at odds with the self-characterised languorous dilettante who appears in his memoirs, set about changing that.

Leywood was very much a man of the theatre. During lunch he would potter off to Berwick Street in Soho where he knew the greengrocers and barrow boys, using them as a sort of weather-vane for theatre business. Having consulted what he called 'the oracle', he would sometimes announce on his return to the office: 'Doors will be good tonight on the Avenue', and almost always he was right.

Willie, the new boss of Jack Waller Ltd, inherited two shows, both very much traditional theatrical fare of the time. *Meet the Cousin*, a comedy by Alan Haines and Al Nestor, which opened at the Lyceum, Edinburgh, and travelled to Blackpool but not further, was most notable for its cast. The leading man, Anthony Tancred, was a childhood friend of Willie's (and twenty-five years later would become ingloriously involved in a row over Willie's TV series *Root into Europe*) and Claire Gordon, the ingénue, was to be Willie's second wife.

From the French, an imported comedy adapted and directed by Hubert Gregg, and starring the French actor Claude Dauphin, opened at the Strand on September 16, 1959.

It was a misfortune for the production that its opening coincided with a considerably more dynamic example of the new theatre, written by JP Donleavy and starring a twenty-five-year-old actor who had been discovered in Joan Littlewood's theatre company, Richard Harris.

The Ginger Man, though, was also co-produced by Willie. Its director, the American Philip Wiseman, and designer Tony Walton had set up a company called Spur Productions and rented an office at Jack Waller Ltd. Although the novel of *The Ginger Man*, published in 1955 by Maurice Girodias's Olympia Press, had acquired considerable *succès de scandale*, Walton and Wiseman had been unable to raise the capital necessary to put it on in the West End. It was Willie who came up with the £3,000 required, and for an oddly sentimental reason which emerged shortly before the play opened at the Fortune Theatre.

During the interval of the dress rehearsal, Donleavy, Walton and Wiseman were having a drink at a pub next door to the theatre. When Donleavy and Wiseman returned for the second half, Tony Walton remained at the bar to settle up. Walton, now an eminent director in New York, recalls the scene. 'There was this guy at the end of the bar who suddenly looked at me and said, "You don't remember me, do you?" and I said, "I don't." He said, "I've invested £3,000 in your show. I'm the biggest investor. We went to school together." I asked why he would do a thing like that, and it turned out to be Willie Donaldson. "I owe you a debt of gratitude," he said. "We were both in the same dormitory at Woodcote House. Do you remember my elephant that the older boys had torn apart?" '

Harold Hobson, doyen of theatre critics, reviewed *The Ginger Man* with *From the French* in the *Sunday Times*. Donleavy's was 'not a pretty play. There were phrases in it that shock,' he wrote. 'It is far more outspoken than, for example, *From the French*. Yet *From the French* was booed almost before the echo of the cheers for *The Ginger Man* had died away. And I am afraid that this difference in audience reaction was right and proper.'

The boos for *From the French*, interestingly, followed an ill-conceived striptease with which it ended. 'The play is bedevilled with the notion that bawdiness, in itself, is something that the public likes. Thousands of pounds are humiliatingly lost in the London theatre through this assumption every year.' Willie stuck this notice into the scrapbook which he had begun to keep, but showed no sign of having taken any notice of Hobson's warning.

By now he had a partner at Jack Waller. Tony Walton's younger brother Richard had recently returned from France where he had attempted to earn a living as a folk singer. In return for an investment of £1,000, Richard bought himself a ten per cent share in the business.

His memory of Willie the fledgling impresario was of dash and enthusiasm. Every morning the two partners would have breakfast at the Lyons Corner House next to their office. 'He was at his very best over breakfast,' Richard Walton says now. 'Very entertaining, full of ideas. He never stopped talking.'

The ideas were not just theatrical. Willie, in partnership with Walton, Richard Dynevor and Jonathan Radcliffe, had acquired a photographic studio above a sweat shop in Marshall Street, Soho.

It was called Panaramic and, although it had an unpromising management structure – five directors and one photographer – was the first professional home of Lewis Morley, a young photographer who over the next decade would be responsible for some of the most memorable images of 1960s London.

With the studio and the contacts, Willie entered the world of photojournalism. In the late 1950s, *Tatler* magazine was still covering hunt balls, geranium dances at the Hurlingham Club, and pretty gals in nice frocks, but it was becoming faintly aware that the young were up to something. It had begun to take the occasional rather nervous glance at social change ('Princess Margaret visits Keele University'), scientific progress ('the latest in man-made fibres') and the arts ('Oh, and Salvador Dali is up to something extraordinary again').

Toffs with attitude: it was a world in which Willie felt at ease. When Lewis Morley caught *Tatler's* attention after taking photographs of some freshly fashionable young playwrights, Panaramic Studios became involved. With Morley and Richard Walton, Willie advanced the idea of a series of photographic features, in which the text would be in extended captions. It was hardly at the dangerous cutting edge of the new photojournalism – its themes including 'The American's London', 'Where Shall We Meet?', 'The Day of the Swot at Cambridge' and 'Strangest Sidelines. An insight into the hobbies of the famous.'

The Panaramic crew did not stray far from their own world. Among the London Americans, there was a portrait of JP Donleavy. The London meeting place issue featured Jonathan Radcliffe meeting up with Mr and Mrs Donaldson, Anthony Tancred at the ICA and Richard Walton waiting at the Festival Hall for a date with Miss Judi Dench. Those whose strangest sidelines were recorded for *Tatler* readers was Willie's rival producer Henry Sherek with a rather less than exotic list of hobbies – cooking, orchids and visiting East Africa.

The Cambridge feature, which was written by Willie, is largely a celebration and defence of the privileged, hedonistic and silly way of life of which part of him disapproved. A member of the True Blue Club complains that 'Cambridge does seem to be

Wʜʏ not pick up the girl at home? Chances are she has a job these days and won't be there. Miss Lucinda Roberts (*left*) works as a fashion model, so Mr. Johnathan Radcliffe suggested the Berkeley Buttery, where they met up with Mr. & Mrs. William Donaldson. It's a place where you don't get pressed to stay for dinner

Tʜᴇ Chelsea set congregate in the Markham Arms, in King's Road, discover which parties are on and decide which ones to crash. That makes for plenty of atmosphere, which may be why Mr. Hugh Davies (*opposite*), who works sedately in the City, met Miss Wendy Weldon there. Also if a girl arrives alone, they won't think the worst

'Where shall we meet?', *Tatler* 1960.

losing its character, becoming more toned down', while a Trinity man, Peter Crutwell, complained that 'There are too many people here incapable of being anything but worksweats ... Most of them would do as well on a Pitman's course or at a polytechnic'. The Old Wykehamist Nick Luard revealed that the previous week he had been to five five-course meals offering excellent food and civilised conversation ('This is as it should be') while David Cammell, Willie's successor at *Gemini*, argued that 'the good full-time playboy deserves as much credit as the scholar'.

Willie would always have a weakness for the world of *Tatler* but it was not in his nature to belong to it. For all the froth and laughter of his life as an impresario and man about town, he hankered after something less safe, more challenging. It was time for him to bring a great ground-breaking satirical review into the West End of London. In his impresario's camel-haired coat, he returned to Cambridge in 1959 to buy rights in a show that would, he was convinced, be a revolution in theatrical satire.

The Last Laugh was the first Cambridge Footlights revue to be overtly political in tone, and the last. Written and directed by John Bird, it also starred Eleanor Bron and Peter Cook, who had been attracting attention at 'smokers', or smoking concerts, at his college Pembroke and who had appeared in Bird's production of NF Simpson's *A Resounding Tinkle*. 'It was time to break from the camp tradition of Footlights,' Bird has said. 'It felt absolutely imperative that this creaky, old, outmoded political structure, with a self-serving ruling class, should be attacked.'

An entertainment around the theme of nuclear destruction, *The Last Laugh* was not notably cheerful. It opened with a news report of an atomic bomb falling on Britain and closed with a song called 'Goodbye World'. In between there were attacks on apartheid, a lung cancer routine called 'The Last One', a scene in which morris dancers turn into members of the Ku Klux Klan, some capital-punishment jokes and a parody of television DIY programmes which involved a man making his own coffin. A running gag throughout the show had a soldier appearing at the end of each sketch and shooting someone.

Donald Langdon, agent to both Bird and Cook, suggested that the producer Michael Codron and Willie should come to Cambridge to see the show with a view to transferring it to the West End. They did, and both were impressed, though in different ways. Codron commissioned sketches from Peter Cook which were to make *Pieces of Eight*, a West End hit for Kenneth Williams and Fenella Fielding that launched Peter Cook's post-Cambridge career; Willie bought the rest of the show, which never reached London and all but bankrupted him.

The professional production of John Bird's show, which was renamed *Here Is The News*, was the kind of debacle that makes an appearance in amusing books of theatrical anecdotes – William Donaldson's 1984 work *Great Disasters of the Stage*, for example – but it was also one of the few of his productions which Willie would talk about with any degree of pride.

Atomic humour is brave at any time and, three years before satire became acceptable, it was bordering on the reckless. Nor was *Here Is The News* exactly produced on a shoestring, having a top-flight professional cast, led by Sheila Hancock, Valentine Dyall, Lance Percival and Roddy Maude-Roxby, and also a full jazz section, which included Cleo Laine and John Dankworth. There was a complicated lighting arrangement by Sean Kenny, the production designer of the moment, choreography by the American Rhoda Levine, original music by Patrick Gowers, and an unusually sophisticated set.

Soon it became clear that even Willie's wealth was not going to be enough to launch this breakthrough in topical comedy. He found a new backer as a result of some inspired casting. A young South African stripper called Kathryn Keeton had ambitions to make her career in the straight theatre. She also, fortuitously, had an extremely rich boyfriend rumoured to have heavy underworld connections.

Willie and John Bird were summoned to the boyfriend's flat, overlooking Regent's Park. The deal, they were told, was simple: if Kathy could be the star of the show, the backing would be there. There were certain practical problems: Kathy was not a comedienne, and had a hip problem which meant she was unable to dance. There was no part for her and, as it later turned out, the boyfriend would never come up with the money. But, emerging from their meeting, Willie was triumphant. 'We've got him over a barrel,' he told Bird.

Here Is The News was rewritten with a part for Kathryn Keeton. There were times during rehearsals when her boyfriend suspected that she was not being taken seriously by the director and other members of the cast and sent along a few friends to keep an eye on the production. Roddy Maude-Roxby remembers rehearsals being unusually tense.

Even with a quality cast, Cleo Laine and a jazz band, *Here Is The News* should probably not have opened on a bank holiday Monday in Coventry. The opening scene, during which a screen showed a mushroom cloud and a placard was lit up, instructing the audience, 'Don't laugh. It may be happening outside', somehow failed to strike the right holiday note.

Willie's account of that first night has suggested that there was no lighting: 'Bird thought that the designer, Sean Kenny, was doing it; Kenny thought Bird was; and I, being new to the dodge, didn't know there was such a thing as lighting.' Unusually, he was understating the scale of the catastrophe.

There were, in fact, lights – expensive, state-of-the-art lights – but they had been brought from Germany and arrived too late for the rehearsals. Because much of the show involved back-projection, Bird had arranged that motorised trays would slide in front of the projection. Only once the show was under way was it discovered that the heat of the lights was too strong for the glass plates. Each scene was punctuated after a few seconds by a loud pop as the light went out. There were spotlights to replace them but they tended to illuminate the actors a few seconds after they had started speaking.

Another problem involved the complicated set. There were no counterweights at the Coventry Theatre to help move large items of scenery on and off the stage, and so the production relied on strong men pushing things on and off. 'As a result,' says John Bird, 'the sets followed several seconds behind each act. At one point, three sketches were going on at the same time. In one, Robin Ray was meant to be a scuba diver descending on a treasure chest. He would be lowered on a wire and, when he reached it, a soldier would step out of the chest and shoot him. Unfortunately, the wire got stuck so that he was left there, dangling. The stage manager decided that the best thing to do was to put on Cleo Laine and Sheila Hancock in the next sketch. They were halfway through their sketch when the soldier in the treasure chest thought he had better do something and so he stepped out and shot Robin Ray. Cleo Laine and Sheila Hancock were so thrown by what was happening that another sketch came on. Robin Ray had to deliver his lines for the first half of the show, hanging from a wire.'

The walkouts began before the finale number, 'Goodbye, world'. 'Bye!' called out several members of the audience as they made their way towards the exit. Sheila Hancock and Cleo Laine were spotted outside the theatre and chased down the road by enraged theatregoers.

It was 'the angriest reaction from an audience I ever had,' Sheila Hancock was to recall years later in her memoirs. It needed a hypnotherapist, twenty-six years later, to help her recover from the experience.

The walkouts made the news pages of the *Coventry Evening Telegraph* but the revue received a relatively sympathetic critical press: 'One thing I can guarantee about *Here Is The News*. You will never have seen anything like it before. It is wicked and witty, an example of brilliant lunacy combined with some material which it is kind to describe as drivel.' By the time it reached Oxford, the show seems to have improved. It was 'quite brilliant', said the *Oxford Times*, while the *Oxford Mail* announced that 'it deserves to run for a couple of years when it reaches the West End'.

Encouraged, Willie and Richard Walton invited a leading producer to see the show in Oxford, with a view perhaps to an eventual run on Broadway. He lasted one half of the show. 'You call this a fucking review?' he said to Walton during the interval. 'There's no fucking girls. There's no fucking dancing. There's no fucking staircase. I'm fucking off back to London.'

Here Is The News never reached the West End. The pressure told on John Bird who became ill during the week in Oxford. Belatedly the choreographer and director Eleanor Fazan was brought in, but three weeks before it was due to open at the Cambridge Theatre in London, its run was cancelled.

Willie remained faithful to *Here Is The News*, and even when his production of *Beyond The Fringe* was the most successful show in the West End, he would say that it was John Bird's revue that he was most pleased to have put on. 'It was very experimental and just not glossy enough to reach London,' he told *Queen* magazine in November 1962. 'If it had, *Beyond The Fringe* might not have made the impact it did.'

It was in a sense the quintessential Willie Donaldson production: daring, unusual, extravagant – and doomed. With the enterprise and courage that he proved in putting on the show, Willie also revealed some significant flaws as an impresario. He was incapable of denying the director what he wanted and he had no control over production costs. If there was a problem, his solution was to throw more money at it.

A few months after the collapse of *Here Is The News* critics were welcoming *Beyond The Fringe* as the dawning of a new age of satire. Michael Frayn later expressed the generally held view: 'Revue had more or less strangled itself on its own clichés; the Fringe people were the first in this country with the genuine originality to make their way back to first principles and start all over again.'

Almost the first. The official opening of the satirical Sixties had been a more shambolic, less glorious occasion at the Coventry Theatre in August 1960, thanks to John Bird and Willie Donaldson.

9

An innocent abroad

There was no doubt in Willie's mind as to who was the most considerable of the four contemporaries whom he produced in *Beyond The Fringe*. Jonathan Miller was the oldest of the four and the leader of the pack; it was his brilliance upon which the critics commented.

Later in life, Willie's respect and reverence for Miller grew as it lessened, curdling into a sort of witty contempt, for Peter Cook. In his mind, Cook was 'silly', a bit like him, whereas Miller had always been one of the grown-ups.

Although they were different in many important ways, there were odd similarities between Jonathan Miller and Willie Donaldson. Both were uneasy with money, and hopeless at dealing with it ('To him it's as foreign as a foreign language,' Sir Jonathan's son William has said). Both have spoken and written obsessively about the better, more serious life they might have lived. Both had a talent for humour and yet developed a sort of distaste for it. Both grew older, restlessly disapproving of their younger selves. Both have a jaundiced view of the great success that was *Beyond The Fringe*.

I was told that Sir Jonathan Miller does not like to talk about the days when he was young and compared to Danny Kaye. Too many books had been written about *Beyond The Fringe* and its influence. He had moved on, some time ago, to more serious things. He might agree to talk to me but it was sensible to be wary, perhaps to ask his opinion of the psychological complexity of Willie Donaldson. He liked that sort of question.

I called. I left a message. A few weeks later, I tried again. Then, one day as I was just about to go out, he rang me. I explained my mission and asked if it would be possible to meet. 'No,' he said. 'I'll talk about William Donaldson now.'

Time has not mellowed Sir Jonathan's view of his former producer. 'He sort of seemed plausible and amiable but, as we later discovered, he screwed us really. He had the charm that is associated with that sort of trickster. We were innocents abroad and he was simply a confidence trickster. He was a crook.'

It was not just that they were paid £110 a week ('£90! £90!' said his wife Rachel in the background) which annoyed Sir Jonathan, but the fact that later Willie and Donald Albery, the owner of three West End theatres, whom Willie introduced as a co-producer, 'exulted in what they had pulled off. He boasted about his behaviour in print'.

Feebly and without any particular evidence, I suggested that Willie was too financially incompetent to be a con-man or a crook, but my defence seemed to make Sir Jonathan angrier, not only with me but with his young, gullible self.

The four of them had been slightly in awe of Willie, he said. 'He was a sort of upper-class inheritor of money and we were bowled over by the urbane charm of what looked like a man about town.'

In fact, none of those involved in *Beyond The Fringe* received much of a press, forty-five years on, from Sir Jonathan. Peter Cook and Dudley Moore were 'showbiz types', the director Eleanor Fazan was 'an amiable go-between when there were problems between the cast'. Willie's co-producer, the one-legged theatre manager Donald Albery has been described as 'a self-regarding patrician, a prick'. John Bassett, the man who brought the team together has been characterised as 'the man from Porlock', having diverted Miller from his medical vocation.

I asked whether Willie had contributed anything to the production. 'He gave us the wonderful pleasure of watching a porn film for the first time,' said Sir Jonathan, the famous voice heavy with sarcasm and distaste. 'He took us to a tart's place in New Bond Street and we were shown a film with Cubans who still wore their socks while having sex.'

There was more along these lines. At some point in our

conversation, Sir Jonathan moved on to his relationship with *Private Eye*, to the distrust that the English feel towards someone with talents and interests in different areas, the sort of person they could call 'a polymath'.

It seemed odd to me, the intensity of these feelings. Almost half a century on, Sir Jonathan is now a revered member of the arts establishment, part of England's select aristocracy of intellectuals, a knight of the realm, and the subject of a biography. Like Willie, he has travelled a long way in his life, but in the opposite direction. His resentment, fresh and raw, towards a man who had recently died impoverished and alone seemed a touch out of proportion, perhaps even ungenerous. That unwillingness to remember a time of youthful success with any degree of pride or pleasure was familiar, but while Willie looked back with lacerating self-hatred, Sir Jonathan saw in his young self a victim, 'an innocent abroad' – in spite of the fact that he was a couple of years older than Willie and had been appearing in the West End while Willie was still serving on HM Submarine *Alliance*.

Our conversation was drawing to a close. Foolishly, in retrospect, I asked him whether he had ever read anything Willie wrote later in his life. He had not.

'He wrote that letters thing, didn't he? I always knew he had a flâneur's talent, and a flâneur's talent would lead him to write that sort of thing. He had no real abilities to do anything really. He was a sort of idiotic, fly-by-night flâneur who had some sort of pleasure at his own bad behaviour and thought it was all rather charming and forgivable. He was typical of the Sixties, really.'

10
Fleecing the Fringers

It was a revolution in revue, the moment when theatre came of age. After years of effete drawing-room comedies and anaemic revues, the critics were almost tearful in their relief at the arrival of *Beyond The Fringe*, which opened at the Fortune Theatre on May 10, 1961. 'We audiences have tasted our own blood and we like it,' wrote Alan Brien for the recently-launched *Sunday Telegraph*. In an uncharacteristic moment of silliness, Bernard Levin in the *Daily Express* declared, 'I shall go and see it … once a month for the rest of my life. If I live to a hundred, it will still be there.' Kenneth Tynan, in the *Observer*, announced that it was 'the moment when English comedy took its first step into the second half of the twentieth century'. Other critics despaired of finding enough superlatives.

Almost half a century on, the varying successes and glittering reputations of Jonathan Miller, Peter Cook, Alan Bennett and Dudley Moore have added to the sense that *Beyond The Fringe* was more than a theatrical landmark. It was a great turning point in comedy, the moment when it became fashionable to laugh at the established order of things. None of Britain's great institutions of satire of the second half of the twentieth century – *Private Eye, That Was The Week That Was, Spitting Image,* Chris Morris – would, it has been said, have been quite the same without the Fringers.

The story of how two stars from the Cambridge Footlights and two brilliant men from Oxford were brought together by Dudley Moore's friend John Bassett, how their revue was put on at the Edinburgh Festival by its artistic director Robert Ponsonby, its subsequent triumph in the West End and on

The Fringers – Peter Cook, Jonathan Miller,
Dudley Moore and Alan Bennett.

Broadway, has inspired a large number of books and articles but in one respect, that which concerns the show's main producer and the subject of this book, the official, generally accepted version is partial and inaccurate.

There is only one person to blame for this distortion. For the last twenty-five years of his life, Willie recounted his involvement as producer of *Beyond The Fringe* to a number of historians, biographers and makers of TV documentaries. The story recurred in his column for the *Independent*, and in several of his books. Unlike other events from his past, which ripened and changed colour over the years, his account of how he blundered into producing the most successful revue in modern theatre and then fleeced its stars remained pretty much consistent. Those who interviewed him, or wrote his obituaries of him, believed every word of it. After all, who would seriously present his own role in a great success as that of a lucky, over-privileged shyster of private means and no sense?

Willie's version went like this. The agent Donald Langdon had been unenthusiastic about his client Peter Cook joining up with three relative amateurs for an Edinburgh fringe show which had been put together by the Oxford graduate John Bassett, but then changed his mind when eighteen producers made their way to Edinburgh, each desperate to buy rights in *Beyond The Fringe*. Belatedly alert to the fact that the show might be a success, he persuaded Willie to produce it. Having flown to Edinburgh, Langdon locked the four Fringers in a room for twenty-four hours and bullied them into appointing him as agent to them all and Willie as producer.

> On looking back on it, it was complete madness and I don't know what they thought they were doing. They auditioned me – I took them out to dinner. There was some sort of audition. I don't know what it was. He told them something – somehow they clearly passed the audition and I had this show. So I was still the only person in London who hadn't seen it. Totally unqualified.

Later, worried about not getting a theatre, Willie said that he introduced Donald Albery, who owned the Criterion, Wyndhams, the New and the Piccadilly theatres, into the deal. Albery disapproved of the show, wanted to sack Alan Bennett from it, failed to provide a theatre, and, with Willie, conned the writers and cast out of their just rewards. The Fringers were making £75 a week while Willlie and Albery were taking home £2,000. It was this kind of thing, 'exulting at what they had pulled off', which had so enraged Sir Jonathan Miller down the years.

Was Willie's role in *Beyond The Fringe* really so peripheral and morally despicable? Alan Bennett has marginally fonder memories of him than Sir Jonathan Miller. He was 'a deceptively gentle and kindly figure', Bennett wrote, weighing his words carefully, in the *London Review of Books*. 'Willie was never condescending as Albery invariably was and seemed as much at sea in the world of showbusiness as we were … By the time he came into our lives and though he was not much older than us he had already lost one fortune.' (Willie was in fact two years younger than both Bennett and Jonathan Miller.) Willie had, on the other hand, been genuinely amused by *Beyond The Fringe*, Bennett told me, and had refused to 'shoot a lot of crap about its prospects'. He was 'laid back and lazy, not showbiz at all ... probably as villainous as Donald Albery but more likeable. Even if we had been told he was going to rip us off, he was so gentle and funny that it would have been difficult to change.'

The truth is that it was not chance or chumminess with Donald Langdon that brought Willie the right to stage *Beyond The Fringe*. Langdon, who now lives in America, had been increasingly bewildered and annoyed by what he calls Willie's 'egregiously false narrative' and is keen to set the record straight. He had, in 1959, been impressed with what Willie had done with his client John Bird and that 'glorious failure' *Here Is The News*. 'I thought he would be the ideal producer for another show that was about to open in Edinburgh with equally inspired content but much simpler in concept. It needed a producer who would allow the same complete freedom of expression to the authors as had been given to Bird, and its very simplicity was proof against the problems that had beset its very complicated predecessor. And to be honest, I also believed I could control Willie. I introduced Bennett, Miller and Moore to Donaldson and everyone was happy.'

Willie matched the offers of other producers but he was flying by the seat of his pants. Unable to raise the £4,000 himself, he received three-quarters of it from fellow producers Peter Bridge and John Gale.

It was Willie who introduced Eleanor Fazan as director, with the brief to adapt the Edinburgh show for the West End. It was a clever move. Fazan, known in the theatre world as 'Fiz', was only in her twenties, had been a dancer and choreographer and had acquired a reputation as a director who could bring shape and pace to productions that lacked both those things. Importantly, she had the tact and lack of ego to work the brilliant, confident amateurs of university revue.

In a fascinating unpublished essay, Eleanor Fazan recalls being approached about *Beyond The Fringe*. The show was a proven success, Willie explained, so it would be a small job: a sort of umpire-cum-production manager with a fixed salary of £20 a week. Seeing the show in a London rehearsal room – it was Willie's first viewing, too – Fazan received something of a shock.

I could well understand their personal success, but the show was badly put together, and their attitude was typically undergraduate. To reach any sort of London standard, they would have to work hard; I wondered if their rebellious spirit, which was a valuable part of the show, could tolerate hard work. I doubted it, and told Willie of my misgivings: some of the material would have to go, and as the show was only an hour long, a great deal more written. It was going to be a huge job. Willie was delighted. He'd had his misgivings too and had been afraid that I might have found *Beyond The Fringe* as wonderful as everyone else. On this basis I agreed to take on the job. No extra money, of course. There was none.

They began to rework the show first at Fazan's flat, then at the bar of the Prince of Wales Theatre, which Willie had booked. He made it all as easy as possible, Eleanor Fazan remembers today. Every night he would ring her up to ask how the work was going.

It is a rather different portrait from the one Sir Jonathan Miller had painted of the Fringers' idiotic flâneur of a producer and of their director, the 'amiable go-between'.

Fazan, Donald Langdon says, has never had the recognition she deserves. She worked with the four, shaping and changing the running order, adding new material, introducing a designer John Wyckham. It was not easy. They were competitive, Eleanor Fazan writes – 'There was still more rivalry between them than friendship, and removing solo spots was a tricky and delicate task' – but she soon realised that it was a serious mistake to treat the show and its cast in a normal professional way. 'To be caught working was more than their English education would allow, and God forbid that they should be taken for actors in need of instruction … They were going to succeed because they were NOT professional – they were brilliant.'

Eleanor Fazan was asked by Willie to approach Donald Albery. 'He did have a short circuit,' she writes. 'An upright and established man could put the fear of God into him. Someone like Donald Albery could reduce him to a stuttering schoolboy.'

Albery was unenthusiastic but was persuaded over dinner to invest. He drove a hard bargain with Willie, matching the original producer's £4,000 but mysteriously becoming the senior partner in the arrangement. Langdon had argued strongly, but unsuccessfully, against the involvement of Donald Albery and was proved right when Willie quickly resigned himself to his co-producer's bullying authority.

After disastrous reviews and several walkouts during the show's week in Brighton ('the satire has as much sting as a blanc-mange', reported the *Brighton and Hove Herald*), Anna Deere Wiman, the owner of the Fortune Theatre, came to see the show in Brighton, got drunk, alienated the four stars and annoyed Eleanor Fazan. Fortunately, her solicitor David Jacobs liked what he had seen enough to bring it as a filler at the Fortune. On the opening night Willie sent a telegram to the cast which indicates what an unusual producer he was. It read: 'Good luck tonight girls. You may not be good but at least you are cheap!'

The portrait of Willie that begins to emerge is not the goofy hanger-on, clumsily exploiting four brilliant young innocents, but of a producer who kept his nerve on the creative (but not the financial) side, made all the right decisions, who was one of the team. Writing of a later show, Fazan presents a portrait of his contribution as producer that is startlingly different from the official, Willie-created version.

> Should I ask him to a run-through, he was always there, sitting in the shadows at the back of the stalls in his long, dark overcoat, quite unperturbed by the chaos that surrounds first runs. At the end of it he'd give an intelligent and sensitive appraisal that was always encouraging. He seemed almost embarrassed to intrude. This may not seem a great deal, but it was. An ability to be both objective and artistically involved is very unusual in a producer.

The famous visit to a tart's boudoir in New Bond Street to which Sir Jonathan Miller refers so scathingly has been widely written about, most recently by Alan Bennett in the *London Review of Books*, but, significantly, was never one of Willie's comic routines –

indeed, he denied that the trip had been his idea. At the technical rehearsal, the quartet, in the words of Eleanor Fazan, 'slumped and mucked their way through. When Willie had asked what treat they would like, the answer came back, "Porn".' An article written shortly after the opening of *Beyond The Fringe* confirms Fazan's account. The four young stars 'can pretend to be eccentric because they are not', reported the magazine *Man About Town*. 'The producer stopped them clowning at rehearsals by promising them a special showing of blue films after the dress rehearsal.'

So off they went to a New Bond Street boudoir: Willie and the boys, Sonia, Jonathan's wife Rachel, Peter's fiancée Wendy, and John Bassett. During the show Bassett recalls Alan Bennett hiding under the bed, a detail which Bennett himself denies although he remembers their middle-aged hostess being shocked by how young he looked. They were asked to leave singly, to avoid the attention of authorities.

Under the sober gaze of the many historians of satire, who themselves have been influenced by the icy disdain of Sir Jonathan Miller and Willie's own inaccurate accounts, it is easy to forget that these were larky and rather innocent days. Miranda Skillman, a pretty, unworldly nineteen-year-old Australian who had come to work for Jack Waller Ltd and the firm he established to deal with *Beyond The Fringe*, W & D Plays Ltd, a month before the revue opened at the Fortune, recalls the quartet coming around to the office and joking in Willie's office. 'They were showing off to each other but I think they were mainly showing off to Willie,' Miranda Skillman says. 'One day when they were in the office, Jonathan Miller said the word "fuck". I was so shocked that I left the room and began writing a letter of resignation in the next-door office. Willie found me in tears and explained that it was only because Jonathan was a medical doctor that he used that word – it was part of his everyday work. He gave me the rest of the day off to recover.'

The sense of their own producer being in tune with their skittish and subversive sense of humour, of his understanding, like Eleanor Fazan, that dealing with them was different from managing professional actors, has somehow been lost in the various accounts. Four years after *Beyond The Fringe* opened Willie told his new girlfriend Carly Simon that, before each performance, he would visit each of the quartet in his dressing-room and assure him that he was the true star of the show.

How cheap were 'the girls'? I had hoped to discover in my researches that Willie's account of the Fringers losing out so badly to Albery and himself was one of his self-destructive stories. Willie, after all, would be bankrupt within three years of *Beyond The Fringe*'s opening, whereas Jonathan Miller and Alan Bennett had managed to buy the houses in Camden where they still live. Neither of the authorised biographies of Peter Cook mention discontent at their rewards at the time. The evidence of a great management rip-off seems slim, and largely based on Willie's account.

But it is there. Even before the opening, the four writers and actors seem to have been aware that they were getting a bad deal – Eleanor Fazan remembers Willie hiding in the lavatory on one occasion when 'the boys' came round asking for more money. Jane Shilling, who was receptionist at Jack Waller, later in the show's run recalls that the four were 'absolutely livid' with Willie about the money.

Willie a skinflint? It is an unconvincing story. Unfortunately, he was now in partnership with a brutal theatrical manager of the old school of whom he was frightened. 'I have the feeling it was an uncomfortable relationship with Albery,' says Miranda Skillman. 'I got the sense that Albery wasn't being gentlemanly. I sometimes had to go down to get cheques signed and I always had an uncomfortable feeling. There was a sense that he was the bad guy. I definitely had the impression that he was lording it over Willie.'

Albery emerges from these accounts as a hard-nosed bully, and a snob into the bargain. He believed that no directors should become friends with actors. At one meeting with the cast and their agent Donald Langdon, Alan Bennett remembers that he had addressed remarks to Donald and Albery thought he was referring to him. 'A spasm of rage crossed his face because he thought I was talking to him and actors didn't use a producer's Christian name.'

Willie was hopeless at confrontation and afraid of Albery. 'His dominance over Willie never stopped,' says Donald Langdon. 'When the request for a raise after the show recouped was rudely rebuffed by Albery, Willie expressed contempt for him and sympathy for the cast, but completely failed either to endorse their case or unilaterally to make a gesture … He would shrug and say, "What can you expect from an arsehole like Albery?"'

Albery went on to be knighted for his services to the theatre and it is in his papers, collected at the Harry Ransom Centre in the University of Texas, where the true story resides of what happened to the Fringers' money.

In a letter from the Golden Theatre, New York, misdated February 13, 1962 (in fact, it was 1963), the four members of the cast wrote to Albery, asking him to confirm their account of the history of *Beyond The Fringe*. There had been interest in the story, they said, from the press. Their summary of the production, which incidentally explains that the reason why Willie had been selected as producer was 'largely because he had expressed interest in the show before it was produced in Edinburgh', revealed that the original contract for the West End show had granted them £70 each as performers (about £1,000 in today's money) and seven per cent of the gross, to be divided between the four of them.

In return for writing and performing the show eight performances per week the cast had been receiving some £114 a week each, while the management, having raised an investment of £8,000 – £5,000 above the actual production cost, the letter claimed – was now sharing £1,300 a week net profit. After six months, the cast had approached Albery with a view to a raise in salary, which had been granted in return for their co-operation in their eventual replacement by other actors when the original production transferred to Broadway. So the four cast members were now receiving £120 a week plus ten per cent of profits from the London production.

The profits from the London production, the Fringers concluded, had been £150,000, of which the management had received £60,000. Each of the cast had received £9,500.

Albery replied five days later. He was angry about the threat to go to the press but seemed to accept, in characteristic fashion, the Fringers' version of events. Their grievances were foolish, he wrote. Otherwise they were soundly based.

I have some difficulty in seeing the four stars of *Beyond The Fringe*, whose careers were launched so spectacularly, as victims. Although the earnings of each of them over the first twenty-one months of the show's run was small compared to the profits being made (£9,500 is the equivalent today of £140,000), those who helped significantly on their way did far worse.

Eleanor Fazan, on a flat salary of £20, was written out of the deal when the play went to New York. John Bassett, the man who first brought them together and put them on at the Edinburgh Festival, was put on a paltry one per cent of the gross, worth £30 a week, when it came to London and even that was ended when the show transferred to Broadway.

Bassett, a gentle man, remonstrated with Willie, who suggested, in typically evasive fashion, that he should sue him. In desperation, Bassett wrote a series of letters to the four stars who were now the toast of New York asking them to sign a statement confirming his right to one per cent of the gross. They never signed.

The backers of the show made huge profits. Philip Wiseman, Donleavy's director, put in £1,000 and made back £33,000. David Gale, one of the original backers, reduced his stake to £100 which nonetheless earned him a £7,000 profit. 'It turned out to be the best investment I ever made,' he told Ronald Bergan, author of the show's official history *Beyond The Fringe ... and Beyond*. Whatever Willie made from the show – probably very little – it was not enough. Facing bankruptcy in 1964 he sold his share to Donald Albery, who, true to form, squeezed him dry.

The great breakthrough in British comedy is remembered in different ways by those who were part of it. Jonathan Miller has frequently moaned about his involvement – 'I still fiercely regret the decision. I think that was a bad thing I did. Much better to have been a funny undergraduate and forget about it – but I got on to this terrible treadmill,' he said. 'I look back on those years without nostalgia, remembering chiefly the frustrations and the embarrassment,' Alan Bennett has written.

Dudley Moore and Peter Cook were less lugubrious about the experience. 'I don't think I ever had such … excitement. It was everything I ever wanted,' wrote Moore. 'I look back on the show with nothing but pleasure,' said Cook.

Willie's view of his involvement remained consistent throughout his life. 'It was a miracle,' he said in an interview in 1962. 'One minute I'm a bankrupt idiot, the next minute I've got *Beyond The Fringe*. I just think I was lucky.' Interviewed forty years later about Peter Cook, he repeated this view word for word.

11
Freewheelin' with Bob

Willie had a definite taste in music, but it was somewhat limited. For as long as I knew him, he only admitted to liking three songs, Stevie Wonder's 'I Just Called To Say I Love You', which reminded him of his Princess, 'Tie A Yellow Ribbon Round The Old Oak Tree', and 'Oh Baby, Baby', his preferred title of the Cat Stevens' hit 'Wild World'. He was also quite partial, when in the mood, to the disco sounds of Donna Summer.

But there was a time, during his days as an impresario, when music management seemed an eminently suitable direction for his entrepreneurial talents. He set up a firm called Players and Writers and began to look for clients. A band called The Harriers from his old school, Winchester, mentioned in the *Daily Express*'s William Hickey column, was signed by Players and Writers, and signed a record deal with Decca. An album was made but never released, and later one of the band's line-up, David Mallett, went to work for the agency on a salary of five pounds a week.

There was a revolution in music going on, but Willie was not part of it. He put a jazz band called the Temperance Seven on at The Establishment Club in Soho's Greek Street. He represented a folk singer called Weston Gavin. Mallett seems to remember the famous actress Sarah Miles, who had become Willie's girlfriend, recording 'I Who Have Nothing'. A young girl group called The Simon Sisters, visiting London from America, also signed up with Players and Writers.

Then there was Bob Dylan, whose relationship with Willie played an increasingly important part in Willie's various memoirs.

> One day I returned to the office after lunch to find a small man sitting on my sofa, strumming his guitar and with his hat on back to front.

'Fuck off,' I said.

It was no good. Every day when I returned to the office he was sitting on the sofa with his hat on back to front. In the end, I tried to get him work but to no avail. My old friend George Martin at EMI courteously listened to a tape but expressed no interest, and Dick Rowe at Decca and Tony Hatch at Pye were equally unimpressed. Only Peter Cook came to my rescue. He put Bob Dylan on at The Establishment – unpaid but with a meal thrown in. Dylan made no great impact and shortly returned to America where things went better for him.

This anecdote served Willie well. After he died, the obituaries solemnly recorded that he was the first man to put Dylan on stage in the UK.

Unfortunately, when I began to look into the Dylan story, those who ran The Establishment, notably Peter Cook's first wife, Wendy, had no recollection of Dylan playing there. There is no record, among other clients of Players and Writers, of a man with a guitar and a baseball cap round the wrong way hanging around Willie's office. Carly Simon, who knew both men well, cannot remember Willie mentioning Dylan but, on hearing that Willie later developed a fondness for crack, speculated: 'Hey, perhaps it was Bob who first turned Willie on.'

I longed for Willie's version of his meeting with Dylan to be true. Few events in this account of his life would have been more enjoyable to see at first hand than a conversation between Willie Donaldson and the young Bob Dylan.

Just as I was about to dismiss the Dylan story as one of Willie's wilder anecdotes, Don Langdon startled me by expressing his disapproval of the way Willie distorted his past. It was not, for example, Willie who had put Dylan on the stage at The Establishment, he said, but him.

Dylan had been brought to London to appear in a BBC play *Madhouse on Castle Street*, directed by Philip Saville, who was Langdon's client. During his stay in London, Bob would hang out at Langdon's office which he shared with Willie. 'One morning when I was late coming in, he wandered off to Willie's suite which he rented from me,' Langdon wrote to me. 'This is how Willie met him but I don't recall them ever hanging out together.' It was Donald Langdon who arranged for Dylan to play unpaid during an interval at The Establishment Club.

Even though Willie did not ring around his music business pals to get the struggling folk singer some work – something Dylan's notoriously ferocious manager Albert Grossman might have had opinions about – it seems that Bob and Willie did indeed spend some time together during the winter of 1962.

How did the voice of a generation react to the West End's wildest impresario? Could the experience have inspired some of Bob's lyrics on his next album *Freewheelin' Bob Dylan*? It is time for the great cohort of Dylanologists to start digging.

12

Nudes and peacocks

'It seems to me that 1961 must have meant a lot to all of us,' Willie wrote in a letter to Miranda Skillman (by then Mrs Miranda Walker and living in Australia) some twenty-eight years after she had been secretary at his offices at 5/6 Coventry Street. Although he never talked in any detail about his years as a producer in the early Sixties, they must have been an exciting time.

The people who, while at university, had believed, as John Bird put it, that they would rule the world were at the gates of the enemy. They had announced their arrival with books, plays and now with a satirical revue (music lagged behind by about three years). They had the nerve and the power to begin doing things in their own way, without asking permission of their powerful elders. The Establishment Club, which Peter Cook set up while sharing Willie's office, became the place where fashionable young Londoners hung out and was in its way as big a breakthrough as the show in which Cook had appeared and which, in spite of the worst efforts of Donald Albery, had helped fund it.

Yet, excitingly, the control of the real Establishment was still in the enfeebled grip of the old guard. Politics was stuffy and out of touch. The theatre, in spite of repeated shock waves of new productions, was still in thrall to tradition. Book publishing, although shaken up by the Lady Chatterley trial in 1960, remained dusty and patrician in its outlook.

'It's impossible to know, if you weren't around back then, the extent to which things needed knocking down,' says Elisabeth Luard, whose husband Nick, a Wykehamist like Willie but a couple of years younger, set up The Establishment Club with Peter Cook and, also with Cook, took over the ownership of *Private Eye* magazine.

People like Nick Luard, Willie, the producers Michael White and Michael Codron, the agent Donald Langdon were all working with the established order of things and subverting it. 'We were two kids playing at being grown-ups,' Willie would later say to Langdon, who neatly sums up the double game Willie was playing. 'A part of him wanted to join the adult world while still holding it in his childlike contempt.'

Class still mattered, yet the old assumptions and snobberies were under siege. The sexual revolution was under way, although it would take a couple more years to break cover and become official. While a secretary could still consider resigning because someone had said 'fuck' in the office, the Pill's availability from 1959 had changed everything. 'People had decided sex should be satisfying in itself in the early Sixties,' says Elisabeth Luard. 'We had begun to see it as recreation. For the first time we didn't have to pick up the bill.'

Through this confusion of old and new, starchiness and freedom, Willie must have been perfectly at home. He had both background and subversiveness. He was in business and yet free, married but not noticeably so. Turning twenty-six in January 1961, he was to all appearances a dashing and successful impresario.

But not an entirely conventional one. Miranda Skillman's most enduring memory is of Willie, during slack periods at the office, flicking water out of the window on to the heads of the people on the street below. 'With his flair, the swirling camel-hair coat and soft, loose hair,' the Willie Donaldson she remembers from those times was 'wonderful, sweet and kind'.

From those closest to Willie, there emerges a picture of easy generosity which is startlingly at odds with his own later self-portrait. His recruitment of dancing girls for his shows, for example, was hardly that of a leering sexual opportunist, according to Jane Pullee, who worked for him after Miranda had returned to Australia. 'He would sometimes take them on if they were single mothers or if he simply felt sorry for them,' she says. 'Apart from the odd f-word, Willie was the kindest man you could ever hope to meet.'

The management at Coventry Street had changed in 1961. Willie's fellow-director Richard Walton had discovered that working with Willie Donaldson, while in many ways a delight, had its problems. Walton had set up W & D Plays Ltd with Willie but, tragically for his bank balance, had opted to invest personally in *Here Is The News*.

But that, annoying as it must have been, was not the reason for his departure. 'I hadn't realised that W & D Plays really stood for Willie and Donaldson,' he says now. While his fellow director would make all the key decisions, it was Walton who had to face the music when they went wrong. If Willie had done a ridiculously stupid deal with the Cambridge Arts Theatre, it was Richard Walton who had to ring them and ask them to reduce their share of the gross. When the two top American producers, Alex Cohen and David Merrick, were in London to discuss the transfer of *Beyond The Fringe* to Broadway, it was Richard Walton who negotiated with Merrick when it became clear – 'humiliatingly clear', he says – that the intention had always been to go with Cohen. One day, quite soon after the opening of *Beyond The Fringe*, Walton decided that he had had enough of being W & D Plays' resident fall-guy and flak-catcher. He resigned, selling – or perhaps giving – his share in the firm to Willie's friend from Cambridge, Richard Dynevor. 'In the end,' Walton says now, 'life was just too short to work with Willie. He was a loveable rogue and I was delighted not to be in business with him any more.'

Money, as far as Willie was concerned, was a means to amusement rather than profit. When an entrepreneur called Eric Hatry approached him and Nick Luard with the idea of taking over a chain of sandwich bars in the West End, they were both intrigued. Hatry took them on a taxi tour of central London's sandwich bars, impressing them both by leaving the meter running while they met the bar managers. It was a great investment, they agreed, and parted with £2,000 each. Hatry, one of the West End's better known con-men, disappeared, having no doubt paid off the sandwich bar managers, each of whom was in on the scam. The chain had never existed.

Another scheme involved Willie putting up the money for a Rolls-Royce which would then be driven to South Africa, where it could be sold at a huge profit. As Willie's associate drove through France, there were occasional calls to England requesting money – the Rolls had a surprising number of mechanical problems – before silence descended. The associate and the Rolls had vanished as completely as Eric Hatry had.

Willie seems to have taken these setbacks in good part. When Nick Luard set up a new magazine called *Scene*, he naturally turned to Willie for a loan. Later, Elisabeth Luard overheard Willie asking her husband whether there was any possibility of being repaid. Luard replied: 'Willie, if you're going to talk like that, I'm simply not interested.' And they both roared with laughter at the idiocy of it all.

This attitude towards money is probably not ideal for a young theatrical impresario. 'Who was his general manager?' the doyen of theatrical producers, Michael Codron asks today. 'The problem was that there was no one in Willie's life to say, "Hang on, this two and two makes five ...".'

Willie's record as a theatrical producer bears out this analysis. The idea may have been good, and the writer talented, but somehow the productions tended to lose money.

JP Donleavy's *The Ginger Man* won rave reviews but was obliged to vacate the Fortune Theatre because the lease ran out, relocating to Dublin where its run ended in controversy. Donleavy's next play, *A Fairy Tale of New York*, won the author the *Evening Standard* Newcomer of the Year award in 1961 but was struggling to reach the break – that is, sell enough of the required percentage of seats each week night to hold its place at the Comedy, owned by Donald Albery.

There is a highly illegal and irregular process by which a producer can keep his play going. Called 'papering the house', it involves buying up tickets in bulk in order to disguise the decline in sales. For Willie, it seemed an obvious way out of his difficulties.

The house-papering for *A Fairy Tale of New York* was comprehensive. Bert Leywood trustingly distributed money among the barrow boys who worked near the office, instructing them to buy themselves tickets – for several days, his office was full of melons, bananas and oranges that had been given to him.

Richard Dynevor remembers giving some tickets to a Catholic priest who, disastrously misunderstanding the nature of JP Donleavy's fairy tale, distributed them to a group of children. 'Halfway through the second act, there was this terrible click of seats as the children were taken away.' Willie did his bit by handing out money for tickets at a nurses' hostel in Charing Cross.

Then resident in the Isle of Man, JP Donleavy heard that the production of his play was in trouble – or, as he puts it now, 'everyone had run and ratted on me'. Only Richard Dynevor was fighting his corner. Willie would later claim that at one point Donald Albery's son Ian, having been alerted as to what was going on, appeared in the foyer and, seeing Donleavy, accused him of malpractice, and was laid out by one of the writer's famous right hooks, but the story is denied by Donleavy himself.

There were other brave failures. In 1962, Willie put on a satirical evening at a club called Room at the Top, bringing together a new generation of Oxford satirists, which included Willie Rushton, John Wells and Richard Ingrams, and, somewhat bizarrely, Barbara Windsor. Ned Sherrin saw the show and, on the strength of it, recruited Rushton for a TV programme he was planning called *That Was The Week That Was*. (Ingrams, he says, 'did not catch the eye'.) John Wells decided, after appearing at the Room at the Top, to give up teaching to become a writer and performer. One night, the Kray twins were in the audience.

But somehow the revue never quite overcame the venue which Willie had chosen for it – above a furniture shop in Ilford. Later, he would write that an enraged audience had burned the club to the ground, but the truth is more prosaic. The Room at the Top is still doing business as a nightclub in Ilford, although its flirtation with political satire was not repeated.

In contrast to his professionalism when he became an author, Willie the producer was bad at following through a production, attending to the details and making it work. Sometimes he seemed to lose interest at the worst possible moment. A show called *So Much To Remember*, starring Fenella

Fielding and written by her with her friend Johnnie Whyte, was such a hit when Willie put it on at the Establishment that it was given a transfer to a West End theatre.

Well before its opening night, Willie had let things slip. The director was working on another play and was unable to direct rehearsals. With no one in charge, one of the older actors had disastrously expanded his own role. At the dress rehearsal, Fenella discovered that the set had been painted pink – a problem, since her character wore pink throughout. Publicity, Willie had decided, would be done by a PR firm from the wine business. 'He said they couldn't do worse than theatrical PR,' Fenella Fielding says now. 'Well, he was wrong. I'm amazed that Willie allowed the play to stay on as long as he did.'

Still benefiting from the reputation of *Beyond The Fringe*, Willie was playing the part of the theatrical impresario to the hilt. In November 1962, he was interviewed in the glossy magazine *Queen*. Photographed moodily lighting up a cigarette against the neon-lit background of the West End, Willie declared that there was not enough money to be made in the theatre and that he would like to go into films and TV. It was difficult to finance a straight play, he complained: 'I'm constantly writing ridiculous letters saying: "It's a marvellous play but I can't conceivably do it".'

It was true, but only to a certain extent. Willie discussed with the young playwright Clive Exton the possibility of putting on a play about an old English fascist called *Land of My Dreams*. He gave John Wain, one of the best of the new generation of novelists and author of *Hurry on Down*, some money to write a play called *The Restaurant*. Nothing came of it. In 1963, he put on Trevor Howard, by then a notorious boozer, in Strindberg's *The Father*, taking great care to ensure that the star's alcohol intake every night was enough to get him on to the stage and through the performance. Perhaps to keep Bert Leywood happy, there were productions of more traditional West End plays like *The Glad and Sorry Season* and a play unpromisingly entitled *A Cheap Bunch of Nice Flowers*.

In the same year, he set up a theatrical agency with Donald Langdon and another agent Moya Lennox-Pierce. William

The man in the camel-haired coat – conversing in Soho with JP Donleavy (top), profiled by *Queen* magazine (centre), and startled in the offices of Jack Waller Ltd.

Donaldson Associates was quite a hip agency for a while, according to one of their first clients, the actress Gaye Brown. 'Willie sort of knew all the right people,' she says. 'He appeared to be completely confident and was always on the verge of asking your opinion – you really felt part of something. When I got really down, I'd ring Willie and he'd tell me about these terrible things that happened to him, all with a sort of sad jokiness. I found his spirit extraordinary.'

Over these years, Willie discovered what he truly liked in the theatre. He could take or leave the traditional West End play and had seen that even satire could quickly be absorbed into the mainstream; *Beyond The Fringe* was such a West End favourite by this time that the Fortune Theatre had not only been graced by the Prime Minister Harold Macmillan but also the Queen ('The Queen has at last got off her Royal behind and is coming to see it,' Willie wrote to Miranda Skillman in February 1962).

His true passion was for the sort of show which his mother had taken him and his friends to – something with a comedian, with music, stunts and turns, dancing girls. The Sixties were just about to start swinging, the modern and the new was all the rage and so, with the unerring instinct of the boy who turned left at Winchester when the rest of the parade was turning right, he became increasingly interested in old-fashioned revues.

They were 'perhaps the most interesting thing to do', he told *Queen* magazine. 'You can get away with anything in a revue.' His ambition was to mount *The Royal Commission Show* by Spike Milligan, a theatrical event which would at one point have the band of the Coldstream Guards appearing on stage. It never came off, but he would remain determined to achieve his ideal theatrical experience, 'a large, vulgar, slapstick revue with nudes and peacocks'.

He had in fact been an early fan of Spike Milligan and, while in partnership with Richard Walton, had discussed various projects with him. Over lunch one day, Willie had given Spike a cheque for £1,000 (the equivalent today of around £14,000) to write a play. Some time later, *The Bed Sitting Room* was announced as appearing at the Mermaid Theatre.

'Wasn't that our play?' Willie asked Walton. It was but, too nice or perhaps too polite to make a fuss, Willie agreed to a small percentage and a credit as co-producer when it transferred.

In 1963, Willie discovered that the young writer Marty Feldman, whose *Bootsie and Snudge* was one of Willie's favourite TV sitcoms, wanted to put on a show which combined jazz and slapstick. 'I was extremely excited, since I admired Marty unconditionally. We met and got on extremely well,' he wrote later. The result was a hugely expensive extravaganza called *Wham Bam Thank You Ma'am*, which starred the black American jazz singer Oscar Brown Jr, Annie Ross, a twelve-piece orchestra, the veteran comedian Fred Emney and some dancing girls, which would include Jacqui Daryl, briefly the love of Willie's life. 'The show,' Willie would later write, 'embraced every comic tradition from pre-Monty Python surreal to picture-postcard slapstick, and achieved only a mystifying confusion.' It closed almost before it opened.

Another act, tailor-made for Willie, was The Alberts, the brothers Douglas and Tony Gray who, with 'Professor' Bruce Lacey, were a jazz band with a difference. Their image was of velvet-jacketed toffs, playing traditional jazz but they were natural stirrers and iconoclasts. Appearing at clubs like The Establishment and the Satire Club, they had gained a reputation for spreading unpredictable comic mayhem wherever they went. The Alberts had made records, produced by George Martin, with Spike Milligan and Peter Sellers. They had appeared with the Bonzo Dog Doo-Dah Band and were said to have been a formative influence on the band's most famous performer, Vivian Stanshall. But they shared with Willie a talent for self-sabotage and a taste for going too far.

Their act was heavily dependant on explosives, custard pies and absurdly tatty props. Halfway through 'Ragtime Cowboy Joe', a battered, badly-made pantomime horse would be dragged on stage. While a large and dignified lady singer sang the Edwardian song 'Pale Hands I Loved', Tony Gray would measure the distance from her to a machine which projected custard pies, firing it as the song reached its climax – and hitting his brother Douglas. During another number, the cello played by Douglas would explode.

With a slightly nervous Michael Codron, Willie put on *An Evening of British Rubbish* at the Arts Theatre. There were no nudes or peacocks and the band of the Coldstream Guards was not involved but, nonetheless, it went some way to being the big, slapstick revue to which he had aspired the previous year. There were certain regular acts – the programme mentions 'Dustbin Dance and Song', 'Yellow Bird and Custard Pie Machine', 'Indian Fakir and Oriental Orange Joke', 'Victorian Striptease' and 'Try Your Strength Machine and Mess' – and the strangely brilliant poet Ivor Cutler was part of the line-up, but at every performance the confusion would be slightly different. One night, they invited a mixed bag of celebrities, including David Frost, Lynn Redgrave, Joan Littlewood and the boxer Henry Cooper, on to the stage and gave them a champagne dinner on stage as the show proceeded. On a night when Princess Margaret and a number of European royals were gracing the theatre with their presence, The Alberts pretended to be doormen greeting the VIPs. On stage, they grumpily compared the tips they had received.

An Evening of British Rubbish received an ecstatic review from Bernard Levin, on the strength of which Don Langdon invited the two great Broadway producers David Merrick and Alex Cohen to London to see the latest revue from the producer of *Beyond The Fringe*, by then a huge hit on Broadway. 'I shall never forget the look of dismay on their faces,' says Langdon. Nonetheless in his view, the show was 'a great farting, dirty post-card of anti-chic absurdity'.

It almost certainly lost Willie money but he had enjoyed the experience of working with The Alberts so much that when, a couple of years later, they came to him with an idea for their peculiar version of Alexander Dumas's *The Three Musketeers*, the fact that his money was beginning to run out deterred him for not one moment. He brought back Eleanor Fazan as director, and this time managed to introduce a nude into the show during a bath scene, which was said to be the first time West End theatres would enjoy a brief, full-frontal moment.

It was during the rehearsals for *The Three Musketeers* that there was an accident backstage with The Alberts' explosives, which detonated, blowing the door off the gents', knocking, Willie would later write, the TV cop Stratford Johns off the lavatory.

The Alberts on parade in *The Three Musketeers*.

What exactly was Stratford Johns of *Z Cars* doing on the lavatory backstage at the Arts Theatre? The answer, of course, was that, if anyone was blown off the seat by The Alberts, it was not him. He was, on the other hand, a perfect comic choice. No actor could have been a funnier lavatory victim than the irascible, pop-eyed TV detective who somehow always wore the absorbed expression of a man sitting on the loo.

The Three Musketeers closed after two weeks.

Gangster backers, explosives in the lavatory, an Ilford satirical revue in front of the Krays: there are moments when it seemed that Willie's relatively brief career as an impresario was a protracted attempt to provide all the material for his later volume *Great Disasters of the Stage* single-handed. But no Donaldson disaster quite measures up to his personal favourite, the 1964 production *Nights at the Comedy*. It was, says Richard Dynevor, 'the only production that I know Willie really truly enjoyed producing'.

In his memoirs *Empty Seats*, Michael White takes a more caustic view, describing his involvement in the show as 'a major disillusionment', but that perhaps is understandable. White, who had agreed to co-produce the show with Willie, made the mistake of going on holiday for a week. Willie, looking for a theatre, sold White's share to Bernard Delfont. As Willie later used to tell JP Donleavy, it is important in life to know when to rat on people.

Nights at the Comedy was highly ambitious, pioneering a sort of avant-garde nostalgia. The idea was to transfer a number of ancient, rackety and outrageous music-hall acts from a pub on the Isle of Dogs called the Waterman's Arms, which was run by showman, broadcaster and man-about-town Dan Farson. There would be a troupe of Red Indians, a fire-eater, a woman with a very large snake, a formidable singer called Ida Barr, a Polish boxer who would take on members of the audience, Demetrius the Gladiator whose act involved blowing up hot-water bottles, a man called Bob who hit himself on the head with a tin tray while singing 'Mule Train', and, most notorious of all, a drag act called Mrs Shufflewick, famous for her outrageous routine and for her alcoholism. ('See this?' she would say, stroking a fur coat that she was wearing. 'It's made of untouched pussy. You don't get much of that in the West End.') Youth was represented by the young Jimmy Tarbuck, making his first West End appearance, and age by the great Jimmy James, making his last. As if the line-up was not combustible enough, the notoriously difficult and truculent Nicol Williamson was booked as presenter. 'This is going to set the West End back ten years,' Willie promised.

Each evening the audience was promised an 'astonishing guest artist' but, in an uncharacteristically masterful way, Willie vetoed Dan Farson's choice, Joe Brown and his Bruvvers, preferring what Farson would huffily describe in his memoirs as 'a "comic" group of middle-aged men with beards, top hats and large musical instruments'. Yes, The Alberts were back.

Williamson fell by the wayside during rehearsals and had to be replaced. A central idea of the show, that members of the audience could buy a drink from a bar at the back of the stage, had to be abandoned when the Comedy Theatre declined to remove the two front rows of seats. The bar, however, remained, allowing Mrs Shufflewick to tipple throughout the performance, making an increasingly scurrilous commentary about her fellow performers. 'Funny-looking fellah,' she said after a singer called Kim Cordell had sung 'If I Were the Only Girl in the World'. During the act with the snake, Mrs Shufflewick muttered loudly, 'Make a nice hand-bag, that'.

Ida Barr refused to sing through a microphone. The Polish boxer was knocked out cold by a member of the audience. The snake pissed on the stage. On the third night, Mrs Shufflewick collapsed after an excess of gin and purple hearts and had to be taken to hospital. She was back for the curtain call.

'It was a wild, wild evening,' reported the *Daily Mirror*. 'The only clean crack all evening was made by an Indian with a whip.'

It was too wild for the West End. Willie had done well with the second fortune he had made, his controversial profits from *Beyond The Fringe*, but after *Nights at the Comedy* the cupboard was pretty much bare. He had sold his share of *Beyond The Fringe* to Donald Albery and now Jack Waller Ltd went into receivership.

Willie's career in the theatre, which was now spiralling downwards, had mattered to him at the time, although even then he preferred to present himself as a dilettante – lazy, unreliable, morally unscrupulous. This assumed lack of seriousness, glossing over any achievements and apparently taking pride in disasters, has once again hardened into the accepted version of events. In accounts of the great and historically revered explosion of satirical talent in the early 1960s, Willie plays the role of an amiable hanger-on, a chancer with charm. Ned Sherrin, who worked with so many of those Willie helped launch into the public eye, remembers him principally for having had 'a lot of money and a lot of jolly friends'. To Richard Ingrams, he was 'a comic impresario'.

One of the few letters to have survived from the 1960s was from Penelope Gilliatt, who, in addition to being married to John Osborne, was one of the most respected theatre critics writing at the time. Willie had sent her an invitation to something which she had politely declined, adding:

> Your letter is an excuse for me to say that I think you've put on some of the best things in London for years. Not just *Beyond The Fringe*; the lot. There isn't another management

that comes within miles of you as far as sense of humour's concerned. I'm bad at writing fan letters and I'm always afraid that they may sound patronising but I really am a great admirer of what you're doing.

Yours ever,

Penelope Gilliatt

She was right. Beyond the anecdotes about collapsing sets, back-stage explosions and financial confusions, there is the sense of a real, unusual and prescient taste in revue and humour. It was Willie who staged John Bird's ground-breaking, over-adventurous satire *Here Is The News*, who backed the Fringers and, by daring to present them in a spare and confident way, contributed to their success. He was one of the first to recognise the talent of Marty Feldman, the promise of Terry Jones and Michael Palin, the unruly genius of Spike Milligan. Indeed when, a few years later, Willie was under attack from *Private Eye* for being, among other things, 'dissolute', 'disgusting', and 'an appalling little shit' – Milligan wrote a letter for publication:

> Zounds!
>
> I must say a word of defence for 'appalling little shit' Donaldson. He gave lots of beginners a break, ie *Beyond The Fringe, An Evening of British Rubbish* – when no one else would touch them and off the record I know quite a few actors who owe him money.
>
> Love,
>
> Spike Milligan

It was not only those who benefited from Willie's easy way with money when he was in funds who had cause to admire what he was doing. Michael Codron, who co-produced *An Evening of British Rubbish*, and has become one of our most distinguished theatrical managers, notes that Willie had the courage to pursue his own judgement. Buying Jack Waller Ltd had been shrewd but Willie, says Codron, 'had the greatest misfortune that could befall a producer – one of his first shows was a hit'.

13
The Love show

Willie's personal adventures during the first half of the 1960s were not unlike that of any other wealthy, confident bachelor with a powerful sex drive. Unfortunately, he wasn't a bachelor.

Songey's suspicions about her husband were correct. He was behaving badly even after – perhaps, especially after – his son Charlie was born in 1960. The young family moved from Hans Street to a larger flat in Queensgate. There were those parties at which Sonia was treated as a guest by the beautiful actresses swanning their way through Willie's life.

From the time he was at Cambridge, Willie had never had problems attracting women; an erotically lethal mix of wit, sympathy, manners, sexual confidence, and a whiff of danger served him well throughout his life. Not conventionally good-looking, he had an intriguing and distinctive style, square-shouldered and correct but with the air of someone who didn't quite fit into the world to which he should have belonged. With the camel-hair coat which Richard Walton had once given him, he gave the impression of someone playing at being an impresario and enjoying every minute of it.

Sarah Miles mentions in her memoirs *Serves Me Right* how he had seduced her while adjusting his cufflinks, but that he was never really one for showy nonchalance. 'He didn't have to seduce,' says Sonia Hobbs, who during that period was Sonia Dean, a supermodel and socialite.

Sonia had been a regular at The Establishment Club since the age of fifteen, becoming something of a mascot to the club. 'They were all after me,' she says, as unimpressed now as she seems to have been then. 'The charm of Willie was that he wasn't. He was a gentle, kind man – a guardian angel to me. We'd meet in cafés and, when I was in trouble, he'd come up with the right advice for me.'

With others, he was less angelic. There was the young leading actress appearing in one of his productions with whom he had an affair. During one intense romantic scene in the play, she would sink her hands into the pockets of a dressing-gown she was wearing; one night Willie complicated the scene by filling the pocket with condoms. A producer was startled to be told by Willie what some of the actresses would do for him at auditions in order to be cast.

Many of these stories were a tease. Although Willie's sexuality was already complicated, and would become considerably more so, he was never a cheerily promiscuous shagger, a quick-blow-job-from-the-ingénue man. In his extra-marital affairs at this time, a strong, sad sense of frustrated romance emerges. Part of him yearned for the straight, conventional pleasure of love, of a relationship.

In 1962, the actress Jackie Ellis, then married to Jeffrey Bernard, followed Willie to his hotel room during the provincial run of a play and, in Willie's version of the romance at least, they 'held hands all the way from Torquay to London, telling each other everything would be all right, even though we knew it wouldn't. I was going to leave my wife.'

Years later, he wrote that he left Songey, crying on the doorstep with two-year-old Charlie in her arms, to go and wait (in vain) for Jackie at the Basil Street Hotel – but that was a typically self-punishing dramatisation. In fact, it seems as if he slipped away quietly.

He had rented a flat and waited for Jackie. After a few days, she rang and told him that she was staying with Bernard, that she and Willie had been ships that passed in the night. It later emerged that a small fleet of ships had passed through the Bernard marriage at that stage. Willie went home.

A rather more serious love was another Jacqui who, to complete the coincidence, would also marry a celebrity alcoholic. Jacqui Daryl, the future Mrs Oliver Reed, was appearing in

Wham Bam Thank You Ma'am, when Willie fell head over heels for her. 'If one woman could have fulfilled my every fantasy it would have been Jacqui the Dancer,' he wrote years later. 'I looked at her and almost fainted with desire.' The affair with Jacqui the Dancer may not have lasted long, and it might not have meant too much to Jacqui, but it would stay with Willie for the rest of his life. Twenty-two years later, he would write: 'I haven't been hurt since 1963 when Jacqui the Dancer went off suddenly with a comedy tenor.'

But already, in his late twenties, Willie was becoming aware of a fault line in his intimate life. He was effortlessly attractive to beautiful, bright women who were perfect for him in every way, except one. They were not tarts. Willie was hooked from an early age on a world where desire was wicked and playful and, above all, uncomplicated by relationships or a future.

Willie was increasingly fascinated by sex as show, as business. Several of his friends from Winchester and Cambridge recall Willie as their guide into the world of prostitutes and by the early 1960s, he seems to have come to terms with this side of his character. At the time of *Beyond The Fringe*, the girls whom John Bassett calls 'Willie's naughty contacts' were known collectively as 'the Blues' and individually as 'A Blue', 'B Blue', 'C Blue' – Willie's Blues reached the end of the alphabet.

It was only a matter of time before this fascination with sex as show would influence his professional life as a producer. One of his very first production, *From the French*, staged in 1959, had been criticised for a striptease gratuitously included in the play. 'All successful dramatists know that indecency is valuable only as a spice,' Harold Hobson had written in the *Sunday Times*. 'It gives a flavour to other things, but you cannot make a play of it alone, any more than you can dine solely on cayenne pepper.'

Now the moment was clearly approaching for a full cayenne-pepper meal. Willie had been on to something when he had told *Queen* magazine that one could get away with anything in a revue. The script for a play had to be submitted to the Lord Chamberlain's office, where any words or deeds deemed too shocking or corrupting would be excised. In an unscripted show, the possibility of pre-emptive censorship by the Lord Chamberlain was reduced. Willie may not have had, as he later claimed, one of Noel Coward's drawing-room comedies typed up and sent in, but he certainly took a few liberties.

Now, with a new mood of sexual liberality sweeping the land, the days of the Lord Chamberlain were numbered, and Willie had a plan to take advantage of that moment of freedom. It was to be a revue that was entirely about sex. He called it *The Love Show*.

Or perhaps it was not his idea at all. The producer Michael White has written that the idea for a post-censorship erotic revue was inspired by the American producer David Merrick 'sometime before 1969' and developed by himself. White was sharing an office with Willie (everyone seems to have shared an office with Willie at some point) and, when the two of them fell out, he alleges that Willie stole the idea and approached Kenneth Tynan with it. Tynan and Willie certainly corresponded and even had an exploratory meeting with a potential director, the eminent, serious-minded and, one would think, absurdly inappropriate Peter Brook; he declined. Unfortunately, by the time Tynan had put together what would become *Oh! Calcutta!*, the most successful erotic revue of all time, Willie was once again on the run from his creditors. ('By this stage Willie Donaldson had disappeared from the scene,' Kathleen Tynan wrote in her biography of her husband – words that might have been a suitable epitaph for Willie.) Tynan went on without him, teaming up with none other than Michael White.

Willie was never slow to blacken his own reputation and others, with a more secure sense of their own part in history, have been quick to assume the worst of him. He was never, though, an ideas thief and the evidence suggests that, if anyone provided the original inspiration for *Oh! Calcutta!*, it was Willie Donaldson.

In 1965, a year before his conversation with Ken Tynan, Willie had approached Terry Jones, a young Oxford graduate who was appearing with his contemporary Michael Palin in a revue called *Hang Down Your Head and Die*. Willie took Jones to a Chelsea restaurant called The Soup Kitchen and asked Jones whether he would like to research and write a revue for him. Willie had little idea of its contents beyond the fact that it would be about sex and would be called *The Love Show*. He gave Jones a cheque for £50.

Obviously the place to start a show about sex was the British Library, where Terry Jones researched different sexual attitudes around the world and throughout history. 'What was in my mind was that this would be about the sexual revolution that was about to happen,' he says now. 'It was very influenced by the Kinsey Report.' Looking for a co-writer, Jones approached Miles Kington, who was not keen on the idea, and then Michael Palin, whom Willie also paid £50. For Palin and Jones, it was their first paid jobs as writers.

Willie must have been serious about *The Love Show* because he had already begun to work on a cast. Ambitious as ever, he had contacted in 1964 Robin Fox, agent of Sarah Miles, the famous and stunningly beautiful star of *Term of Trial*, *The Ceremony* and *The Servant*. As it turned out, *The Love Show* did not appeal to Sarah, but its producer did.

Accounts vary about how Willie and Sarah became lovers – against her suave cufflink-adjusting version, there is another told by Willie to a friend in which their need for each other was so great that they didn't even make it home, consummating their love halfway up the stairs. Either way, it had happened within a month of their first meeting.

They must have seemed the perfect couple. Sarah has always had a weakness for Wykehamists, she says. She came from a smart background, had a wanton, girlish beauty about her. She was outrageous, funny, stylish, driving around London in a sports car with Addo, her Pyrenean mountain dog. Like Willie, she had a complicated romantic past. Her enthusiasm for sex matched his.

Theirs was not exactly a furtive affair. Soon they were seen together at The Establishment Club, at first nights of Willie's shows, at a live performance of Willie's favourite comedian, Tommy Cooper. On one occasion, Sarah drew up outside Willie's house and hooted her horn until he emerged.

Songey was spending more and more time at her family's

With Sarah, 1964.

house down in Shepperton. After a weekend with her parents, she returned with Charlie to find a note from Willie: 'Have gone away'. And that, effectively, was the end of their marriage.

Sarah Miles has written about her love affair with Willie, and sometimes he emerges in an unexpected light. He had 'more fingers in more pies than any other impresario in London', she says, and would spend the day 'with his great nose for business shrewdly sniffing out the greatest acts in town' or dealing with creditors on her front doorstep.

Willie would rise at 9.30, my debauched Burlington Bertie, and dressed with hurried precision – whilst still at it, standing there in a striped shirt, tasty tie and pukka grey suit. How I loved it. I seemed to spend all my Willie D era more or less naked. He'd pull his fingers away so reluctantly before wrapping me tightly in my towel. Then he'd kiss as only a debauched Burlington Bertie could, before sauntering off like a toff. Willie liked making love, a lot, and no two ways about it, so did I.

Willie, Sarah knew, had secrets. 'Though his appetite for erotica bordered on the pornographic he was careful never to bring the latter home. I wondered what he was doing all day,' she wrote. But Sarah had secrets, too. As she explained to me, in words that have probably never been said by anyone else: 'Life with Willie was the straight life.'

Throughout a relationship which, with one highly significant interruption, lasted around two years, Sarah was also conducting an affair, once or twice a week usually, with Laurence Olivier. So far as she knows, Willie was never aware that he was being cuckolded by the greatest actor of his generation and infidelity, anyway, might not have been a problem. Willie recounted in his memoirs a night when Sarah went out to dinner with a French actor called Jean Pierre Cassell. He awoke to find Sarah standing at the end of the bed, her head bowed. 'I am guilty,' she said. Willie claimed that he had discovered that night that it was jealousy that really excited him.

Sarah, on the other hand, is unimpressed by this story. 'I didn't fuck Jean Pierre Cassell,' she says. 'When I came back, Willie was in such a state of rage and so determined that I should confess something, that I confessed just to shut him up.'

By the spring of 1965, the affair was beginning to peter out. Willie was ashamed of his money problems, and that he was living off Sarah. There was one more tranche of Donaldson family money that was due to him and that was in the gift of his aged Granny Grace, who remained stubbornly alive. 'When Granny dies, it will be striped shirts and chicken on Sunday for the rest of our lives,' he would tell Sarah.

Once, rather surprisingly since Willie's contacts with his family in Scotland were not close, his ancient grandmother met him in London. He took her out for an extremely long walk, hoping to hurry nature and his inheritance along. Granny Grace returned as spry as when she had left; Willie was shattered.

According to Sarah's memoirs, she had agreed to appear in a film shooting in Ireland that summer, and asked Willie to leave. There is, in fact, a small mystery connected to the first collapse of Willie's relationship with Sarah. Once, after she had been away, she found a woman's shoe in her flat and reached a decision that Willie had gone too far this time; it was the end of the road. What Willie did not, for his own reasons, reveal was that the shoe belonged to his friend Sonia Dean who had stayed at the flat – quite innocently, Sonia says.

Terry Jones visited Sarah's house in Hasker Street one day to find Willie sitting disconsolately beside his suitcase, thumbing sadly through a leather-bound book. 'I've been thrown out, m'dear,' he said. Jones asked what the book was. It turned out to be a first edition of Pope's poems. 'D'you want it?' Willie asked. Jones has kept the book to this day.

Sarah left for Ireland, where she had an affair with Julian Glover. Terry Jones went to work for the BBC. 'I hadn't thought about this before,' he says now, 'but I realise now that Willie was quite influential in that he showed me that material possessions needn't dominate one's life – that nothing has to be that serious.'

The summer of 1965 was a time of change for Willie, not all of it good. His business affairs were on the slide. He was divorced and saw neither his ex-wife nor their son Charlie. He had drifted away from his sister Jane and no longer worked with Richard Dynevor, although they remained friends. Others he had been close to, like Julian Mitchell, Anthony Beerbohm, Jinx Grafftey-Smith, were going their own way in the world. Sarah Miles had kicked him out. It must have seemed that nothing quite worked: not his productions, nor his marriage, nor even his relationship with a woman who must have seemed the perfect girlfriend.

As dawn was rising in St James's Park on the morning of August 4, Willie confessed to a new friend that 'something was missing with him and it was slowly being repaired'. The friend, who was about to become a lover, was the young American singer Carly Simon.

Willie and Carly: both of them would later refer to their affair glancingly in interviews but, even in Willie's odd life, it is an oddity. Although the affair was brief, it was important enough for Carly to have been on the brink of becoming the second Mrs

Willie Donaldson. 'We were only together for a short time, but he has cast a long shadow,' she says now.

Carly was approaching her twentieth birthday and, with her sister Lucy, had formed The Simon Sisters. She was contacted in New York by someone proposing some gigs in London. There was a contact there, a man called William Donaldson of Players and Writers Agency. She noted in her diary that on July 14 she first had an interview with Willie, visiting him at Sarah Miles's house two days later.

The timing was provident. Carly had been involved with two men and was about to solve the problem by leaving both of them, and Willie's relationship with Sarah seemed to have run its course. 'I feel very close to Willie even if he does call me Simon's Sister,' Carly wrote on July 20. She rented a flat at Wilton Street for ten shillings a week.

Carly, 1965.

At the time, Carly believed that Willie simply liked having her around. 'We were instantly attracted to one another's wit, Willie's being far more everything than mine, but me being a great audience.' Then, on July 26, she notes in her diary that Willie had broken off with Sarah. The timing is so suspiciously neat that it is safe to conclude that Willie actually engineered the shoe incident in order to be given his marching orders – he was never, after all, one to confront a situation head on. He found a flat at 6 Wilton Street, across the road from Carly's place. By the end of the month, Carly was noting that 'Willie has an old man's body. What is it that I want?' and, from the first week in August, they were with each other all the time. 'Oh Carly, watch out,' she wrote in her diary. Willie, rather extraordinarily, soon began to discuss marriage to the girl to whom he had given the nickname 'Little Frog Footman'.

During August, the two of them were caught up in a passionate, happy affair, going on trips to Cambridge to visit Willie's old rooms ('He was very sentimental about it,' Carly says now). Lucy Simon had flown over to join her sister, the flight apparently being paid for by Willie, but in fact by Carly. Lucy took a fancy to Richard Dynevor, whose ancient lineage had earned him the nickname of 'the King of Wales', and, while the Simon Sisters were doing auditions at Take One club and the Rehearsal Room above the Royal Court, the four of them would go out together.

Carly describes Willie as adorable and tender, a very ardent lover. 'It's pretty amazing that an affair can be so intense to halt me in that way. We had a wonderful sex life although, like me, he was shy of the way he looked and didn't want to be seen in the light.'

The Simon Sisters were needed back in America and booked on the liner the *United States* for September 6. Before that, though, they had reached a decision. Carly would put her life in order in America, then return to marry Willie. When she boarded the ship, she found a telegram from Willie, which read 'LITTLE FROG FOOTMAN COME BACK SOON'.

In America, Carly's friends were alarmed by her new plans and attempted, without success, to dissuade her from marrying the strange Englishman with whom she had fallen in love. She received letters daily from him and they spoke on the telephone every other day. She wrote two songs about him, 'You're The One' and 'The Best Thing'.

Then, quite suddenly, the letters stopped. He no longer seemed to be at Players and Writers and failed to return her calls. On October 24, Carly received a letter 'full of empathy and love and telling me how much he loved me', but telling her it was over. She should stay in America, he said. Her career was important. The letter, he told her rather unnecessarily, had been so difficult for him that it had taken four drafts to get it right.

Willie had, in fact, moved back to Hasker Street at Sarah Miles's suggestion. They resumed their affair but in a half-hearted way – not long afterwards, Sarah fell in love with Robert Bolt, whom she later married. By early 1966, neither Sarah nor Carly were part of Willie's life.

Eleven years after their affair, Willie and Carly were in touch with one another and conducted what she calls 'a tortured correspondence' over the subsequent five years during which Carly's two children with James Taylor were born and the marriage began to founder. In 1979, Carly, James, Willie and his girlfriend Cherry Hatrick went out for an Indian meal. Carly wrote from the QE2 liner on her way home: 'James thinks you are nearly perfect which is aided by your thinning hair, as his seems to be heading south as well and he finds you physically very appealing and fully understands why I cannot stop loving you.' In another letter to him, Carly says that he is the only man, apart from James Taylor, that she had really loved. Willie replied, saying that it had been 'marvellous and confusing' to see Carly again. 'There's not a day,' he told her, 'when I don't think about how my life would have been if we'd stayed together.'

Although Willie later upset Carly by reinventing the meeting with James in a comical (to him) and cruel (to her) manner, her emails to me, and occasional telephone conversations, have made it clear that their love has indeed cast a long shadow.

She still loves talking and writing about Willie, she told me.

'It's good to fill in some of the places creating a finer and tenderer gap where my imagination just did not do it justice. I don't think someone can feel so intensely without it altering the soul. Otherwise, what's the point?' Later she wrote: 'I'm so re-falling in love with him, it's hopeless, isn't it? Love through the goddam ages.'

As for Willie, he worried away at what had happened, and not happened, during the mid-Sixties for the rest of his life. In his memoirs, he told the story of how Sarah Miles had discovered in his wallet a photograph of two women entwined with one another. Understandably upset, she was confused by Willie's explanation that, while exciting, this sort of thing had nothing to do with their relationship – indeed, it would be embarrassing in that context. Gamely, Sarah asked why, if that was what he liked, he had not asked her to help out.

> 'You?' I was so startled that I struggled to find the most reassuring words. They came at last. 'Why would I want to do things like that with you? I *love* you.'

The same problem, Willie claimed, had arisen with Carly Simon. She had been 'the answer to any sane man's dreams – funny, quick, erotic, extravagantly talented', but, just before she returned to America to prepare for marriage, she had revealed too much of herself.

> Carly quite embarrassed me. She took a bath and then stretched out on the bed with nothing on. 'What do you think?' she said. She looked magnificent, in fact, but I felt most uncomfortable. She'd slipped embarrassingly out of character... This was a woman I loved and respected, a woman I was going to marry. No doubt I climbed into bed and turned away, thought about silent tall women prowling the stage with nothing on. Carly had confused herself for a moment with a Helmut Newton woman, a woman whose business it was to do this sort of thing, to pose and mock you at a distance, to wear thigh boots and stand in the corner if I told her to.

The fact that none of that, Carly says, actually took place is less important than Willie's need to invent and later present it as a reason that the relationship came to an end.

'The tragedy for Wykehamists,' he wrote, 'is that they try to turn fantasy into reality – but with the wrong people.'

For Willie's personal love show, 1965 represented the closing of a chapter. From here on, things were to become less innocent and more complicated.

14
A bitter insult to professionals

Late in 1965, even as his career as producer seemed damned, Willie continued to pursue ambitious projects. In addition to *The Love Show*, to be written by Terry Jones and Michael Palin, there was a play by the novelist Anthony Powell called *The Garden God*. In spite of its rather dashing theme – the Roman deity Priapus is disturbed by a group of archaeologists and returns to investigate, with some dissatisfaction, their sexual lives – it was a long way from *Nights at the Comedy* or *Wham Bam Thank You Ma'am*.

Powell, through a mutual friend Richard Schulman, had approached Willie, whom he describes as 'a pale fair-haired young man of decidedly raffish appearance'. Willie liked the play and, in spite of the fact that he was now almost completely without funds, behaved as if a production could be mounted at any moment. 'These lunches were thoroughly enjoyable,' Powell wrote in his autobiography *The Strangers All Are Gone*. Unfortunately there had been an unpleasant business in Liverpool, after which Willie had been obliged to go into hiding. 'No one seemed to know where he had gone,' wrote Powell. 'I never set eyes on him again in the flesh.'

The production which brought the curtain down on Willie's days as an impresario was a long way from the world of Greek gods and Anthony Powell. *London Swings* was to be, as one preview put it, 'a lively romp through such 1966 subjects as discotheques, bistros (and their owners), Batman and "fearless exposure" TV documentaries'. There were to be sketches, songs and what were ominously described as 'complicated magical effects'. Written by Peter Myers, who had scripted films for Cliff Richard and contributed sketches to *That Was The Week That Was*, the show had a cast of six, including Moira Lister, Amanda Barrie and Leslie Crowther.

Shortly before the show's provincial tour, it was decided that the title was unlikely to play well in Liverpool and Leeds, where it would be showing first. To ensure local support, its title would change with every venue, containing the telephone number of the theatre. On its opening three nights at Liverpool's Royal Court Theatre, for example, it would be called *Dial Liverpool Royal 5163/4*.

There was no opening night. During the last week of rehearsal at the beginning of September, it became clear that certain key elements – the set, basically – had not been paid for. Willie left a note for Myers at the Adelphi Hotel, saying that he was 'going to London to pick up some dibs. Keep cheerful. I think we have a hit. Love, Willie.'

In London, he rang his Uncle Fred and explained the problem. He agreed to release at least some of the £6,000 that was needed but then, the next morning, changed his mind. Willie went into hiding.

Back in Liverpool, the cast gamely kept going, working on the show into the early hours of each morning. The first night was postponed, and then the second. 'It's just a question of rehearsing the scenery,' Amanda Barrie told the local press. Leslie Crowther explained there were problems on the technical side. Moira Lister said that they all felt it was unfair to put on a show that was less than perfect.

On the third night, when there was still no sign of Willie or his dibs, *Dial Liverpool Royal 5163/4* was cancelled. Michael White who, in spite of his painful experiences with Willie in the past, had agreed to act as the production's guarantor, arrived in Liverpool, saw a run-through of the show and said there was nothing he could do to save it. Equity representatives arrived to help out the actors, who shared the small amount of compensation with the dressers and backstage staff. For several days, the slow collapse of Willie's last revue had dominated the front pages of the local press. Moira Lister returned to London, complaining of 'a bitter insult to professionals'.

Willie was in hiding for several weeks, first with Claire Gordon and then, briefly, staying in Sarah Miles's attic. He was now, at least until Granny Grace had the decency to die, completely broke.

It was in 1966 when Willie met up with his old friend from Cambridge, Mervyn Stockwood, who was now the Bishop of Southwark. The two had had dinner at La Popote.

'I am so glad you felt able to tell me something of the problems and worries of the past few years. I am afraid that you must have had a very sad time,' Stockwood wrote afterwards.

> I know what you mean when you say these things 'coarsen'. That, I suppose, applies to all of us. It's difficult for a bishop, for instance, as he runs his vast administrative machine, to remember that the machine is not an end in itself but an agency for love and compassion. However I have no fears for you. It was the same Willie that I knew at Cambridge – just as honest and sensitive, just as free from humbug and just as ready to mock at pomposity!
>
> Remember the next time you are in the depths – i.e. in a hotel room alone with a Bible – there is always an alternative at Bishop's House. We can even provide you a room without a Bible.
>
> My love
> Mervyn

This sad Willie, confiding in the Bishop of Southwark and talking of being alone in a hotel with a room with a Bible, is something of a surprise, and it would not be entirely unfair to point out that, if things had 'coarsened', then in certain key areas – family, finance, ambition – Willie had played a part in the process.

But it is perhaps significant that only two letters from his days as an impresario remained among his papers: that from the bishop and the note of admiration from Penelope Gilliatt. Willie was always more sensitive that he allowed himself to appear, and envious of those who led more serious and solid lives than his own. He may have chosen, at the time and in later years, to present himself as a dilettante who spent his money as a theatrical producer for the amusement of the thing or for the girls, but the truth was more complicated.

Although it was not the done thing to be seen to try too hard – even in the classless Sixties, the idea of the talented Englishman who wins without breaking sweat remained a potent myth for Willie's class and generation – his chosen career had mattered to him, and humiliating public failure brought a sense of shame that he was perhaps only able to share with the unlikely figure of the Bishop of Southwark.

The previous seven years had been a riotous switchback ride and, at the end of it, the young man who had once dreamed of being a dance critic, a great publisher or an influential producer was now a failed, broke ex-impresario whose last production, a provincial revue, had, in his words, 'been dropped off the end of the pier'. It was not what he had planned.

15
Mr Bear and Mrs Mouse do the sixties

The explosive failure that was *The Three Musketeers* had one positive side effect. Willie found the woman who would be his second wife. He had first worked with Claire Gordon when, at the age of seventeen, she had appeared in his first production, *Meet the Cousin*. Now they met again and it seemed to Willie that she was born to play the sex-bomb part of Lady de Wynter in The Alberts' latest extravaganza. By a lucky chance (or not), the role would involve Claire standing up naked when an ancient butler walked into her bathroom by mistake – 'Excuse me, sir,' he would say before shuffling off. Willie seems to have worked closely with his leading lady. 'I can't believe I'm allowed to fuck Claire Gordon,' he told one of The Alberts during rehearsals.

The affair blossomed into a relationship, much to the surprise of many of Willie's friends. Claire was a 'standard-issue Sixties chick', one of them told me. Taking up with Claire Gordon was 'a very odd thing to do', said another.

But Claire and Willie were important to each other. 'I was a handful, a real case,' Claire says now. 'He was the first relationship I ever had.' Willie was, she once said in an interview, 'just my type – tall, blue eyes and deplorably English!'

As for Willie, Claire was not only a fantasy figure – 'I had big breasts and long legs and was proud of my body,' she later reflected – but was someone with whom he did not feel the pressures and expectations of his class and background. 'Everyone thought Claire was a scatty bimbo married to an intellectual. The truth was exactly opposite,' he would later say. He called her Mrs Mouse and he became her Mr Bear.

Claire is still in showbusiness – when I met her, she had just been appearing in *Aladdin* at Hunstanton in Norfolk – and it is not difficult to understand her appeal. She is funny and sharp, an odd mixture of the knowing and the unworldly, with the air of someone who is in on the joke of her own sexiness and is happy to play along with it. She told me she had met Willie socially not long before she was cast as Lady de Wynter. 'I asked Willie, "Haven't I seen you at a disco?" and he said, "No, I've never been to a disco." Now everyone in those days went to a disco in their suits and beads. Everyone tried it on at a disco. So this was really very unusual.'

During 1966, she moved into his flat in Pavilion Road, renting out her own place to Scott Walker of the hit group, the Walker Brothers. Years later, when talking to the *News of the World* while promoting a fitness video called *Claire Gordon's Chair Aerobics* – 'RANDY SECRETS OF THE REAL MRS ROOT' was the headline – she mentions that she 'found Scott very sexy and when I visited him to collect the rent, we'd lay on the bed, kiss and fondle – with me always wearing a clingy, silky dress with no bra.'

By the time of the debacle that was *Dial Liverpool Royal 5163/4*, she was back in her own flat, fending off the angry calls. 'They would ring up and say, "Everyone's trying to find Willie, where is he?" and I would have to say, "I don't know", and they would say, "He must never ever do this again" and of course Willie was skulking in the background all the time. There was really quite a kerfuffle about it and I thought, well, this is showbiz.'

Broke, at least until Granny Grace died, Willie travelled around the country with Claire, as she appeared in rep at various provincial theatres. 'I think the most enjoyable time we had was Christmas in Blackpool, when I was appearing with Bootsie and Snudge of *The Army Game*,' said Claire. 'Willie loved that.'

During the run of *Doctor at Sea* in Brighton, she took her cat Tennessee to their digs and recalls that Willie was absorbed in James Agate's *Ego 8* – significantly, perhaps, the same book he had been reading over a decade before when he was with Julian Mitchell in the navy. 'He was kind of wonderful then. It was lovely coming home to Willie and Tennessee.'

With Mrs Mouse, 1970.

During 1967 Willie made two half-hearted and distinctly odd attempts at making a living. He taught briefly at a crammer and, when that came to an end, he hired a room in Seymour Street and then took out an advertisement in the *Marylebone Mercury*, offering his services as a masseur, calling himself 'Mr Grant'. Whether Willie was really trying to make a living on the game, or simply had magical hands, we shall never know. One of his first clients, he told Claire, had been David Jacobs, the gay showbiz lawyer who had helped him bring *Beyond The Fringe* to the Fortune Theatre and whom Willie had last seen when they had had lunch together at Le Caprice. Like Willie, Jacobs was operating under a pseudonym. Neither of them, Willie claimed, had broken cover and they transacted their business as if they were strangers.

But what exactly was the business? Claire Gordon recalls only that Mr Grant had four clients in all. 'I don't think any of them were actually ringing him for further appointments,' she says.

The picture that Claire Gordon portrays of her first eighteen months with Willie has a certain beguiling innocence to it. 'He didn't seem to have any ambition and that was why he was so easy to live with. He just wasn't driven by ambition.'

Sitting around in digs, re-reading James Agate, trying his hand as a masseur, unambitious, easygoing, Willie is so difficult to recognise in Claire Gordon's description of the months following the collapse of his hopes as a producer that it is tempting to see them as a sort of breakdown. For the first time, apart from his brief flirtation with *Tatler* journalism in 1959, he started to write, although nothing has survived from this period.

He also became uncharacteristically insecure about his relationship with Mrs Mouse.

From the start, Claire says, he would become enraged and excited when strangers looked at her as she drove around London. He had an obsession, she says, about men looking at her legs. 'It was really one of the things he quite liked, having his bird clocked by other people.' Now, two years after his divorce, he decided that living together was not enough. 'He said, "I've got to marry you – I don't want to lose you",' Claire says. 'I was his sex fantasy. He was marrying his sex fantasy.' At Marylebone Register Office on September 1, 1967, Claire Gordon became Mrs Donaldson.

'Neither of us got what we wanted from marriage,' she later told the *News of the World*, 'I thought I was marrying an intellectual and marriage would make me respectable. But the truth was, all Willie wanted was to be a swinger.'

Willie's version, recounted in his memoirs, is more complex. In about 1965, he wrote, the singer Annie Ross told him that something called the Sixties was about to start, for which he would need a Mrs Mouse. 'I'd do the Sixties with a Mrs Mouse, whom I found too obviously attractive but whom everyone else wanted to fuck,' he wrote. 'I'd have the perfect other woman on the premises. For a year or two, I'd not be bored at all.'

Both accounts agree on one thing. It was after his grandmother died at last, in 1968, that their marriage became more social. 'When Granny did die, it was the root of all evil,' Claire says now. The Donaldson Line had gone into liquidation in 1966 and Willie's final inheritance was worth just under £46,000 (around £550,000 today). He acquired a couple of model agencies, and bought a penthouse flat in a block called Ranelagh House off the Fulham Road.

Soon Willie and Mrs Mouse were organising what they called 'musical evenings' at their new flat.

'Willie was very interested in bad cabaret acts,' Claire explains. 'There was Jack the Tramp who was paid seven pounds to light himself up in ultra-violet and play the saw. Zelda Plum was a rather large lady who used to do a striptease with a chinchilla on her head. One day our Burmese cat nearly caught the chinchilla. Somebody else would do something with an accordion on the stairs. Then there was a man called Richard who could recite fourteen verses of *Eskimo Nell*. It was silly really.'

Willie wrote various scurrilous accounts of the musical evenings at Ranelagh House, not one of which has been confirmed by Claire Gordon. In a *News of the World* interview, she said that it had been distressing for her to discover that her husband was turned on by kinky parties and wanted to use her in group sex games. In the end, the paper reported, Willie's 'sexy antics proved too much for her'.

There are differing views on these musical evenings. Few of those I have interviewed have spoken about them with huge enthusiasm. Willie's former colleague Don Langdon had been disappointed to find they were 'innocent, innocent ... Nothing occurred. I once asked when something was going to happen and I was looked at with great disapproval.' Virginia Ironside, now the *Independent*'s advice columnist, was another guest who discovered nothing shocking at Ranelagh Gardens.

All the same, there is little ambiguity in the way Willie wrote about doing the Sixties with Mrs Mouse. It was a time in that decade when the relative innocence that preceded the Summer of Love in 1967 had tipped into something seedier and more perverse. The evidence is there in the films, in magazines like *IT* or *OZ*. Sex was no longer part of some great universal revolution, a metaphor for freedom; it had become an end in itself.

According to members of the Drugs Squad, who attended the parties as part of their undercover surveillance, soft drugs were an important part of the musical evenings, hash cakes being regularly served to guests, and the police soon had a warrant to search the flat.

The visit of two police constables from the Drugs Squad did not, curiously, occur when a party was in progress. In fact, Willie claimed at the time that, although he did have some pot at the flat, the officers failed to find it and solved the problem by planting the evidence on them. So incensed had he been that he reported them to Scotland Yard, filing an eleven-page statement of complaint.

The bust turned out to have been doubly annoying. Not only did Willie insist that stuff had been planted on him, but a free-lance agency cleaner, who had arrived just as Willie and Claire were being taken to Chelsea Police Station, had turned the situation to his advantage by burgling all the valuables in the flat. When they appeared in court, Willie and Claire pleaded guilty to possession. No further mention was made of the complaint against the police but later, after one of the officers involved was jailed for perjury during a clampdown on corruption in the Drugs

Squad, Willie would write up his version of the incident, a story he repeated in various works over the next twenty-five years. The officer still insists that the drug-planting story was fiction.

It would be a mistake, in view of later events, to see Willie as a serious Sixties pothead. He certainly liked the occasional smoke at the end of the day and always regarded cannabis as incomparably less harmful than alcohol, which he hardly ever touched, but there is no connection, I believe, between his casual use of pot in the Sixties and the Seventies and the crack cocaine habit he developed in the mid-1980s.

In the end, Willie wrote, he discovered that Mrs Mouse was not as contented with this way of life as he was.

> It turned out that Mrs Mouse was a civilian at heart, wanting a dressing table and to give dinner parties for nice people … she failed as the perfect other woman. But she taught me a lot – not least that you must start with the fiction, create the life you want to act and then cast the other parts appropriately. Fantasy comes first, then you fall in love with the created object. It's an act of faith – like religious belief. And you must remain loyal to this fictional object of your love, this perfect other woman. Finally, you must live with her, rather than visit a service flat in the afternoon. Mrs Mouse didn't want her home to become a service flat. But she bridged the gap.

Claire Gordon's view is, as ever, more straightforward. 'Looking back on it now we both loved each other very much but it was a rather sad, naïve relationship,' she said.

16
Blasphemy at the Criterion

Willie's business dealings in 1968 and 1969 involved a flurry of acquisitions, sometimes of agencies which, he discovered too late, brought with them a trail of undeclared debts. He employed and went into business partnership with one or two people whose entrepreneurial soundness would not have stood up to the most cursory examination. Although it all must have made some kind of sense at the time, his behaviour during this period has the air of a sustained, probably subconscious, attempt finally and definitely to blow his last inheritance and to rid himself of the curse of money.

Within months of Granny Grace's departure, Willie had set up two businesses at an office in Albemarle Street. A model agency called Nichol Chaulet was jointly run by Leah Chaulet and a randy, enterprising Australian called Ray Nichol.

Then there was Westminster Artists, a theatrical agency for which Willie employed David Barclay, a man whose ambition far outstripped any sense of reality. Barclay would regularly dictate improbably ambitious letters to Willie's secretary, Cherry Hatrick, who had joined the firm, having previously worked for Tim Williamson, a former colleague of Willie's from his Players and Writers days. Cherry would type up the letters, get them signed and then throw them away.

There were certain in-built problems in the new set-up. 'Diamond Dave' Barclay was unreliable, as was Ray Nichol, whose real name turned out to be Bruce Jenkins. There were too many people working at Albemarle Street. Willie's attitude towards money was more wayward than ever. Although he always liked to work on figures (his files and folders reveal an obsession with doing sums), according to Cherry Hatrick his calculations were invariably wrong, a result of an optimistic form of mathematics which involved rounding up income and rounding down expenditure. Soon the creditors were gathering once more. When the heat was turned on one of the two agencies Cherry would tell those at the door that all the assets at Albemarle Street belonged to the other.

Apparently unconcerned, Willie breezed from one crisis to another. Describing his working day, Cherry says, 'he had coffee with people, then he had lunch with people and then he had tea with people'. He cheerily invested in a new musical called *Lie Down, I Think I Love You*. It ran for one night. 'Get up, I think I hate you,' wrote one reviewer.

In spite of increasingly desperate juggling of the figures, it was reported in early 1969 by the *Financial Times* that Willie was bankrupt. Somehow he must have laid his hands on new funds because he was soon responding to financial crisis in the way he knew best – by spending more money. A theatrical agent suggested that Willie might take over his business, omitting to mention that money to his clients had not been paid for months. Willie agreed. A large respected model agency, Jean Bell Ltd, which had offices in the King's Road, also became available and was quickly snapped up. The firm had been losing money and, when the Nichol Chaulet Agency merged operations in the King's Road, it was discovered that Jean Bell's staff were on lower salaries. They were all given pay rises. The losses increased.

Late that year Carl Snitcher, the assistant director and legal officer of Equity, the actors' union, was sitting in his office when his secretary announced that someone had come to see him. The visitor walked into his office. 'My name's Willie Donaldson,' he said. 'How much do I owe you?'

Willie's last foray into the theatre was an odd affair. He had set up yet another company, called Film and Television Copyrights which, he thought, would finance and develop screenplays. It had always been something of an ambition of his to move away from the theatre but FTC Ltd had not been involved in any projects in the new media. In 1969, though, it came into its own – with a theatrical production.

When Carl Snitcher first suggested to the Equity General Council that Willie Donaldson was proposing to go back into theatrical management, his colleagues were adamant: Donaldson was not going to make monkeys of them a second time. In the end, though, Snitcher managed to persuade council members to relent on two conditions: Willie would pay back the money owed to Equity after the Liverpool fiasco. He would also deposit enough money in an escrow account to act as insurance against a further debacle.

Willie's partners in FTC were Anthony Perry, a film producer with what he describes as 'a reputation for respectability' and Jean Legris, a smooth, good-looking Anglo-Frenchman who was born to an English mother and had a public school education but now worked in France with, among others, Alain Resnais.

It was an unlikely team. Willie and Jean were kindred spirits – dashing, unreliable, ill at ease with their privileged backgrounds – but Anthony was altogether more serious-minded. His involvement must have helped give FTC an air of solidity, although to judge from Anthony's memories today, there was on Willie's part an element of game-playing in their relationship. Throughout his life Willie loved to tweak and tease respectability.

On one occasion, Anthony and his wife visited the Donaldsons and there was what he calls 'a terrible sexual *frisson* when we went there'. They were obliged to watch a porn film before making good their escape. On another occasion when Anthony called round, Willie and Claire were preparing for a party and Willie offered Anthony one of their famous little brown cakes. 'I discovered later that they were naughty. I bloody nearly killed myself on the way home.' Now and then Willie would confide in Anthony, alleged secrets from his casting sessions. 'He told me all the naughty things the actresses did with him. They – and this is not my phrase – went down to him.' (Willie was teasing; the one sexual activity in which he had no interest was the blow job – 'So *boring*', he would later complain to Rachel Garley.)

Jean Legris had seen a production in Paris of a play called *Le Concile d'Amour*, which had been written in 1893 by a German playwright called Oscar Panizza. It was daringly satirical, featuring the revenge of an ill-tempered God on the depraved Vatican of Pope Alexander VI, and, in the French production, stylish and funny. It was also sexually explicit, with an orgy scene taking up much of the second act.

He contacted Anthony Perry with the idea of an English production and Anthony spoke to Willie. They both became 'quite enthusiastic in a lazy way', says Legris. Anthony wrote later that *The Council of Love* 'really did seem a sure-fire winner. "You can't go wrong," everyone said, but actually you can, and we did.'

But what was Willie playing at? His last production, a little over three years previously, had ended in humiliating failure. He was *persona non grata* at Equity and the Society of West End Producers. His reputation was not good – 'I always noticed that the fact that I was working with Willie didn't impress people,' Anthony Perry told me rather sadly – and what money he did have was draining away fast. He was not hooked on the theatre; in fact, apart from his mad music-hall acts, the stage had begun to bore him, even when he was part of that world.

But the model business, while providing a satisfactory drain on his funds, must have seemed tame after the excitements of his evenings of British rubbish, those eventful nights at the comedy.

Since his enforced retirement, there had also been a significant change in the theatre: the Lord Chamberlain, under the Theatres Act of 1968, had lost his power to censor plays. The first theatrical event to benefit significantly from the new permissiveness was that distant relation of Willie's *Love Show*, *Oh! Calcutta!* Kenneth Tynan's production had been an off-Broadway hit in 1969 and was due to open at the Roundhouse in London during the summer of 1970. Extravagant, outrageous, and shockingly sexy, *The Council of Love* must at some point have seemed the perfect vehicle for a great Donaldson comeback.

He looked around for backers among his old friends. Donald Langdon, who had founded the film company Hemdale, obliged, buying up a majority share. Willie, with Anthony Perry and Jean Legris, had soon hired an impressive array of talent. The translator and adapter would be John Bird, by then something of a star of satire on the BBC. The director was Jack Gold, who had an impressive string of TV credits, and who would go on to direct *Goodnight, Mister Tom* and *The Naked Civil Servant*. Eleanor Fazan was back to do the choreography, and original music would be written by Carl Davis. The cast would include Warren Mitchell as the Devil. *The Council of Love* would open on August 20 at the Criterion Theatre.

But things rather soon began to go wrong. John Bird was hopelessly late with the script, in spite of Anthony Perry's increasingly desperate urgings. Although Perry has described Bird's script as 'brilliant', Legris still believes that the text should not have been modernised in tone – Willie's idea, he says. 'It amused him to make it more scandalous and of its time,' Legris told me. 'There was a sort of connivance between him and John Bird to make it as rude as possible. When I contacted Leonor Fini, the designer of the costumes for the Paris production, and asked her if we could use them, she said it was out of the question – not with that crappy script. The problem was that instead of it being visually beautiful, it had a sort of English vulgarity to it.'

That 'sort of English vulgarity' sounds distinctly familiar. It had been what had concerned Kenneth Tynan when Willie had first discussed with him his idea for a love show. Vulgarity tends not to be arousing. Although Willie would later say that sex was the one thing he took seriously, his presentation of it, on the stage and later in his writing, never quite had the po-faced intensity required for erotic entertainments that aimed, above all, to excite. The ridiculousness of sex kept breaking through; some sort of Alberts-like mishap was never far away.

The Council of Love was not a happy production. Jack Gold felt uneasy with this material and once again Eleanor Fazan, Dr Fiz, had to come to the rescue – looking after a tricky orgy scene in

iff and
th this
ng on
to do
and

Gold
vertis-
the
ook a

rival
and
ard
nt.
re

ly

at Willie's expertise in the matter
t consultative role turns out not to
ould watch rehearsals from the back
much too shy to appear on stage.
ut what was being asked of the cast,
stification. 'We wanted the girl who
to get down to business properly,' says
danger of a cast strike at one point, with
g an appropriately devilish role in the
earsed with a view to performing in a big
ly the Criterion was available, had to cut
uce the production values.

that he was unable to visit the Criterion very
doing a TV series at the BBC, but sensed that
remember going down a passage backstage and
an archangel, holding a drink in one hand and
e other, walked towards me, bumping into the
ng "Fucking amateurs" as he brushed past me.'
ar at what stage Willie took to his bed. According
: 'The whole thing was becoming a catastrophe. It
ing with the first director and we had to get in
age to save the situation. I'd go back and see Willie
ing and he would be in bed.'

ne could accuse the production of lacking adventurous-
here were orgies in the papal court, a stark-naked cardinal,
a whining and resentful Jesus, a Virgin Mary knitting a shroud
for her son and a wheezing, knackered God who is enraged that
the church has sent a saint up to heaven on the grounds that she
has been raped two hundred and eight-four times, mostly by
Benedictine monks.

Willie must have been aware that the production was in
trouble by the time it opened in August 1970, but all the same
he wrote a touching letter of thanks to Eleanor Fazan.

Dearest Eleanor
    At least I'm glad I've got another opportunity to write
one of my embarrassing letters of gratitude to you. I think

you know how I feel about you, although I'm too s
paralysed to say it to your face. I hope we get away wi
one so that I can do another show, with you directi
your own and with us strong enough to allow you
what you really want, unsurrounded by confusions
compromises.

    Very much love
    Willie

The reviews for *The Council of Love* were not good. Jac
departed on the day of the opening. In spite of lurid ad
ing which played up the evening's sexual content
production was already in trouble when things suddenly t
turn for the worse.

    Within a week of the play's opening night, high-minded
producer Geoffrey Russell, managing director of Linnit
Dunfee, was reported on the front page of the *Evening Stand*
to have complained to Scotland Yard about the play's cont
The producer William Donaldson was quoted as saying, 'We
not taking this complaint too seriously.'

    A rather more serious threat came from the Dowager La
Birdwood, a nutty fascist who had just been pronounced by th
Guardian as 'the sharpest thorn in the side of the permissiv
society'. Having unsuccessfully reported the immorality of
Oh! Calcutta! to the police, she was tipped off that significant
blasphemies were occurring every evening at the Criterion
Theatre. With a small group of morally minded folk, she attended
one show, barracking some of the ruder scenes, then returned for
three more nights to confirm that what she had seen was as shocking as she thought. Hymns were sung outside the theatre. Lady
Birdwood then reported the production to the Director of Public
Prosecutions for breaking the laws of blasphemy.

    It was an unusual charge. With uncharacteristic thorough-
ness, Willie had consulted a lawyer at an early stage. Although
the original play's author Oscar Panizza had experienced a few
problems on this score, being jailed for two years for blasphemy, counsel had reassured Willie that the most recent case

had taken place in Britain in 1883 and that the danger of prosecution was slight.

He under-estimated Lady Birdwood. The peculiarities of the
blasphemy laws meant that it was the people deemed to be directly
responsible for what happened on stage, the director and the
choreographer, who would be prosecuted. Jack Gold and Eleanor
Fazan faced a charge of having directed a performance of *Council
of Love*, 'which performance was blasphemous in that it did
violently and ribaldly vilify, ridicule and scoff at the Christian reli-
gion and did in like manner impugn its doctrines'. Months after
the show had closed following its brief run, they were ordered to
appear before Bow Street Magistrates on February 18, 1971.

They had the good sense to consult a barrister with a reputation for taking on cases that concerned freedom of speech – John
Mortimer. Brilliantly, Mortimer convinced the court that, in
order to be guilty of blasphemy, Gold and Eleanor Fazan would
have needed to be physically present in the theatre, supervising
the actors' every sinful move. They were not, and therefore had
no control over what happened on the stage, Mortimer argued.
Birdwood's barrister was so awestruck by the presence of
Mortimer and the cleverness of his argument that he virtually
conceded the case. The prosecution was slung out. When Lady
Birdwood asked leave to bring a case against the producers and
the author, the magistrate angrily waved her away.

At it happens, they might have had difficulty finding one of
the producers, Willie Donaldson. By the time the case reached the
court, he was not, as he would later claim, counting his earnings
in a foreign bank account, but nor was he to be found in court.
Willie had bolted yet again, leaving his adored Fiz to face the
music alone.

It was not his finest hour, but it now emerges that his behaviour might have been even worse than even he has admitted to.
Who was it who tipped off Lady Birdwood in the first place?
Donald Langdon remembers that Willie had planned to leak
news of the disgusting immoralities taking place at the Criterion
to those who would be most outraged. The row that followed,
he had thought, was bound to be good for business.

It would be entirely typical for Willie to alert the very guardian of public decency who would cause him and the play most trouble. Throughout his writing career, he was forever grassing himself up to the authorities, at various points in his career inviting the attentions of the police or the press or libel lawyers upon himself; it was the only form of self-promotion that really interested him. 'Whenever I've tried to invade someone's privacy – not least my own – my efforts have been humiliatingly rebuffed,' he once complained.

Why, though, had he failed to turn up at the trial of Eleanor Fazan and Jack Gold? He was in the company of Richard Dynevor and they were both staying in Paris with Jean Legris, but he would have known that the trial was taking place. A clue is contained in Julian Mitchell's diary entry for May 1971. 'Willie Donaldson came for lunch – what little hair he has left down to his shoulders. I *am* fond of him... He's had a dreadful time – with wife, with the police, with his hopeless business ventures. He had a breakdown in the winter, he says, and I can well believe it.' Willie told Julian that he had been unable to see him or any other of his 'intellectual' friends for feelings of shame. 'I think he's desperately lonely, probably. This breakdown took the form of just not going out, just sitting, being depressed. And he's so ashamed of himself: I think it drives him to do things to make him even more ashamed.'

Willie, Julian concluded, had reached 'that interesting age when men break with their past lives, and start again, if they're going to'. He was right about that.

17
Through the bottom of a glass-bottomed boat

The firms which Willie had bought with the Granny Grace inheritance were snuffed out, one after another, at the end of 1970 and the beginning of 1971. He was back in the doghouse at Equity. The newly powerful voice of public morality, *Private Eye*, began a sustained campaign against him which it would pursue pretty much until the day he died. Ranelagh House was sold. He was completely, utterly and definitively skint and no more Donaldson Line money was going to come his way.

He was free at last.

In Paris that February, Willie and Richard Dynevor began to plan for the future. They visited the Left Bank bookshop Shakespeare and Company and hatched the idea of opening a secondhand bookshop for English-language books in Ibiza.

They took the train south and Richard remembers Willie's mood of elation, his sense of a new beginning. For most of the journey, and at a restaurant in Barcelona, there was exuberant talk of his new plans. He was going to be a writer. They would live in Ibiza with their bookshop. 'He was very optimistic about it all,' says Richard. 'Really on top of things.' There would be no more limited companies or agencies or theatrical productions. Willie, Julian Mitchell later recorded in his diary, 'had a moment of utter happiness – just being with a friend, talking, away (I presume) from his idiotic, bungling life. Then he felt immensely sad because that wasn't a proper life, either.'

The Donaldson marriage was in difficulties by now, but, when he returned to England after the exploratory trip, Claire agreed to accompany Willie to Ibiza. Although the flat at Ranelagh House had been sold, not much of the money can have survived Willie's financial earthquake, because by the time he arrived in Ibiza with Claire, he was low in funds.

At first it all went well. Ibiza had become a place where, from the late 1960s onwards, a hippie aristocracy would live or stay. 'Ibiza was discovered by the Beautiful People,' Damien Enright, who lived there at the time, has written.

> Nico (of the Velvet Underground), Nina van Pallandt and Baron Frederik (of Nina and Frederik fame), Terence Stamp, Charlotte Rampling, Terry-Thomas, pieces of the Beatles, bits of the Stones, jet setters and groupies arrived in velvet, lace and delirium, hot for a cool time. Restaurants and boutiques burgeoned. By the early 1970s, Ibiza was the hippest place in Europe for drugs, sex and style.

'Everything became marvellous in Ibiza,' Richard Dynevor recalls. Willie had found possible premises for his bookshop which was to be called Shakespeare & Son, but soon an even better plan emerged. Willie would spend his last £2,000 on a great business venture. He bought a glass-bottomed boat.

'I have one epigram for you this lunchtime.' Thirty-five years later, Willie's contemporary Andrew Sinclair recalled those years, amusement bringing his normally lugubrious face to life: 'You cannot see your future through the bottom of a glass-bottomed boat.'

As it turned out, very little could be seen through the bottom of a glass-bottomed boat. Sinclair's brother, who lived in Ibiza and who sold the *Capitan-Wylly*, as by happy chance it was called, to Willie for £2,000, failed to inform him that the lease on its berth expired in early 1972. He did well at first with his team, a *capitano* in whose name the boat had to be registered and a Yugoslav deckhand, or *marinero*, called Gabriel. But when, after the winter, he had to take the boat to a town called Portinax in the north, everything began to go wrong. The currents around the north coast ensured that the water was thick and brackish, rendering the *Capitan-Wylly*'s glass bottom an irrelevance.

Gabriel returned to his alternative career, making leather goods. The money stopped coming in.

All was not well between Willie and Claire. Their rows became more frequent. Willie the impoverished boat-owner seemed to have been rather less enjoyable company than Willie the theatrical impresario. At some point relations deteriorated to such an extent that Claire threw his suitcase out of the window and asked him to leave. He would later claim that he slept like an abandoned dog, under the window of her flat for some days.

The early months of 1972 were an extraordinarily grim period for Willie. With no place to live, he slept on the beach under his boat. The business was no longer making any money. He was alone, homeless, and with only the clothes he stood up in. For two or three months, he was close to starvation. It was, says Richard Dynevor, 'absolute hell for Willie, a really shocking experience'. When Richard learnt the gravity of the situation, he paid the rent on a small flat in Ibiza Town which Willie then shared with Gabriel, the *marinero*, with whom he had once again become friends.

Even now, as the Ibizan dream faded, Willie continued to believe that something could be salvaged. In the autumn he wrote to Richard Dynevor to say that his books were on their way from London to provide the basic stock for what would be a library in Ibiza Town. But by the time the library stock had made its slow progress from London, Willie was moving on.

It is time to introduce Emma Jane Crampton.

A pretty, nicely spoken girl from the Home Counties, Emma Jane had worked as a temporary secretary in Willie's office during the late 1960s when she was in her late teens. She had attended one or two of her boss's musical evenings and had been having an affair with him when the business folded. Finding herself out of work, she had taken up a new career as a call girl. She had proved good at this new job and had found that the freedom and variety it offered suited her temperament. Emma Jane Crampton is, of course, not what she is called, but is the name Willie gave her when he came to write about her.

In the early autumn of 1972, Emma Jane received a brief and unexpected letter from her former employer. Shortly afterwards, he rang her and invited her out to Ibiza. She flew out and, for the first two days of her holiday, the couple stayed at a hotel in Talamanca. It was at that point that Willie confessed his financial situation. For the rest of the two weeks of her stay, Emma Jane lived with Willie, and Gabriel, at their small flat in Ibiza Town.

After she had left, Willie reached a decision. He found the *capitano* in whose name the ownership of the *Capitan-Wylly* had been vested. It was agreed that the *capitano* would take back the boat, paying Willie the sum of £250. He bought a ticket home.

In October 1972, there was a ring at the door of Emma Jane Crampton's flat off the King's Road. Standing on her doorstep carrying a small suitcase which contained all his worldly possessions, was Willie.

Capitan-Wylly revisited. This photograph was taken in 1984.

18
How many pupils of FR Leavis have ever become ponces?

The way Willie told the story, he had, for once in his life, landed on his feet. He had no responsibilities because he had no money. Apart from a small number of close friends, nobody knew where he was, or even that he was back in London. He was out of contact with his sister, his first wife and his son, with all the problems and expectations that families bring. Mrs Mouse was living her life away from him. He lived in a flat in the part of west London which he loved. Emma Jane Crampton, who kept him, had a way of life which was perfect for a voyeur. He was a ponce, a man who lives off immoral earnings. There were contacts with the underworld, outrageous stories of bent policemen and pervy politicians. Attractive, misbehaving women were all around him.

Another, less comical way of looking at his situation was that he was on his uppers, that the man who had once had money, influence and a sort of reputation now had nothing. He was in his late thirties, with no obvious professional skills and, as he had discovered that morning in 1958 spent at Mather & Crowther, little capacity for being an employee. Poncing, in real terms, meant accepting handouts from his girlfriend.

Willie had always been diffident about his writing skills. When in 1960, a collection of Cambridge and Oxford writing was put together in anthology, he was the only editor (the others were John Fuller, Julian Mitchell and Robin McLaren) not to contribute himself. Now though, he had little to do with his time, and was surrounded by the perfect material for his particular talent.

'He's really only interested in two things – sex and the police,' Julian Mitchell recorded in his diary of September 13, 1973. Perhaps, Julian had suggested, Willie was leading such an extraordinary life that he should consider writing it all up. 'How many pupils of FR Leavis have ever become ponces?' he asked. Willie replied that he couldn't write but, Julian added, 'I suspect he rather does want to'.

He did. The distance that he maintained from his own life ('He observes it all, as it's happening, with his old wry – no incredulous – detachment,' Julian Mitchell wrote) was a positive asset when it came to writing about it, tweaking, twisting and generally sprucing up reality for better comic effect.

'What of the role of the ponce?' he pondered in the account of his life that he was now beginning to write.

> In many ways it ought to be one of the most desirable. It has little public status and as a convenient label at a cocktail party it's pretty much a non-starter. Thanks to this role, the surface facts of my life are better than they've ever been. The grub's good; there are two colour television sets; cash is distributed like Monopoly money; nobody harasses me; sensual stimulation is more available than it should be to an old fart; for the first time in my life I have a job that doesn't require me to traffic with unacceptable people. I have no problems.

The opening line of Willie's first book – 'Living in a brothel isn't everything it's cracked up to be', was not entirely accurate. The brothel to which he was referring was the flat he shared with Emma Jane, who for a while worked from home but later hired a room elsewhere, which she shared with another working girl.

Emma Jane, with her private-school background, shared Willie's amusement at the world in which they now found themselves. He was proud of what she had made of herself, seeing her and her call-girl friends who, in his books, went under such names as Dawn Upstairs, Pretty Marie, Scatty Sally, Dopey Linda and Stella Who Stutters, as not only funny and charming but as incomparably more honourable than, say, policemen or politicians. 'They were *excited* by themselves,' Julian wrote, having met Emma Jane and Dawn Upstairs. 'They seem to have an amateur for-kicks attitude, tho' it is what they do for a (goodish) living.'

A guest who had been invited, with his wife, to dinner with Willie and Emma Jane recalls that there was a lengthy interlude between the first and second courses while Emma Jane popped upstairs to turn a trick in Dawn's flat with a client. Work completed, she returned and served up the chicken.

Willie seems to have been hovering about on the fringes of Emma Jane's activities. He attended meetings of neighbourhood ponces where matters of common concern were discussed, cutting an unlikely figure among his young, sharply dressed colleagues. When a Sikh client of Dawn Upstairs required an Englishman to accommodate his large wife while he was with Dawn, Willie manfully volunteered, but drew the line when she requested a repeat booking.

Meanwhile there was a brief revival of his entrepreneurial fantasies. He was working within the sex business. He had a track record as an impresario and producer of theatrical events. What could be more logical than to bring these two strands of his life together and lay on a series of swap parties, orgies or, to give them the name which he preferred, *partouses*?

Emma Jane was unimpressed. 'You'll lose money,' she told him.

Willie went ahead anyway. The plan was to rent a flat at the Knightsbridge end of the Fulham Road where he would put on regular parties for sexual sophisticates. Tickets would be £10. It was the early Seventies and everyone was now obsessed with sex. It couldn't fail.

Yet, as the first *partouse* approached, a somewhat predictable problem became evident. Male partygoers had bought tickets enthusiastically enough but women, for their own peculiar reasons, were more cautious. In fact, there were hardly any of them.

A couple of days before the first *partouse*, Willie turned to the professionals. Pretty Marie, Dawn Upstairs, Emma Jane herself were hired to help out at the party. Suddenly Willie's profit line was looking distinctly unhealthy.

Several of Willie's friends attended one of his parties but, perhaps for understandable reasons, their memory of what went on at them is a little hazy. 'It was all incredibly awkward,' one of them told me. 'I spent most of the party cowering in the bedroom. When I did emerge, there was very little going on – one couple were fucking but very little else was happening.'

Willie's series of *partouses* folded after a couple of months but were not a total failure. As he wrote in his first book, he must have discovered a fact which would stand him in good stead as an author: the worse that life gets, the more material there is for the work. A shambolic orgy may indeed be 'incredibly awkward' in reality but, by the time Willie had finished with it, it would also be incredibly, and perhaps unrecognisably, funny.

'W has written a book about being a ponce, which is being published next year, & has thrown him into a great state,' Julian Mitchell recorded in his diary. 'He's half-proud of his caddishness, shocking himself, which excites him … No parents, so he shocks himself and loves the thought of shocking his old life.'

Willie's first experience of being a published author started quietly. When he had completed his manuscript, he mentioned it to a friend called Hugh Murphy who in turn recommended it to an independent publisher called Mike Franklin. The publisher was immediately interested – 'I didn't think it was anything remarkable but it was fun,' Franklin says today – and eventually offered Willie the modest but fair advance of £750. Willie accepted. Publication date was fixed for the end of February, 1975.

Franklin ran a small publishing house called Talmy Franklin, established in 1969 with the rock producer, Shel Talmy. Based in Knightsbridge, the firm had a reputation for cool, faintly outrageous books, among them Jenny Fabian's *Groupie*, Luke Rhinehart's *The Dice Man*, Xaviera Hollander's *The Happy Hooker*.

Shortly after agreeing a deal with Mike Franklin, Willie, with his natural talent for causing confusion, appointed a literary agent, David Bolt of the Bolt and Watson agency. Bolt was keen to renegotiate, but Franklin persuaded Willie to ignore his new agent and sign the contract as it was. Understandably, Bolt withdrew in a huff.

Willie's proposed title *Both the Ladies and the Gentlemen* was an adaptation, and small misquotation of a WH Auden poem (the original refers to 'both the ladies and gentlemen'). Franklin was not keen on this title (the American publisher later replaced it with the ghastly *Don't Call Me Madam*) but it neatly captures one of the strengths of the book, an unlikely combination of an author who can quote Auden with an inside account of working in the sex trade.

Willie's opening lines set the tone.

Living in a brothel isn't everything it's cracked up to be. This struck me late yesterday as I tramped up and down the Fulham Road, banned from the premises until the last visiting fireman had been tipped into the night.

Perhaps I should have thought twice before accepting the job. That it was the first position of any sort offered to me in competitive circumstances no doubt over-impressed me. And the timing of the offer was most fortuitous. Determined to hang on in Ibiza, I was in a state of some uncertainty as to how best to do so. Should I promote a *Scrutiny* revival on the island by opening a library with books miraculously hung on to since Cambridge? Or should I run an Indian restaurant in a bicycle shed behind the bull-ring?

It was fifty-fifty. Then providence in the shape of Miss Crampton the temporary secretary drops out of the sky with the not unforeseen circumstances that she's now Emma Jane the call girl, with a place for me on the firm. The terms offered were the air fare back to London, full board and upkeep for the duration of the agreement, a small dress allowance and enough mad money to take my cronies out to lunch. This sounded like life with some of the problems removed, so I accepted.

It is the truth, more or less, but a memoir adjusted and shaped just enough to be funny, outrageous and to make a libel lawyer roll his eyes with appalled delight.

A man from Hickson, Oswald Collier & Co, the first of many legal firms to have been enriched by Willie's brand of non-fiction, read the manuscript and was worried, pointing out, with some justification, that 'it is not always clear what is true, what is half-true and what is purely made up'. There followed a long list of potential litigants. Willie made some adjustments, and all parties agreed (wrongly, as it happens) that it was now safe to publish.

A letter to Mike Franklin about the jacket blurb, dated November 11, 1974, is explicit about his approach to truth and fiction. 'I think it most important that it (the blurb) sets the tone of a world gone disgracefully wrong and the protagonist doesn't seem to realise it', he wrote, going on to suggest that he should be credited not only with producing *Beyond The Fringe* but with 'some more heart-warming moments of live theatre during the Sixties'. It would be very dangerous, Willie continued, to refer to Emma Jane as his *protégée*.

> It only makes it seem that I put her on the game, which is a very different kettle of fish to merely living on immoral earnings. (It's also very against the gentleman ponce image.) For similar reasons I think it v. dangerous to say that 'Willie runs the show'. Finally I think it would be better not to put 'true' in final line. Let me explain. I have every intention of sailing as close to the wind as possible. I intend to clown around to such an extent that the authorities *have* to take notice. I want to make a prosecution for living off artistic earnings a real possibility. Should I find myself standing in the dock before you know who, my defence will be, roughly, that the book's a joke, a work of the imagination, I'm mad, drunk, can't tell fact from fiction etc etc. I think the whole thing should be launched in such a *confusing* way that the authorities simply don't know how to react or how to handle it. Actually to boast on the blurb that I have been influencing the movements of prostitutes (which I haven't) would be a terrible mistake, I think. Likewise to emphasise that it's true. People reading the blurb will assume it's true without our actually saying so. Please be patient. All the above is v. important to me.

The publisher sensibly removed the word 'pimp' from the blurb (in vain, because the description attached itself to Willie even in the obituaries for him) and deleted the word 'true' from the final sentence, which then read, 'It's the funniest and most outspoken story ever to hit the market.'

In fact, the main action described in *Both the Ladies and the Gentlemen* was very near the truth. There is Emma Jane and her working-girl friends, punters who included a Tory MP and a man called the Wanker. Willie's friends – Allen Scott, John Bassett, Richard Dynevor – play their parts. His old colleague Tim Williamson and his wife Christina were mentioned several times, the fact that she was daughter of Sir Robert Mark, head of the Metropolitan Police, proving to be irresistible. Williamson later sued for libel and forced changes in the text before it was published in paperback.

Of course, Willie was sensible enough to give pseudonymous cover to his more outrageous characters. In addition to Bruce Jenkins/Ray Nichol, who was now Ken the Australian Horse Player, Sonia Hobbs became Sarah 'arding and David Conyers was Toby Danvers.

Most of Willie's concerns and obsessions are in place with his first book. Decency, humour and honesty are represented by tarts and villains; corruption and moral compromise by politicians, the police and establishment figures. There is a cheerful curiosity about the private lives of call girls and ruminations about pornography, public image and philosophy interrupt the storyline. Willie himself is presented as a lazy, amused onlooker, significantly less addled by guilt and haunted by his background and his past than he would be in later books.

An element of bewilderment was evident in some of the reviews when the book was published. David Holloway, in the *Sunday Telegraph*, welcomed a book that was funny but 'written with remarkably little offence'. *Time Out*'s Peter Ball took a more serious line. 'Although the career of ponce undoubtedly pre-dates the specialised work situation produced by industrialism, it is not a well-documented area in literature,' he wrote. 'On those grounds alone, *Both the Ladies and the Gentlemen* is fascinating reading.'

A combination of Willie's smart yet rackety background and his book's subject matter was a gift for promotion. There were diary items in the *Sunday Times,* columns in the *Guardian.* Interviewed in *Men Only,* Willie complained, not for the last time, that he was shocked by how unshocked the reaction to his book had been. He had expected scandal, disgrace, if not arrest and a stiff fine – indeed, he had reported his disgraceful behaviour to the *News of the World* – but nothing had happened.

The publicity surrounding *Both the Ladies and the Gentlemen* did, however, catch the eye of the Vice Squad, one of whose detectives, Frank Pulley, contacted its author. Once it had been established that, to Willie's disappointment, he was not about to be nicked for poncing, the two met occasionally. Pulley wanted to congratulate Willie on his book – 'It was a very shrewd observation of the pond life of London,' he says now – and also to see whether Willie could help him with some information. Apparently he did, unwittingly, although Pulley's suggestion to him that he might like to be a professional grass for the police was turned down flat.

Willie had not been afraid to use his contacts. Julian Mitchell wrote him a congratulatory card, and a new friend Professor Anthony O'Hear, a philosophy don at Hull University, sent him a fan letter: both found their words appearing in the publisher's publicity.

'My book's been out for a month now and judging by my mail it's tickled the public palate with all the zest of unset jelly,' Willie was to write. 'Until this morning I had received precisely four letters: three from creditors suddenly alerted to the fact that I was still alive, and one from a naval architect in Devonport wondering whether I had yet formed an opinion of a play he sent me in 1966.'

There is a large element of truth here. A small metropolitan circle may have found the idea of a posh former theatre-producer emerging as a ponce piquant and amusing, and quite a few of them enjoyed his writing (mostly in the tentative, slightly baffled manner of the critics). In the big outside world however, *Both the Ladies and the Gentlemen* made little impact. A bestseller needs, above all, to be recognisable, to be clear and confident about the readers to which it wishes to appeal. It might be funny, or sexy, or satirical, or opinionated but, if it is a riotous confusion of all these things, it will fall between the cracks when it reaches the market. Most of the paperback houses turned it down, a couple complaining that they had been expecting more sex in the book. In the end, the relatively new firm of Futura acquired paperback rights from Mike Franklin for £1,500.

Journalists met Willie and filed their stories for publication – or, in the case of the *Daily Mail* and the *Sunday Mirror*, both of which deemed Willie's story too sleazy to publish, for the spike. Kenneth Tynan, by now something of a waning power in the theatre, praised Willie's book whenever he could, choosing it as his book of the year in the *Observer* and comparing Willie's prose to that of Evelyn Waugh.

Such was Tynan's enthusiasm that, with the director Clifford Williams, he expressed an interest in stage rights, news which helped the book's publicity no end. A deal for the modest sum of £250 was struck and Tynan began to look around for someone to adapt the book for the stage.

His choice of would-be authors was eccentric. He turned first to Alan Bennett, who rejected the idea of working with his former producer, sensing, probably rightly, that a mixture of Donaldson and Bennett humour was likely to curdle rather badly. Tynan then approached Clive James, who was making his way in the world as the *Observer's* TV critic and a poet. James took on the job, explaining that he would be writing the play in heroic couplets.

He met up with Willie and Emma Jane and then Emma Jane on her own, expressed a lively interest in the world to which she belonged, but soon the heroic couplets dried up. As Ken Tynan recorded in his diary on June 25, 1975: 'Clive James has called to say he can't continue the Donaldson adaptation, doesn't like what he has done and is giving it up. Won't be dissuaded and is coming over to apologise.'

In fairness, it should be pointed out that James's memory is rather different from the accounts by Willie, Emma Jane and Ken Tynan. His 2006 memoir *North Face of Soho* records that Willie was a 'bull artist' who had once been 'a tycoon of upmarket sexual commerce', his book was a dishonest erotic fantasy, and his girlfriend (who was a pretty twenty-five-year-old at the time) had 'a sour face on the surface of a veteran grapefruit' and an old sticking plaster where she had nicked her leg shaving. In this version, the young Clive James completed the play and delivered it. Concluding an account out of which he alone emerges with credit, the master of the unreliable memoir bids farewell to Willie on a hilariously mawkish note. 'I liked him. He forgave me for being as square as a brick under my air of exuberance, and I forgave him for peddling fake petrol. We had to forgive each other because we both pulled our cons using the same device: the spellbinder sentence, the little castle in the air.'

Willie was becoming something of a fringe celebrity, appearing in May 1975 on a late-night ITV discussion programme called *Ideas in Print* ('some strange items turn up in what is supposed to be the religious slot', the *London Evening News* commented coldly). A few months later he would be Melvyn Bragg's guest on *Read All About It* where he would discuss his writing with a panel consisting of Billy Connolly, Frank Muir and the novelist Angela Huth.

It was all going much too well. Something had to go wrong. Mike Franklin was friends with the Australian media magnate Clyde Packer. Described by Franklin as 'a sort of failed Howard Hughes', Packer was a great twenty-two-stone gorilla of a man and, off-puttingly, an enthusiast of paid sex. When Franklin gave him a copy of *Both the Ladies and the Gentlemen*, Packer loved its humour and its subject matter and immediately offered to buy film rights.

Under normal circumstances, and with any other author, Packer's interest would have posed an insuperable problem. Dramatic rights had already been sold to Tynan. It was Michael Winner who suggested that, under the Copyright Act of 1956, film rights might be exempt from this clause. Recklessly, Willie agreed to attend a meeting with Mike Franklin and Clyde Packer at the Savoy. Willie was under strict instructions from his new agent, a quiet, grey, powerful man called Jonathan Clowes, to listen politely and sign nothing.

There are differing accounts as to how much money changed hands that night. Mike Franklin recalls Packer calling for a brief-case containing £10,000 in notes. The version that Willie was later to write suggested a more modest £750 against an overall deal of £7,500 and this is borne out by later correspondence. As Franklin and Packer haggled, Willie began to work out in his mind what the deal would represent. Pretty Marie and French Simone fourteen times, he reckoned, plus a suit and a Polaroid camera. When Packer actually produced the cash, it was too much for him. 'Fuck it,' he wrote later. 'I sign Mr Packer's laundry list, grab the money and scram.'

The consequences of this moment of madness are to be found in two folders, bulging with letters, statements, minutes and depositions that were among Willie's papers. Lawyers became involved, representing Packer, Tynan and Clifford Williams, Mike Franklin and Willie. Threats were made, meetings held, letters and telegrams came and went from England, America and Australia. Everyone fell out with more or less everyone else. In the end, a vast document of agreement, involving all parties, was drawn up. Whatever money was ever received from Packer must easily have been swallowed up in legal fees.

Neither the play nor the film was ever made. After Clive James had bowed out, Tynan commissioned another writer, the unlikely figure of Warren Tute, a veteran writer of war thrillers, to write the play under the pseudonym of Jack Sweden. By 1977, a play with the rather good title of *Whatever Happened to Willie?* had been written and the producer Eddie Kulunkandis planned to stage a London production. Another lucky lawyer was employed to go through the text, raising the usual questions about which character was real and which invented, but in the end, nothing happened. Packer had lost interest and Tynan was a sick man. He had, according to the biography written after his death by his wife Kathleen, never been 'passionately involved' in it.

In the long term, none of these confusions caused the slightest rift between Willie and the others who had been involved. Just as Michael White continued to view Willie with affection after being left in the lurch by him on two separate occasions in the mid-1960s, so now Tynan remained such good friends that he would soon contribute an introduction to Willie's next book, in which he made humorous mention of Willie's 'Savoy Sell-Out'.

Why did Willie break agreements like this? Because money meant so little to him? Because, bored, he wanted to see how badly he could behave? Because he was a writer looking for material? Perhaps Ken Tynan's explanation is nearest the mark: 'He hates to disappoint people'.

Some time before his first book had been published, a change had occurred in Willie's romantic and domestic arrangements. The woman known in print as Emma Jane Crampton returned to the world of respectability which, a few years before, she had deserted. Perhaps for this reason, her relationship with the man who had given her notoriety began to cool. Another girl from his past, Cherry Hatrick, his secretary at Westminster Artists and the Nichol Chaulet Model Agency, had reappeared and they had begun to see each other. It is unclear whether Emma Jane knew what was going on, and she is unwilling to talk about the end of the affair to this day. Whatever the precise circumstances, she was soon gone and Willie was living with Cherry at her flat at 139, Elm Park Mansions. He would be there for the rest of his life.

19
Just a pensée

It was not entirely true, as Willie claimed, that the only response to *Both the Ladies and the Gentlemen* had been letters from three creditors and a play-writing naval architect. An article by Alan Brien in the *Sunday Times* caught the eye of Willie's Aunt Eve. She contacted Brien, who passed the letter on to Willie. Soon he was in contact once more with his sister, formerly Eleanor Jane, now simply Jane.

She was, and is, an extraordinary woman. Jane was known to Willie as Bomo, and in his books is called Bobo. Willie had drifted out of her life ten years previously, had squandered two large portions of family money, had abandoned his wife and child and had now reappeared on the scene, boasting of how he was living off immoral earnings. In spite of all that, she was delighted to see him again when they met for lunch, and was proud of her brother, the author.

Her husband Christopher Downes was less pleased. He had never been a fan of Willie's, even when he was a passably respectable midshipman on a submarine – an incident in 1955 when Willie and his pal Julian Mitchell had hidden Christopher's new company car was 'seriously unfunny', he told me – and events of the subsequent twenty years had not improved his opinion. He instructed their children Harry, Gerard, Simon, Tom and Claudia to have nothing to do with their wicked Uncle Willie, who immediately became a subject of fascination to them.

For someone living a life of comfortable respectability in Hampshire, having a close relation who appears in the press and on TV to discuss living in a brothel and is forever making silly-arse jokes about hard-working politicians, the Metropolitan

Police and Mary Whitehouse can be tricky. From 1975 until the end of her brother's life, Jane would become aware of an odd tension among some of her friends: they were intrigued by Willie's notoriety, yet disapproved of him.

It was thought in respectable circles that Willie Donaldson, though amusing in his way, was something of a bad lot. Anyone who made the mistake of becoming involved with him was in serious danger of being corrupted. The terrible tale of what happened to the Major when he met Donaldson was a lesson for anyone who might be tempted.

The Major, as he was carefully described when Willie wrote about him, was living near Christopher and Jane Downes in the mid-1970s. He was an Old Wykehamist, married to a JP, and was a former Guards officer and member of White's. Having read *Both the Ladies and the Gentlemen* he wrote to Willie.

> Dear Mr Donaldson
>
> I am writing to you on two counts – first to congratulate you on your recent book which occupied me for the whole of a non-working day and which I found most informative. I was extolling its virtues to a couple who live nearby in the evening when I was interrupted by my hostess, who transpired to be your sister Jane. I fear that her husband did not share my enthusiasm for your work!
>
> I am like yourself an Old Wykehamist (1943–1947) and the current economic problems have forced me to turn my attention to getting paid employment.

The letter went on to suggest that the Major was rather interested in setting up a brothel under the cover of his obvious respectability. When Willie met him at his club to discuss this proposal, the Major came up with an even more audacious plan. Being a trusted member of the community, he was aware of precisely when his various well-heeled neighbours were away and where the keys to their houses were kept. Would Willie happen to have any useful contacts within the burgling community who might go into partnership with him?

Willie was rather shocked by this idea and, beyond noting that it would be useful for his next book (in which a version of the Major, a goofy old cove whose catchphrase was 'Just a pensée', became a leading character) he thought nothing more of the letter.

A few weeks later, another invitation to break the law came Willie's way, this time from a rather different direction. A local drug dealer who knew Dawn Upstairs, had asked her whether she knew a solid-looking gent who could help him transport some drugs from Thailand to Stockholm via London. The plan was that an Asian carrier would fly into Heathrow. There the gentleman courier would be waiting, having met the dealer at the airport and been supplied with a ticket. An exchange of suitcases would follow and the gentleman-mule would then take the drugs on the last part of the journey.

Dawn immediately thought of her friend Willie, but drug-running was no more attractive to him than burglary had been, and he turned the offer down flat. It was Cherry who came up with the idea that the Major might be excited by the idea of being approached by a real drugs-runner, not thinking for a moment that he would be stupid enough to agree. The Major – a sporty old spiv – was delighted by the idea.

On the day of the operation, the dealer was, by an unlucky chance, detained by the police in London and was unable therefore to make his way to Heathrow, where the Major was waiting for him. Being a trained military man, the Major used his initiative. He went to an information desk at the airport and had his contact paged on the public address system. Alerted by the helpful announcement, customs police followed the Major as he picked up the suitcase and got on to the plane. He was arrested in Stockholm. Under interrogation, the military poise of an officer and gentleman slipped rather quickly, and the Major sang like a canary, providing full details of those he claimed were behind the heist – Willie, Cherry and Dawn Upstairs.

The police raided 139 Elm Park Mansions later that night. By another unhappy accident of timing, it was the evening when Songey rang to say that she needed to discuss their son Charlie's future. Willie explained that he was in the process of being raided by the customs police. Unperturbed, Songey said she would be there in a few minutes' time.

The Major was tried and eventually sent down for three years. Willie who, when the police arrived, had handed in a small amount of pot that was in the flat in order to avoid Cherry being accused, was later fined for possession. His day in court became rather more irritating and expensive when it was discovered that he owed hundreds of pounds in unpaid parking fines.

What is interesting about the Major's story is that, in the mysterious way of things in Willie's life, the blame quickly attached itself not to the drug-running would-be burglar of his friends' houses, but to the person who had done nothing more than put him in touch with a true villain. Willie the corrupter: a central part of his myth.

20
Charlie Donaldson

Willie had a tremendous time writing up the meeting of his first wife with members of the customs police at his flat. The scene, in which Sonia was portrayed in conveniently cartoonish fashion – 'a sensible, house-holding woman dressed by Hermès and with a voice that could have pierced a labrador's eardrums at a distance of five furlongs' – was a staple in his books and was re-told two or three times in his *Independent* column.

When Sonia arrived at the flat, the police had asked her to wait in the bedroom until they had completed their work. Later, as Willie was about to be taken down to the Chelsea police station to account for the pot in his possession, he explained to his ex-wife that it was not a good time to talk about their son's future, since he was being arrested for possession of drugs. Sonia said she would wait. An hour or so later, they did indeed discuss what was to happen to Charlie.

For some time Willie had wanted, in a rather feeble way, to catch up with the son whom he had not seen since 1963 – according to Julian Mitchell's diary in 1971: 'He says he couldn't lift the phone to make the arrangements, he'd simply dissolve into tears'. In 1975, under Cherry's encouragement, he had contacted Sonia with a view to catching up with Charlie at last. When he did, it turned out that, as Sonia had said, he did indeed need a father's influence.

Charlie Donaldson is something of a black hole at the heart of this story. Over the years that I knew him, Willie would be reluctant to talk about his son. He would make occasional references to him in his writing, but it would often be in the form of savage, uneasy jokes.

I met Charlie, briefly, after Willie's funeral when neither of us was feeling conversational. Now a man in his forties, he is darker than Willie but has his father's eyes and mouth, and exaggerated eyebrows. After I had agreed to write this book, I assumed that he would want to contribute: he had always been proud of his father. He failed to pick up the telephone when I rang. I left messages with mutual acquaintances but he never contacted me. Eventually, Cherry Donaldson convinced him that he should meet me; he agreed, but only if she were also present. Two meetings were arranged. He failed to show up for either.

When I spoke some weeks later to his mother Sonia, she told me that Charlie had told her he could not face seeing me to talk about Willie. In a slightly unnerving echo of Julian Mitchell's diary entry about his father, he had said that 'he would burst into tears and cry all the time'.

There may not have been much for him to tell me. He saw nothing of his father during those exciting boom-and-bust late Sixties and early Seventies. A trust had been set up on his parents' divorce, which paid for his education. He did well at prep school – like Willie, he went to Woodcote House – and then was sent to Eton.

By the time he was fifteen, he had become the perfect public school anti-hero. He was handsome, funny, bright, charismatic. He was a good runner and gymnast. A talented guitarist, he had formed a group. He was also uncompromisingly rebellious. It was not that he broke the rules, his Eton housemaster would say, so much as the rules simply didn't exist for him.

'We thought he would rule the world. Everyone loved him,' says his best friend from that time, Kim Kindersley. 'He was one of the most talented musicians I have known.'

Kim, like Charlie, came from a wild and privileged background. Between them, the two boys must have been every public school's nightmare.

One of Willie's first acts as a born-again father was to drive down to Eton to hear his son's housemaster express his concern about the way Charlie was going. The warning was too late. A month or so later, Willie and Cherry received a call from Sonia. Charlie had run away from Eton. Twenty-four hours later he turned up at Elm Park Mansions. Not long after he had returned, with his mother and father, for the formality of being expelled, he moved in with Willie and Cherry.

Living in a flat off the Fulham Road with a dad and his girl-friend who took a relaxed view of discipline must have suited the sixteen-year-old Charlie pretty well. It must also have been a trial for Willie and Cherry.

The Elm Park Mansions flat was small: a sitting-room, a small kitchen, a tiny bathroom, a bedroom and, across the small front hall, the room, which he called 'the literary room', where he wrote and where Charlie now slept. In the best of circumstances, which these were not, a sixteen-year-old boy takes up more phys-ical and spiritual space than almost any other kind of human being. The domestic concepts of making oneself scarce, or fitting in, rarely, if ever, register on the teenage radar.

Willie and Cherry did their best. Don Langdon, who saw Willie at around this time, describes him as 'very much the concerned father'. When Kenneth Tynan invited Willie around for a drink, he declined on the grounds that Charlie had just moved into his flat. Young Donaldson had just been expelled from Eton, Tynan wrote in his diary, 'in the hope that exposure to Willie's paternal example will be beneficial to his moral health. I am not clear whether the authorities at Eton are aware that Willie is a pimp.'

A letter sent from Eton by Charlie's friend Kim Kindersley suggests that, in their way, Willie and Cherry were sympathetic in their dealings with the two problem boys. 'I enjoy my chats on the phone with you because it makes me feel normal again,' Kim wrote. 'However the real point of this letter is to thank you for adopting me and for allowing me to spend so much of my time in 139, also for the money, telephone calls, ringing up Uncle Bobby for me, the list is endless. I hope to see you very, very soon (very lonely here). Love Kim.'

Willie was certainly a liberal father, his only knowing act of discipline being to turf the boys – and occasionally girls, according to Kim, who became a regular visitor – out of the literary room in the morning so that he could work. 'I used to see that face in the morning,' he recalls. 'There was nothing nonchalant about it when he was about to work. He would walk into this nightmare of suede and sex and ask us quite firmly to move out.'

When Willie was not working, he was rather less steely. Cherry had agreed with Willie that it would be setting a bad example if the grown-ups smoked pot in front of the boys but, says Kim, he would occasionally roll joints with them once the coast was clear. When, after some misdemeanour, Charlie was brought back to the flat by a policeman and presented to his father, it was Cherry's authority he invoked. 'I don't know *what* your Aunty Cherry is going to say,' he said.

Kim recalls that time with real fondness. 'Willie was always very kind to me and I think he enjoyed those days,' he says. 'I really did see him as a sort of surrogate father. He wasn't a great father but he was a fucking great party dad.'

In his late teens, Charlie drifted away. Kim had fallen out with him, after Charlie had run off with his girlfriend while he was away – 'The great betrayal of my young life,' Kim says – and Charlie spent more and more time away from Elm Park Mansions.

Over the subsequent twenty-five years, Willie was a distant figure to his son. 'I could do without children, I must admit – particularly my own. I don't find it sad, which is odd,' he said in an interview shortly after the publication of *The Henry Root Letters* and, from 1984 onwards, that is pretty much what he did.

Charlie kept track of his father's career and, according to neighbour Mike Hanford, would regularly send cards to Willie during the 1990s. There was no sign of any of them in his papers. Charlie is hardly mentioned in the memoirs and then only with a shifty, guilty joke, the book's emotional charge being invested in Willie's various babies and princesses.

Charlie was in a sense abandoned by his father as completely, and at the same stage in his life, as Willie was left by his own father, when Charles Donaldson drank himself to death.

The final scene of *The Balloons in the Black Bag* closes with Willie being summoned to the office of his son's housemaster. The Eton man, though, is given the name of Mr Altham, who was Willie's first housemaster at Winchester, and as the scene goes on the adult world and the school world are increasingly confused (particularly when, in Willie's version, he lights up a joint). Finally, they are not discussing Charlie at Eton but Willie at Winchester and beyond. The problem is no longer misbehaviour in class or on the football field, but is selling rights twice in a book, putting on dodgy theatrical ventures, worrying his sister Bobo, interesting the Vice Squad, getting involved in a nasty business involving two trollops. Charlie and his problems seem to have been forgotten. Or, perhaps, the father has seen rather too much of himself in the son.

Willie had a profound allergy to responsibility. As soon as someone needed something from him that was not drugs or sex or amusing company, he was off. Nothing was more appalling or frightening to him than the fact that his own son did indeed need a father's influence. So he ran, hiding behind the occasional joke. In every area of his life, it was important for Willie to be in control, Rachel Garley, the last great love of his life, told me. 'And that was the problem with being a father,' she says. 'Children are something where you have no control. There's no game with children. The game is over.'

A few days before Willie died, Adam Bellow, son of the novelist Saul Bellow, wrote a tribute on the birthday of his dead father.

> Most people have a rich fund of shared experience to help them keep their dead alive. My memories of my father are much sparser. But I do have one advantage over people who knew their parents in the normal, daily sense. Over years of separation I developed a connection with my father that did not depend on physical proximity. I did this, I now realise, by wilfully incorporating aspects of his being in myself: ways of thinking, particular expressions, a certain way of looking at the world.

Therefore it seems fitting on his birthday to affirm my belief in this improbable connection, a bond that transcends time and space, and even death, because my father, though absent, is deeply, unpredictably, stubbornly present in me.

21
The cry of a bull moose caught by the knackers in a trap

Soon after the publication of *Both the Ladies and the Gentlemen*, Willie began to write letters to public figures and to the letters pages of newspapers under the name of Emma Jane Crampton. From his days at Winchester, when he communicated with the advice columnist Evelyn Home under the pseudonym of Miss Donaldson, he had enjoyed sending out spoof letters. Occasionally, trying to get himself into trouble, he had impersonated enraged members of the public and had written to the Lord Chamberlain, TV companies and moral crusaders. When *Private Eye* had attacked him following the closing of *The Council of Love*, he had considered getting some fake notepaper printed and sending off embarrassing letters, supporting all the wrong causes, under the name of Richard Ingrams.

Now, as a writer, Willie saw the potential of the letter form. Not only could it stir things up nicely, but it also allowed him to develop a voice and character that was not his own. There was a limit, he must have realised, to the extent that he could mine his own life for material, and he lacked the confidence – and perhaps the interest – to write a conventional novel with a made-up narrative and invented characters. In letters, there would be a fictional character whose interaction with public figures, in their way also playing a role, would lead in all sorts of interesting and revealing directions.

Neither the idea of a book of Emma Jane's letters, nor the sequel to his first book, *The Balloons in the Black Bag*, interested Mike Franklin, who was anyway running down his publishing business and spending more time in America.

Willie's new agent Jonathan Clowes paired him up with an editor who in many ways was perfectly suited for the job. Geoffrey Strachan of Eyre Methuen had not only successfully published a number of funny books, including some highly successful book tie-ins with *Monty Python's Flying Circus*, but he knew Willie. In fact, as a young undergraduate, Strachan had contributed a poem which had appeared in the first edition of Willie's and Julian Mitchell's magazine, *Gemini*.

Now the former poet was to publish his former publisher. Strachan's approach was as different as can be imagined from the instinctive seat-of-the-pants style of Mike Franklin. Elegantly presented, and with a preface contributed by Kenneth Tynan, *Letters to Emma Jane* conveyed the seriousness which Willie always liked. The joke rather lost its point, he felt quite rightly, if it announces itself in advance. For the same reason, he hated to be described as 'a humorist'.

No longer a bit-part player in the fictionalised life and misadventures of Willie Donaldson, gentleman ponce, Emma Jane Crampton took centre stage. Still working as what Tynan calls 'a charming young call girl', she was also an advice columnist, dispensing wisdom and gossip to those who wrote to her. Jane had also become more involved in social issues, becoming rather obsessed by the women's movement, an organisation called PUSSI (Prostitutes for Social and Sexual Integration) and the Metropolitan Police and shows a startling sophistication in philosophical matters, replying to Anthony Bryson of the University of Warwick (who later takes her to the Aristotelian Society). Now and then she provides little cameos from her life with Willie, described sometimes as her 'young man' and sometimes as 'the old boy'. On one occasion, she and her young man celebrate FR Leavis's eightieth birthday by bicycling around London, listening to a tribute on the radio before he asks her to write out a hundred times 'I will not commit the intentional fallacy'.

Letters to some public figures, from Lord Longford to Anna Raeburn and Esther Rantzen, were included in the book and, more riskily from the legal point of view, there was invented correspondence from real people, including a vulgar come-on to Emma Jane from 'Richard Ingrams' in which he makes various intimate boasts, one of the more innocent of which was that he had 'the best loving technique you ever experienced, sweetheart!' and signs off 'Yours for mutual pleasure'.

The fragile defence Willie used to protect against legal action was a series of po-faced notes, usually in the form of corrections, at the back of the book. 'I take this to be another of Emma Jane's jokes,' he writes of the Ingrams letter. 'If she ever received such a letter, I think we can assume it came from a prankster, not from Mr Ingrams.'

Around publication, he tried, as usual, to get himself into trouble. After he had appeared on TV to discuss the book, he wrote letters of complaint to the TV company, but without success.

In 1978, he had better luck. The magazine *Penthouse*, under the editorship of Nevile Player, was a perfect home for Emma Jane Crampton's unusual mix of salaciousness, cultural opinion and silly jokes. Among its contributors, the magazine had Kingsley Amis writing about drink, Stirling Moss testing cars and, more surprisingly, the show-jumping Yorkshireman Harvey Smith as travel correspondent. It was also, Player says now, 'rude for its time'.

One of the Emma Jane columns included a photograph of Nigel Dempster the gossip columnist, who at the time was writing under the name of 'Grovel' in *Private Eye*, with a girl who, it was claimed, was Emma Jane, and a whiskery old routine about Dempster arriving home to his young bride after some 'late-night drinking and sleuthing'.

Dempster rose to the bait. He threatened to sue. As Emma Jane, Willie contacted the press, earning a mention in Anthony Holden's Atticus diary in the *Sunday Times*. Letters, from an innocent call girl under brutal legal attack from Dempster and in desperate need of help, were sent to newspaper editors, including Charles Wintour of Express Newspapers.

Dear Mr Wintour

Forgive me for writing to you out of the blue, but I am utterly distraught. I am being sued for libel by Nigel Dempster over a tiny joke I made about him in my column in *Penthouse* and I'm afraid this action may be the end of me. I cannot possibly afford a long battle in the courts with someone of Mr Dempster's great power and wealth, and I am compelled, therefore, to form the 'Nigel Dampstain Fund' in order to pay for my defence. I will be organising various money-raising japes, such as late-night poetry and jazz recitals, comical variety bills starring turns like Peter Cook, Stanley Moon and Julie Covington, and a humorous darts match in which a team of *Sun* Page Three Lovelies will play a team of topless hacks captained by Richard Ingrams.

Needless to say, I am near despair and while I realise that you are a very busy man, I wonder whether you would consider sitting on the Fund's management committee? I expect to be raising a considerable sum of money, and it is of paramount importance that this money is seen to be disbursed with the utmost probity.

I enclose a copy of the matter Mr Dempster is complaining about, and I think you will agree it's really very innocuous.

I look forward to hearing from you and I hope very much you can help.

Yours sincerely,

Emma Jane Crampton

Dempster eventually seems to have lost interest, but Willie must have been encouraged by the spasm of mischief that he had achieved. For years, it was one of his proudest boasts that he had been sued by Nigel Dempster in his *Private Eye* days.

Willie liked the persona of Emma Jane Crampton. It allowed him to be, by turns, worldly and intelligent, eye-wateringly rude

RECIPE, Here's a useful:

Cut it out and keep it by the telephone. It's called 'Bill's kedgeree' and I pinched it from the 'Bill's Cuisine' column in Gay News. I'm sure Bill won't mind. (Loved your recipe for cottage pie, Bill!!)

    8 tbsp f ckd rc
    6 z ckd hddck
    3 tbsp lv l
    1 lrg nn chppd
    1 rd pppr dsdd nd chppd
    2 stlks clr mncd
    1 tbsp sltns
    jc f lmn nd glss f wtr
    nb f bttr
    3 hrd bld ggs
    2 tbsp crsl chppd prsl
    slt nd pppr
    1 qtrd lmn nd sm mng chtn

Fr th nn, pppr nd clr gntl ntl th nn s trnslcnt. Str n th crr pwdr nd cntn ckng fr tw r thr mnts. Dd th wshd sltns, th lmn jc nd th wtr nd ck fr nthr tn mnts. Dnt lt t stck, nd mk sr y'v bt hlf a cpfl f lqd whn y dd th r nd thn th hddck. Str nd ht thrgh. Dd slt nd bck pppr t tst nd trn nt a ht srvng dsh. Str n nb f bttr nd sprnkl th chppd ggs nd prsly n tp. Srrnd wth lmn qrtrs nd srv th chtn.

REDGRAVE, Brother Vanessa:

One of the four fabulous Fonda children. It is one of the best kept secrets in show business that her father, the distinguished mime Sir Henry Redgrave, has refused to speak to her since she tried to raise money for the International Revolutionary Party of North London by dancing in the nude in a series of porno movies.

A revolting Trot who has done much to relieve the plight of film buffs everywhere by refusing to make any more films, she once refused an Oscar in an amazing scene in which she punched Big 'John' Wayne as a sign of solidarity with Red Indians everywhere. She is now married to an Eskimo.

A useful recipe from *Emma Jane's Reference Book*.

or simply to tell jokes. Although *Letters to Emma Jane* had not been particularly successful he had two more ideas for her. There would be a diary, for which Auberon Waugh would write the introduction (and was indeed paid £500 to do so) and then there would be *Emma Jane's Reference Book*, which Willie completed, striking for the first time the note of false authority that would later become the hallmark of some of his most successful books.

OLIVIER, *Sir Lawrence of*

Thirty years on, there's still a kind of kinship that separates those who saw Larry's Oedipus from those who didn't. I didn't, because I hadn't been born at the time, but for the fortunate few, it was a shared, never-to-be-forgotten experience, forging an unbreakable bond between them, as though they'd been on the Somme together. It was as heavy as that.

Will anyone who was there ever forget Larry's ear-splitting

scream of anguish which all but took the roof off the New
Theatre? I once asked Larry where he'd discovered that terrible noise. It was the cry of a bull moose caught by the knackers
in a trap, he told me, a ghastly high-pitched wail of agony he'd
first heard when hunting in Canada as a young man.

Larry gives each word of a part a unique rasp of danger
which is his and his alone, and yet – and this is the really
extraordinary thing about him – when he's sitting quietly on
the train to Brighton, if it wasn't for his enormous false
nose, his stage make-up and his habit of suddenly bellowing
like a bull moose caught by the knackers, he could be
mistaken for any other commuter on his way home after a
hard day at the office.

But Willie's career as a writer was in trouble. *Letters to Emma
Jane* made the smallest of splashes in 1977 and *The Balloons in
the Black Bag*, a brilliant comic version of events around the
publication of his first book, was almost completely ignored.
'Most literary editors simply seem to have funked it', Geoffrey
Strachan wrote gloomily. *The Diary of Emma Jane Crampton*
never saw the light of publication and nor did *Emma Jane's
Reference Book*.

On April 5, 1979, Geoffrey Strachan turned down the diary
and confessed that the two books he had published had not sold
well. 'I do feel your range is potentially much greater than that
of the books I have seen so far,' he wrote. 'There are so many
subjects you could be tackling. Anna Raeburn and Sir Robert
Mark are only a part of it. I agree, however, that it is no good
asking a Serbo-Croat poet not to write about his village in
Yugoslavia if that is where he happens to live and breathe.'

Unable to sleep one night early in 1979, Cherry Donaldson
reached for one of several books that had been sent to Willie
from America by his ex-publisher Mike Franklin. It was called *The
Lazlo Toth Letters* and was written by the American comedian
Don Novello. It made Cherry laugh enough for her to suggest

to Willie in the morning that he read it. Soon he would be working on what would become one of the most successful books of the 1980s and one which has lived on as a classic in a category of its own.

The Henry Root Letters were, Willie would later write, 'a straight rip-off of a much funnier book', *The Lazlo Toth Letters* and, in a simplistic sense, he was right. There was the idea of an irritating patriot and over-enthusiastic defender of traditional values writing unwelcome letters of support or protest to the famous and self-important, the inclusion of a small bribe with some letters, the stamp of 'No Reply' at the foot of the letters to those who refused to rise to the bait.

When Willie's book became Britain's number one bestseller Victor Lownes, the chairman of the Playboy Club in Britain and friend of Don Novello's, sent the author of *The Lazlo Toth Letters* a copy of the book. Replying, Novello seemed at first to take Willie's *homage* in good part. 'I'm not mad at him at all. I figure we stole their language, we shouldn't be upset if they steal a book from us now and then,' he wrote, but later in the letter, a certain white-knuckled sarcasm creeps in. 'I wonder how he ever thought of putting those lines on the top and the bottom of the No Reply stamps,' he wrote. 'I also wonder why he has no blank pages at the end of the book.'

But while the idea was stolen, and provided a useful publicity hook, it was Root himself – a beaming, good-hearted, monstrously insensitive self-made man – who brought the book its enduring success and popularity. It was 'one of the funniest books I have ever read', Auberon Waugh wrote. Another brilliant columnist, Colin Welch, then deputy editor of the *Daily Telegraph*, said that he had been unable to read some of the letters for tears of laughter.

With the creation of Henry Root, Willie truly hit his stride as a comic writer. His previous narrators, himself and Emma Jane, had been relatively urbane and well brought-up – their good manners were part of the joke. Now, as the appalling, bustling Root, he could let the mad energy and aggression in his writing off the leash. There was a new bounce in his writing, an intoxicated love of language and of jokes that is only partly explained by his delight at tweaking and teasing those in public life. Willie was having fun. 'With Willie's writing there was this great electricity,' says Craig Brown. 'Most good writing is about poetry – it's a question of putting words together so that they have this intense tension. There was a sort of poetry to Willie's wit.'

Quite where the perfect, no-nonsense name of Willie's most famous character originated is something of a mystery although he may possibly have plundered his past for inspiration – the fifth issue of *Gemini* in 1957 had contained a letter from the moral philosopher HE Root.

By profession a wet-fish magnate, Willie's Henry Root was as far from his last persona, Emma Jane Crampton, as can be imagined. 'Here are the facts of my life in a nutshell,' Root wrote to a Mrs Joan Pugh, when applying for the job of programme researcher for London Weekend Televisions 'Minorities Unit':

> Born January 4, 1935. Left school at sixteen with one '0' level in geography (so I know my way around the world), but continued my education at the University of Real Life, than which, you will agree, there is none better.
>
> From the age of sixteen to eighteen worked as a porter in Billingsgate Fish Market. Gained invaluable experience of the English working class's dislike of ethnic minorities and so-called intellectuals. From eighteen to twenty did my National Service in submarines under the legendary Captain 'Crab' Myers VC. Commissioned.
>
> On being demobbed, started my own wet fish business. Worked like a black (but paid myself rather better) and was able to sell the business for a tidy sum in 1976. Now find myself with time on my hands. Looking for new challenges with a societal bias.
>
> Personal details: 5ft 8¾ ins, 15 stone, English on both sides of the family as far back as can be traced (1904). Expert

shot. Front upper denture due to boxing mishap sustained during National Service. (Seventeen fights, two convictions.) Married Muriel Root (née Potts) in 1958. Two youngsters – Doreen (nineteen) and Henry Jr (fifteen).

May I say how much I'm looking forward to joining your team and to flushing out the ethnic woodworms from the fixtures and fittings of our society.

Yours Against Minorities!

Henry Root

Apart from sharing a date of birth and National Service in the submarines, Root has nothing in common with his creator, nor do his family, with the possible exception of Henry Jr – who sleeps in his make-up, dreams of being a pop star and takes on a job at the Embassy Club – bear any resemblance to Willie's. Root has all the hallmarks of a monster, being bigoted, randy and simultaneously corrupt and moralistic, but there is something inescapably endearing about him. He is an outsider, like the man who created him and, because he can be relied upon to say precisely the wrong thing at all times, he will always remain so. But he is an optimist and nothing can dent his bluff self-confidence. There is a telling generosity in the way Root is portrayed which transforms what would otherwise have been an unkind joke at the expense of busy, important people, into something more human and interesting. The kindness which Willie worked so hard to keep hidden in his autobiographical writings emerges in spite of himself.

From March 1979 onwards, Willie started sending out letters from Elm Park Mansions under the name of Henry Root. The beneficiaries of his impeccably ill-judged support included senior policemen, politicians, publishers, Esther Rantzen, business magnates, lawyers, newspaper editors, the Queen, model agencies, columnists, judges, football managers and Leslie Crowther. Because he was always utterly sincere, his targets would often reply, choosing to ignore or put a positive gloss on his maddest claims, his most insulting insinuations.

The Henry Root Letters, one of those rare writing projects which seemed to have a charmed life from start to finish, was timed to perfection. As the first letters went out, Mrs Thatcher was about to come to power. She had the full support of Henry Root.

'Dear Leader!
    So they said a woman couldn't do it! They were forgetting Joan d'Arc, the maid of Orleans! She put it over the French with their bidets and so-called soixante-neuf and so will you!

Promising to keep his leader in touch with doorstep opinion, he signed off, 'Avarice is patriotic! Here's a pound. Your man on the doorstep, Henry Root.'

Avarice, of course, was indeed about to become patriotic. Well before the Eighties slipped into its greed-is-good cliché, Willie had created a character who was the perfect Thatcherite. A languid, fat-bottomed anti-intellectualism was back in fashion, represented week by week by the *Spectator*. A quote by the journalist George Gale, 'Common sense is a sturdy plant and self-interest a great fertiliser', encapsulated the mood and attitude so perfectly that it was included at the foot of Root's later letters. There was also a whiff of Lady Birdwood-like moralising in the air, with the first of many reactions against the permissiveness of the Sixties. 'One last thing,' he wrote in his second letter to Mrs Thatcher:

Mrs Root and I have recently formed 'The Ordinary Folk Against Porn Society'. We meet once a week with some of our friends (Dr Littlewinkle and his good lady, the Smithsons, Major Dewdrop and Fred and Rita Snipe, who live opposite, form the hard-core nucleus) to discuss sex, drugs, nudity and violence. While I know these are all subjects that interest you, I expect you'll be too busy at the moment, what with one thing and another, to address us yourself. Don't worry. We understand. However, a signed photograph and message of encouragement would mean a lot to our members.

A signed photograph and polite note from the new Prime Minister arrived at Elm Park Mansions within a few days. When Cherry had seen some of the early letters before they went out, she had worried that they were too obviously comic but she underestimated the vanity of those in public life.

The joy of the letters format for Willie was that it generates its own story, one reply – or lack of reply – leading to another. A letter to the *Sunday Mirror*'s correspondent suggesting that, since there was said to be a shortage of 'royals', there should be introduced a system of Life Royals who 'like actual Royals, should be ordinary but exceptional folk up to whom lesser folk will naturally look but with whom they can relate', was copied and sent to the Queen and two potential Life Royals, the editor of the *Sunday Express* John Junor and the columnist Mary Kenny, both of whom were busy defenders of old-fashioned family values.

Writing to ask the highly respectable Lucy Clayton model agency whether they would provide models to jump out of a cake at a Rifle Brigade dinner and 'mingle' with the guests ('I naturally don't want to be too specific in a letter'), he is threatened in a reply from the agency to be reported to the Provost Marshall. 'I don't understand,' he replies. 'It was the Provost Marshall who recommended you.'

When there was no response, Willie was quite prepared to live up to his creed of never letting the truth stand in the way of a good joke by doing a bit of none-too-subtle cheating. The sequence of letters sent to Esther Rantzen, becoming increasingly rude, to which Rantzen replied, 'Thank you very much indeed for taking the trouble to write to me. Hearing from viewers like yourself is a tremendous boost for us all,' was a fake. Willie received a single acknowledgement, and changed the date on it for subsequent replies.

There were several publishers among the recipients and one or two of them even sniffed an opportunity, but it was Simon Dally, the editor of Arthur Barker, an imprint of Weidenfeld & Nicolson, who was the most decisive. Here Willie was in luck again.

Dally, an Old Wykehamist, not only was attuned to Willie's

sense of humour and his view of the world (not everybody was, or is) but he also had considerable courage as a publisher.

The Henry Root Letters is now accepted as one of publishing's great success stories, but it could easily have been a disaster if packaged and promoted differently. There were libel and copyright risks which might have convinced other editors to play safe and take off the essential edge of the letters. Conventionally, humour books presented themselves facetiously, with cartoons and silly title (or at least sub-title), a puff on the cover from a well-known funny person, and a blurb containing at least one mention of the word 'hilarious'.

Weidenfeld's format and cover, a photograph of a fish on a slab, was as straight-faced and self-important as the book's title. A sensible legal report from Paisner and Co, warned that, while unauthorised reproduction of letters was a breach of copyright, the main risk was of libel. Willie made minor adjustments to the text and, unusually for him, there were no more legal excitements. The blurb was perfectly judged in its po-faced seriousness.

> This work will not be favourably reviewed in the columns of the *Guardian* or the *New Statesman* or other so-called intellectual organs staffed by lounge-room revolutionaries with long hair; nor will it appeal to homosexuals, BBC2 producers, Jonathan Cape Ltd, the National Council for Civil Liberties, weirdos and other minority groups Mr Root is against. It will, however, produce a warm glow in the hearts of ordinary folk everywhere as one common man's exceptional perceptive and illuminating contribution to the Great Debate.

The potential of *The Henry Root Letters* became clear to Weidenfeld & Nicolson months before publication. A large marketing budget of £8,500 was allocated. Book club and serialisation deals were done. Willie had kept sending out Root letters during the autumn of 1979, so enabling him to sell a second volume to Weidenfeld for £5,000 in August. It would appear the following autumn, six months after *The Henry Root Letters* had been published to become the number one bestseller for several months.

Willie was a model author. He followed his editor's advice, made the changes suggested by the libel lawyer. The manuscript is remarkably free of his usual obsessions: only a few mentions of Richard Ingrams, virtually nothing about brothels and, with the possible exception of a tweak at Leslie Crowther, one of his complaining actor-victims from *Dial Liverpool Royal 5163/4* in 1966, no settling of old scores.

There were lunches to attend, sales reps to address, book-sellers to suck up to, books to be signed – on one day in the warehouse, Willie added his signature to 2,000 copies for a book club. He was popular with those promoting and selling his books, sending out notes and magnums of claret to those who were doing particularly well. He even agreed to be a celebrity auctioneer at a British Heart Foundation benefit event.

A record producer wrote to him suggesting that a Root record might be released. Richard Curtis, a writer of *Not the Nine O'Clock News*, wrote a treatment for a Root TV series, which would be a sketch show about contemporary events fronted by Ken Campbell or 'a less famous Leonard Rossiter'. It reads well even today, even though it was necessarily vague ('Generalising about comedy has killed men,' Curtis wrote). Nothing came of it and Curtis went on to writing stardom with *Four Weddings and a Funeral* and its successors.

In the spring of 1980, Henry Root was everywhere. The book's reception delighted Willie. Those whose judgement he valued enthused, while several of the public figures who had been goosed by Henry Root chuntered on pointlessly in the press. Jean Rook, who had not been pleased by her letter from Root – 'You seem like a sensible old trout,' Root had written, going on to describe her as 'the thinking man's Anna Raeburn' – wrote a huffy response to Root in the *Daily Express* pointing out that it was her job to take letters from the public seriously. Another Fleet Street *grande dame*, Lynda Lee-Potter of the *Daily Mail*, devoted a full-page to the outrage, headlined 'DEAR SIR, YOURS TRULY ISN'T AMUSED.' The *London Review of Books* described the letters as 'a disgrace to publishing'.

Equally annoyed was Alexander Chancellor, then editor of the *Spectator*, whose correspondence with Root had not made it into the book. Chancellor had received a letter from Root following a burglary in which he had lost £185. Root enclosed a pound noting that 'I have calculated that if each of your readers sent you a pound two-thirds of the loss would be made good.' He then went on to congratulate Chancellor for his editorship of the *Spectator*, flushing out the so-called intellectuals and replacing them with 'good sound journalists with their feet on the ground and their thoughts on the relevant issues: *haute cuisine*, good wine, gardening and gentlemanly sports such as cricket, shooting, gaming and fisticuffs'. Chancellor replied, solemnly thanking Root for 'your kind remarks about the magazine'.

As the book soared high in the bestseller lists, Chancellor complained that the first collection of letters were 'silly and tiresome ... I am quite angry with Lord Weidenfeld for publishing them' and then when the *Further Letters* were published, delivered himself of some ruminations which Willie, always a lover of the pomposity of the *Spectator* diarists, might have written himself.

> My objections to Root's first volume were ... warmly applauded by a number of correspondents as serious and high-minded as myself. Several (including Mr Graham Greene) wrote helpfully pointing out that the copyright on a letter belongs to the sender and wondering whether Mr Root or his publishers had sought permission to print the replies he received to his manic outpourings. Good point, I thought. Now in this latest collection I find an elegantly composed letter on *Spectator* writing paper from Clare Asquith, assistant to the literary editor and grand-daughter of Raymond Asquith, whose own letters were recently published to profit and acclaim. Was she asked if they could publish it? Was she offered any money? No, she was not. A fair payment, promptly made, could even at this late stage alleviate our distress and permit us to allow the matter to rest.

Although there was a part of Willie which sympathised with the Chancellor argument that serious people should not have to waste their time on silly jokes, there is little doubt that he enjoyed his moment as a bestselling author. Cherry remembers him going out to buy a copy of the *Sunday Times* knowing that it would contain a profile of him, and returning, having seen the headline, humming, 'I'm the joker of Elm Park Mansions, I'm the joker of Elm Park Mansions.'

Although the critics of *The Henry Root Letters* complained that it was irresponsible, the file of letters not published suggests that Willie was more careful than it might appear. Root sent a letter to a senior policeman who had been jailed for corruption, congratulating him on his release, asking his advice about Henry Root Jr whose ambition was to be a crooner, enclosing a pound to help him with his finances and offering him a job in the wet-fish business as a security guard. The bent cop replied with a sweet and sincere two-page handwritten letter and a photograph. Thanking Root for the £1 – 'It is accepted in the spirit in which it was given' – he went on to advise on the case of Henry Jr.

> As far as your son is concerned, I am sure he will find his own niche in life and settle down to a career which will make you proud of him in due course. The mere fact he wants to be a rock and roll singer at this stage is, I believe, a natural reaction and comparable with people of my generation wanting to become traindrivers and the like.

As for the offer of a job, the ex-policeman was grateful for the offer. 'However at the moment I am adequately fixed up.' Sensibly – and sensitively – Willie kept this letter to himself.

The *Sunday Times* reviewer Miles Kington praised a 'slow-burning yet ephemeral classic', predicting that 'the presence of so many turn-of-the-tide celebrities is going to make it pretty dated by 1990'. Oddly, this has not turned out to be the case and, while every publishing season brings another author's attempt to 'do a Henry Root', there has never been anything quite like the original man of letters created by Willie Donaldson. As Craig Brown wrote some twenty-five years after *The Henry Root Letters* were published: 'In a funny sort of way, Henry Root is now all the more robust, and far more real and vivid than the stuffed shirts and charlatans he once addressed.'

22
Failed impresario boasts of friendship with convent schoolgirl

Willie was less social than he had been in the days of theatre and musical evenings and sometimes his books made contact with new and old friends, like bottles containing a message being despatched from a desert island. *Both the Ladies and the Gentlemen* had put him back in touch with his sister Jane, introduced him to his nephews and niece, and established a firm friendship with the philosophy don Anthony O'Hear, 'the Doctor'. Now the two Henry Root books were to bring two rather different people into his life.

Shortly after the publication of *The Henry Root Letters,* Willie received a letter from Cove House, Cove in Devon. It read:

Dear Mr Root,

I think your letters are smashing. It's my birthday today and my cousin is at the moment lying seductively on the spare bed reading out your witty naughtiness.

Anyhow the whole point of this so far dull epistle is that I have a proposition to make to your much exalted self. That is I'm going to ask you, dear sir, to write to me at my catholic convent, whither I shall be repairing in a couple of days. Your wonderful letter will be opened by the nuns and send them into epileptic fits which would be very jolly and dramatic. Then I would be called in to answer for my highly unsuitable correspondence with the disreputable Mr Root. I shall then make a long speech about liberty and injustice and all the other things that catholic convent girls make speeches about after getting letters from Henry Root.

I've just realised that earlier in this silly letter I've said that I had a 'proposition' to make when in fact it's just a plea. Anyhow my school address is St Mary's Convent, Shaftesbury, Dorset, SP7 9LP.

I'm fifteen and called CLAUDIA FITZHERBERT and would be really chuffed if you answered this letter.

Lots of love and admiration

From C F.

PS. Please also, dear dear, dearest Mr Root, send me a signed photograph of your beloved self.

Root, the great letter-writer, received hundreds of fan-letters himself – his address was on almost every page of his book, after all – and eventually Willie had to give up replying to them. Claudia Fitzherbert, though, very quickly received a letter that was both startlingly effusive and distinctively un-Rootlike in tone:

My Dearest Claudia

Your letter thrilled and delighted me – as you knew it would! You're a tempting and capricious young lady! And only 17½! How will you be in another year I tremble to think! Sorry about all these exclamation marks. There's something about the memory of your loveliness that brings them out like a rash. And how rash we were! (There I go again!) (And again!)

Root, for it is he who signs the letter, slips back into character for a paragraph about the letters ('There are some who'd argue that there are passages in it that a girl such as yourself should do better not to read till later. I am not of their number') before closing with a dreamy speculation of how, in the summer holidays, they'll go punting together on the River Cam: 'You'll look exquisite lying back in a dear little straw boater and white knee socks! Then we'll take tea in Grantchester.'

Root closes with the exhortation: 'Work hard! All play and no work etc etc!'

At first glance, it is difficult not to conclude that there is something distinctly dodgy going on here: the clammily gushing tone, the slightly laboured joke about Claudia's age, the white knee socks. It was certainly true that Willie was thrilled to be in contact with a fifteen-year-old convent girl. In the two months which followed, the correspondence continued at a feverish pace, with Willie – he had abandoned the Root alias by the third letter – writing once or twice a week and Claudia responding to him within a day or two. Between the end of April and June, a time when the Root letters were at their peak of popularity and the author was in wide demand, Willie wrote ten long letters to Claudia, several of which ran to eight pages of A4 paper. The correspondence was to continue for a year.

It survived a setback which might have done for other pen-friendships. Willie had become aware that, as the country's best-known practical joker, Henry Root would soon be a target for pranks himself. Cherry (who, in all Willie's letters to Claudia, remains Muriel or Mrs Root) suspected that someone might be making a monkey out of him and noticed a similarity in the handwriting and the style of writing paper to those of Auberon Waugh, who was also Catholic and lived in the West Country.

Claudia's reply confirmed that Cherry's suspicions had been half-correct. Willie had not been corresponding with Auberon Waugh, pretending to be a schoolgirl, but the schoolgirl was Waugh's niece. 'It's clear that you've found out something so I may as well put you in the picture like. Auberon Waugh is my uncle, being my mother's brother.' Claudia was mystified at how her secret was revealed but wrote firmly: 'I must make one thing clear, for all my famous uncles (Willie and Bron) I AM WHO I AM, please do not doubt that'.

Willie may not have been entirely reassured, because soon afterwards, he had a confession to make:

Now then. I have to tell you of a catastrophe that nearly occurred on Friday. You may have heard already, but I pray not. Suddenly the phone rang (I suppose it always rings suddenly) and a Scottish voice identified itself as belonging to Peter Mckay – Mr Grovel of *Private Eye*, self-styled friend of your Uncle Bron's, ex-Hickey and now gossip of the pornographic *News of the World*. Had anything interesting happened to me lately, he wanted to know, because he was short of copy for one of his columns. Claudia, in my panic at being spoken to by someone on PE I quite lost my head and told him all about you! Wasn't that frightful? As soon as the words were out of my mouth I knew I'd made a frightful mistake. Of course he was fascinated and gave it as his opinion that your Uncle Bron was behind the whole thing. Meanwhile I was imagining nightmare headlines in the *N.O.W.* along the lines of 'Failed impresario boasts of friendship with convent schoolgirl'. Wouldn't that have been dreadful? In the end he promised to write nothing without first speaking to your Uncle Bron, but these popular journalists are not to be trusted and I had to take two valiums before opening the N.O.W. this Sunday. Wasn't that incredibly indiscreet of me? Sheer nerves. I promise that such a thing won't happen again.

Claudia forgave him, even when the story did indeed by an indirect route appear in the press and a journalist rang her parents for a comment. 'Phew! What a horrible episode!' Willie wrote the following week. 'I pray I've learned my lesson. You've been exceptionally forgiving and I doubt I deserve it. While I'm satisfied I didn't act dishonourably, I certainly was a bloody fool and for that I couldn't have complained had you broken off our tremendous friendship.'

There are few friendships between a man and a woman, of whatever ages, which do not have a tug of sexual tension, and it is impossible to imagine Willie corresponding quite so avidly with, say, a fifteen-year-old boy. All the same, the correspondence with Claudia Fitzherbert reveals Willie at his sweetest and kindest. Looking back now, Claudia has no doubts about his intentions. 'He absolutely wasn't raffish with me,' she says. 'I asked him to play the part and he gleefully complied. It was all very innocent.'

Indeed, as he became better acquainted with Claudia – on paper, at least – Willie became genuinely solicitous and concerned about her ('I feel you don't take your writing ability as seriously as I do. *YOU MUST WRITE*'), asking about her exams and encouraging her to work for university.

When Claudia revealed that she and her friend Anna Chancellor (who turned out, to Willie's mock-dismay, to be the niece of Alexander Chancellor, editor of the *Spectator* and scourge of the *Root Letters*), had planned to run away to Australia, he was shocked.

> I'd do anything for you, you understand, except help you run away. Disreputable I may be, but I wouldn't want you to upset those who love you. I'm sure you were only joking. Let me know about this. Plus about the depressions. Do you really get depressed? Is it just impatience? If so, impatience for what?

Much of Willie's own news sees him in comic-defensive mode, but now and then insights slip through which would find no place in a column or book. On a hot summer's day, at a desk overlooking the courtyard of Elm Park Mansions, he wrote:

> How lovely it would be to live graciously which once one did, before entering the theatre … How nice it would be to be seated now on an elegant lawn by a stream, rather than in a dirty yard with cats, pigeons and many examples here and there of what you call common folk.

The idea of the correspondents meeting up was discouraged by Claudia – 'I'm very boring and somehow don't go in for conversation, it's all to do with being a frustrated genius,' she writes, and Willie confessed:

> I know what you mean about conversation being a bore. I find it harder and harder and, like you, have now cut my friends down to about six. I can't be bothered to talk to anyone else at all. However I know I'll enjoy talking to you. You'll make me rock with laughter.

Claudia was certainly a precocious fifteen-year-old and her letters, one of which opens 'Hail, Uncle of the Underworld!' are sometimes as funny as Willie's. But beyond the jokiness there is something else in Willie's letters to Claudia Fitzherbert, a sort of yearning for a straightforward life, in which adults behave well and are concerned about the way young people grow up – something, in other words, he would never have. He does, indeed, do a very good impersonation of a friendly old uncle, rewriting his own history to provide a moral lesson:

> I was as good as gold at school, driven on by the fear of failing in life to work like hell and play cricket for the honour of the house. I was *completely* straight until I went into advertising at the age of twenty-four. *Then* I rebelled and behaved like a twelve-year-old for the next twenty years. Perhaps it is after all healthier to rebel in one's teens.

A running joke in the letters had been how Claudia, self-mockingly devout in her Catholicism, was leading her wicked Uncle Willie towards the path of righteousness. He would never make it there, of course, but there were signs in the letters that, writing to her, he was able to be more direct and serious than he would ever allow himself to be in his published writings. He revered Philip Larkin, he once wrote, second only to Claudia's favourite the Pope (her Uncle Auberon Waugh came third), and so he was going to send her a volume of Larkin's poems. When Claudia received *High Windows*, she had loved it although, she confessed, she had found some of the poems a touch depressing. Willie replied:

> I'm glad you like Larkin, but I am beginning to think it was perhaps not a suitable book to send you. I'd never thought of him as depressing, but I can see why you find him so. It is a very wistful, if not bleak, view of life, but I suppose his poems make me happy because they're so extraordinarily good. It's a marvellous world, I think, which contains a man who writes as beautifully as this.

Willie was proud of his correspondence with Claudia. He discussed it with Cherry and, he told her, showed her letters to some of his friends. In February 1981, almost a year after they had started, the correspondence petered out. Willie took Anna Chancellor, then a teenager, out to dinner to give her some tips about the theatre world ('My advice will be *invaluable*'), but he would only meet Claudia once in person, years later at a launch party. She says that they were both rather embarrassed and tongue-tied.

Willie's other new correspondent was rather different. Scott, now Roy, Stevens, and later to be known in Willie's writings as 'Honest John', first contacted Henry Root when a copy of *The Henry Root Letters* had reached him in Exeter Prison. Today Stevens is an intense, bespectacled man with the studious air of a contestant on *Mastermind*: in the past, his special subject was fraud. He had first contacted Willie at a time when he was much exercised by having been classified as a psychopath and was in touch with Lord Longford, who remained a friend for the rest of his life.

His letters to Willie, on yellow lined paper, suggest someone who was bored by where he found himself, who was intrigued by Willie. Although now rather serious-minded, the man who would become Honest John seems to have liked convention-breaking comedy then. His letters to Willie from Exeter contain plaintive and repeated requests to help him get in touch with Barry Humphries. After his release, later in the 1980s, Stevens had a celebratory lunch at the Gay Hussar with Lord Longford and Willie. Peter Cook was at a nearby table and Longford effected a reunion between Cook and Willie. (It is difficult to imagine a more unlikely foursome than Lord Longford, Willie Donaldson, Honest John and Peter Cook.)

Later, when Willie's life grew considerably darker than in those sunlit days of Henry Root, Roy Stevens would become an important supplier of companionship and pharmaceutical support.

23
You know where you are with plaice

Something rather startling was happening to Willie. He was becoming successful – fashionable even. Money had become less of a problem. The two books of Henry Root letters earned him around £80,000 in the first year or so and continued to bring in royalties. By 1983, his agent Jonathan Clowes reported that so far 182,000 *Henry Root Letters* had been sold in hardback and 62,000 for the *Further Letters*. There would have been book club sales, his share of the paperback advance and other fringe benefits, including a contract with £2,500 down payment for *Mrs Root's Diary*, which was never written.

There was talk of a TV series, deals for *Henry Root's World of Knowledge*, a two-book deal covering a novel and an autobiography. His paperback publishers Futura took advantage of Willie's popularity by reissuing *Both the Ladies and the Gentlemen* and *The Balloons in the Black Bag* (to be re-titled *Nicknames Only*).

His home life, by his standards, was settled. Although he grumbled about it to some of his male friends, living with Cherry suited him pretty well. She enjoyed his jokes, was proud of his books and was undemanding as to their social life, disliking dinner-parties and preferring to socialise within their own circle of friends. They had their cats and were now renting a flat in Ibiza Town where they would take holidays. Willie was not behaving entirely well, occasionally paying for girls to spend time with him in Ibiza when he was meant to be writing, but the excitement of success and the pleasure of writing seem to have kept at bay the old boredom and restlessness for the moment at least.

There were signs, though, that the better things appeared to be going for him, the more depressed Willie was becoming. Always bad at playing the fantasy game required of successful authors, he went out of his way in interviews to exude anxiety, pessimism and doubt and now made it clear that success had hit him very badly. 'I will tell you an odd thing,' Willie told a journalist from the *Birmingham Post*. 'I've been much unhappier since Root came out than I was before – and what that can mean, I can't imagine. I feel much more troubled. I should be happy as a cricket.'

An interview in a magazine called *The Bulletin* was even more revealing.

> I enjoy being down and out. I like the buzz of basic survival,'
> he said. 'I'm having a crisis of confidence with writing. I
> don't believe in what I'm doing but I haven't the energy, the
> discipline or indeed the talent to produce a truly successful
> book. I think I'll gracefully retire. A beach bar in southern
> Spain seems very attractive. Failure is lovely and cosy.

This gloomy view of his life gladdened the hearts of those journalists who had disapproved of him and the disruption he had

With Cherry, 1980.

caused among serious people. 'Willie Donaldson seems long ago to have lost the bounding confidence of the dreadful Root,' Max Hastings declared with some satisfaction in an *Evening Standard* profile. 'Henry Root's amusing little comet has risen, blazed and within a year or two will have died and been forgotten. Donaldson will probably be back in the shadowy, picaresque Chelsea world in which he has lived for so long that he has no real impulse to escape from it.'

Certainly Willie was working hard to convey that impression. 'Nothing has changed,' he told Hastings. 'The books have done a lot for Henry Root but nothing at all for William Donaldson as a writer. All people want is more Root ideas. I still sit in this seedy flat. Nobody asks me to dinner. I don't see anything of my family, although I've got together with my sister again. Her husband disapproves of me for some reason.'

The combination within Willie of a solid background with an unrivalled talent for stirring things up was already making him suspect to those, like Hastings, who sat at the media top table – he was essentially a 'fringe character', to use the description of him once deployed by another self-appointed prefect Clive James – but it is an odd fact of the British establishment that it likes to have the odd court jester in its ranks to amuse and scandalise it. Jeffrey Bernard, reporting blearily on his own decline from the bar of the Coach and Horses in Soho, played the role to perfection for many years. With his wit, politeness and talent for disruption, Willie must have seemed in the early 1980s another perfect candidate. Once again, perhaps for the first time since the early 1960s, he would be at the centre of things.

Tina Brown, the editor of *Tatler*, was a great fan of Willie's writing and decided he would be ideal as a restaurant critic. The magazine was going through one of its skittish phases, tuning in cleverly to the new snobbery – 'Are you being sirred? Hugo Vickers on the graduations of bowing and scraping in the Royal protocol' was a typical feature. It had become quite the thing for restaurant columns to be written by literary mavericks who were given the liberty to be quirkier and more eccentric than mere hacks, and *Tatler*'s man on the culinary front line had been Julian

Barnes, writing under the name of 'Basil Seal'. In January 1981, he was replaced by Henry Root.

From the opening words of the first column ('Henceforth it will be the policy of this column to visit restaurants in the company of *bons viveurs*. I have in mind the Archbishop of Canterbury ...'), it was clear that there was to be not the slightest whiff of the wet-fish business in this column. The byline might have been Henry Root's but the tone, attitude and background are unmistakeably those of Willie Donaldson.

'I'm hating this *Tatler* stint,' Willie was soon writing to Claudia Fitzherbert. 'This week I have to have three disgusting blow-outs and then next week I have to write about them. I have *nothing* to say about food.'

It is not an insuperable problem to be a restaurant critic who is entirely uninterested in food, and Tina Brown must have known that Willie was some way from being a gourmand. When she took him out to lunch to propose the column, she was slightly startled when Willie ordered fish fingers and milk.

There were, in fact, practical reasons for this approach to food and drink. He had bad teeth – or rather a bad set of false ones, having had the original ones removed over a period of two days at the Royal Dental Hospital – and, apart from the occasional roast at home, preferred to eat soft food, particularly fish. He usually chose to drink milk rather than alcohol. But even without these disadvantages, Willie really was bored by food and uninterested by wine, and one of the incidental pleasures of reading his *Tatler* column, which lasted from January to October in 1981, is to see how even the mention of what had been eaten was kept to a minimum. In one column, having noted that he could have bought thirty hardback books or one hundred and ten paperbacks for what he had spent in restaurants that week, he went on to praise one of his guests, Fay Maschler, adding that 'so struck was I by her company that I quite forgot to make a note of what we ate'.

Willie never really enjoyed small talk or making low-key jokes about things which had no interest to him and having to write fifteen hundred words having picked unenthusiastically at a bit of fish – 'You know where you are with plaice' was pretty much the sum total of his culinary expertise – must have been a nightmare for him. But he was always serious about his writing and the *Tatler* column contained some touches which suggest that he had a better time than he let on. The Berkeley Hotel had 'lime-green and Windsor-purple lighting, a truly dispiriting combination which made the thin scattering of punters look like corpses'. Later the place was 'as deserted as Malcolm Muggeridge's annual Christmas party of fellow intellectuals'. Dining with Julian Barnes, or rather 'Basil Seal', he notes that he looked like 'a dyspeptic penguin and is prone to make unfashionably cynical comments, quite out of place in this year of Mary Kenny and the Royal Wedding'.

His guests were at first a roll-call of old friends and new – JP Donleavy, Richard Dynevor, Michael White, Nick Luard, the stripper-turned-author Fiona Richmond and the villain-turned-author John McVicar – but after a few months, it was suggested by his editor that he might care to play host to what were called '*Tatler* sort of people'. The result was a meal with a suitably double-barrelled man from the wine trade – 'red braces, charmingly diffident manner and a ventriloquist's ability to speak audibly without opening his mouth' – and a former deb of the year whose comments on the food ('Absolutely brilliant', 'excellent', 'sheer paradise', 'total bliss') were carefully noted and included in Willie's piece.

Soon Willie was back with the winner of Miss Nude Europe and the manager of a talent agency who had on her books the ugliest stripper in London. 'I see you handle Jean Rook,' Willie said.

Having tried several times throughout the autumn to resign, Willie eventually succeeded, and Basil Seal returned to his old job.

Some of those who knew Willie well might have been startled to read that, when Associated Newspapers announced that it was to launch an exciting new Sunday paper called the *Mail on Sunday* in May 1982, he was to be their gossip columnist. The creator of Henry Root, it was said, would be 'adding a new dimension to the art of gossip'.

What on earth was Willie playing at? Short of becoming wine and cricket correspondent for the *Spectator* or editor of Pseuds Corner for *Private Eye*, it is difficult to imagine a job less suited to him. He would be working for a middle-brow newspaper, staunch in its straight-faced defence of family values. He would be expected to go to smart parties (which he hated), report on the activities of the famous (whom he found absurd), and peep and sneak on private indiscretions and misbehaviour (an activity of which he disapproved).

But there was a side of his character which quite liked respectability. From university onwards, he frequently seemed to go through the motions of joining the straight, grown-up world, only to discover, on the occasions when he succeeded, that he was unable to resist tickling it up and generally behaving in a way that made it inevitable that he would soon be out in the cold once more.

Before the *Mail on Sunday* was launched, Willie took his friend Christopher Matthew to the building where he would be working, pointing where his desk would be, where his secretary would be sitting. 'It was a proper job and he was taking it all very seriously,' Matthew says.

For a while, Willie did indeed add a new dimension to the art of gossip, cunningly introducing his own concerns, obsessions, jokes and stories and passing them off as society news. His first column included the news that the 'brilliant comic novelist and creator of theatrical masterpieces JP Donleavy' was in town ('Over tea at the Dorchester Donleavy reminded me of the days when things went less smoothly for him in the theatre' and soon we were back in 1961 with Willie's production of *A Fairy Tale of New York*). A planned visit of the Pope allowed Willie to invent a call to the philosopher AJ Ayer; news of Rear Admiral Sandy Woodward reminded him of the days when they served together in the submarines. Best of all, he was able to tease Alexander Chancellor, whose *Spectator* column had made a reference to Michael Parkinson's good fortune in being paid to flirt on TV at six-thirty in the morning with his co-presenter Angela Rippon.

How inelegant! It has been my misfortune to witness Chancellor flirt at six-thirty in the evening and a most unpleasant sight it was. The effort caused his face to lose focus with excitement, its features sliding sideways and downwards like the lines of a pavement portrait in the rain.

Willie also introduced something called 'Commonsense Corner' in which the amiable idiocies for which he had such a good eye were recorded. 'Mrs Thatcher's admirable crackdown on so-called academics notwithstanding, the undesirability of being an intellectual doesn't yet seem to be accepted in all quarters,' he solemnly noted, going on to invite submissions from readers of 'the bluff, undeceived, pronouncements of plain men and women'.

Having a full page in a popular Sunday newspaper gave Willie the chance to irritate Richard Ingrams, the editor of *Private Eye*, as much as Ingrams had irritated him in the past. Almost an exact contemporary of Willie's, Ingrams had appeared at his Ilford satire revue and was said to have auditioned unsuccessfully for a part in *Beyond The Fringe* when the famous four stood down.

These days, Ingrams is studiously vague about Willie. They had been acquainted during the Sixties, he says. There had been a story in the *Eye* about a blasphemous play he had put on. 'I always thought he was an addict,' he says now.

In fact, *Private Eye* expressed over four decades a loathing for Willie that was almost visceral, describing him on various occasions as 'a balding, middle-aged fun-lover' (he was thirty-five at the time), 'a disgusting, pot-smoking, self-styled theatrical impresario', 'this appalling little shit', 'a slimy crook', 'the well-known shit and pimp', a 'once dishonest impressario (sic) and latterly a pimp', 'a literary pimp', an 'appalling sleazebag' nd 'the wretch Donaldson'. Willie made sure that he included a few bruising new Ingrams jokes in most of his books.

During his stint at the *Mail on Sunday*, Willie scored several palpable hits at the expense of his old enemy. He produced a letter, purportedly from Ingrams to Penguin, who were to publish an official history of *Private Eye* in which Ingrams, while claiming 'I don't want to be a censor in any way', went on to list 'a few things which will have to come out'. There followed four unflattering items of which Ingrams allegedly disapproved.

'Loyalty is an admirable quality,' Willie concluded. 'But for how much longer can Peter Cook, the *Eye*'s proprietor, resist the growing demand inside the organisation to replace the Editor, a man who has one law for his victims and another for himself?'

A couple of months later, Willie suggested that *Private Eye*'s well-practised defence in cases of libel – that it was just an impoverished little magazine – was bogus.

> The profit in scandal for the year ended September 30, 1981, was so healthy that the directors felt able, even while handing round the begging-bowl among their faithful readers, to carve up between themselves a fat £106,883 as opposed to a mere £39,005 the year before.
>
> Richard Ingrams, a correct Christian whose worldly goods were previously thought to consist of a copy of the Bible, a jock-strap and a photo-album commemorating his days as a Sergeant in the Education Corps, more than doubled his salary, trousering cheques to the sum of £25,587 – £1,000 an issue.

It was good stuff, and *Private Eye* could only respond by claiming that the Ingrams letter to Penguin had been a fake or a joke or perhaps a bit of both. To this day, it is said at *Private Eye* that Willie's allegations against Richard Ingrams are easily explained: the stories were leaked by the *Eye* to Willie in order to discredit him. Ian Hislop, now the magazine's editor, recalls that it was a regular challenge for junior staff to plant inaccurate stories in the Willie Donaldson column, that they would invariably be believed by the gullible gossip columnist, but the records show that only those two stories about *Private Eye* were published in Willie's column. Neither were trivial and neither was effectively disproved.

The problem was anyway soon resolved. After a couple of months, Willie was showing signs of becoming bored of impersonating a gossip columnist for the benefit of *Mail on Sunday* readers. He developed a philosophical point out of remarks by Enoch Powell, and compared him to the footballer Kevin

Keegan. He pretended to be representing The Society of Gossip Writers when responding to an attack on gossip columns by John Osborne:

> Without our revelations – which, believe me, often hurt us more than they do our victims – adulterers, gays and fornicating actresses would often go unexposed. No doubt Mr Osborne, snug in his rural retreat, is so out of touch with the modern world that he fails to see how the very fabric of society is threatened by such people.

Irony and the *Mail on Sunday* are not natural bedfellows (the majority of readers may well have thought the column's campaign against intellectuals in 'Common Sense Corner' was a thoroughly sound idea), and by now Willie must have known that he was living on borrowed time. His column shrank to half a page. For several weeks, he filed his copy only for it to be spiked.

Private Eye was able to report gleefully – and inaccurately – that the newspaper's new editor David English had been trying to fire Willie for some time but had been unable to find his deskless and usually columnless gossip columnist. In fact, the opposite was the case. Willie had only appeared at the office in the hope that he would be summoned to the editor's office and put out of his misery. Eventually the axe fell and he was given a generous pay-off. His replacement was Nigel Dempster.

The feud between Richard Ingrams and Willie was to rumble on for the next two decades as their careers headed in different directions – one towards the heart of the Establishment, the other into the cold exterior. Ingrams, of whom John Wells once said, 'he caresses nothing more passionately than the status quo', has become the Grand Old Man of British satire, admired and slightly feared, while Willie died as he lived, a true and natural outsider.

24
Where not to go, how not to speak, who not to be

Willie had discovered while writing for *Tatler* that writing under the name of Henry Root did not oblige him to maintain the persona of a bellowing, vulgar, right-wing anti-intellectual. Now he delivered an unrecognisably different type of Root manuscript to his publishers Weidenfeld & Nicolson, who, after two best-selling collections of letters, were eager for more product.

With *Henry Root's World of Knowledge*, the bouncy, aggressive bonhomie, the ambition, the scattering of pound notes in the path of celebrities were forgotten; instead Root was a plump, *Spectator*-reading bar-room philosopher whose every opinion was an over-worn cliché of thought or language. Willie had been a great admirer of Gustave Flaubert's exhaustive compendium of non-thought, the *Dictionnaire des Idées Reçues*. 'You would find there in alphabetical order, on all possible topics, everything you ought to say if you want to be taken for a decent and likeable person,' Flaubert had written. 'It would be the historical justification of everything respectable... done in an outrageous style, ironic and raucous from beginning to end.' Root's spruced-up contemporary version, set in 1980s Britain, fully lives up to the ambition of the original. It is a book-length 'commonsense corner'.

Willie had been worrying away at this idea for almost as long as he had been a writer. His second book, *The Balloons in the Black Bag*, had contained several interruptions to what narrative there is by someone called One-Eyed Charlie who had been commissioned by the Cambridge University Press to produce an updated version of Flaubert. Occasionally Willie tests him on his progress:

'GENIUS, Men of,' I said, and I held my breath.
'Men of genius belong to the whole world.'
'NATURE, Human.'
'You can't legislate against human nature.'
'Tremendous!'

Even when One-Eyed Charlie is sent to prison, he continues to compile entries for his dictionary.

A collection of clichés is not an obvious candidate for a publisher's humour lists but, with the name of Henry Root, it earned a £5,000 advance, a respectable publicity budget and, most important of all to Willie, the production values of an authoritative, straight-faced work of reference: designed pages, six full-page diagrams, eighty line drawings and a hundred integrated photographs. In the manner of heavyweight encyclopaedias, its contributors are listed on the book's copyright page. Among those included are Plato, Anna Raeburn, Flaubert, John Motson, St Augustine, Penelope Keith, Michael Parkinson, Niccolo Machiavelli, Barry Norman, General Pinochet, Geoffrey Chaucer, Bertie Wooster and, of course, Richard Ingrams.

> Almost everyone is here: from Sam Johnson and Will Shakespeare to Bill Grundy and Dick West. Yet I make no claims to accuracy. Only the owlish go to their shelves to check each quote and reference. I am a busy man. Generally I have been content to catch a fellow's thrust, more or less.

Henry Root's World of Knowledge was the first book on which Willie worked with a collaborator. His enthusiasm for received ideas dates precisely from when he became friends with 'the Doctor', as he called Anthony O'Hear. It had been the Doctor who, having been introduced to Willie by Julian Mitchell, had responded to the philosophical asides in *Both the Ladies and the Gentlemen* and had encouraged the enthusiasm for ideas which would intrigue (or exasperate) readers when they appeared in his books over the next twenty years. Together they had enjoyed discussing philosophy over a breakfast fry-up on Saturday mornings, had attended meetings of the Aristotelian Society, after which they would have what Anthony O'Hear calls 'a post-match analysis'.

Today, O'Hear sees Willie's interest in philosophy as genuine but also something of an intellectual hobby. 'Willie didn't have an original mind but he wanted to get the arguments right,' he says. 'When it came to the minutiae of arguments, he had far greater stamina than I did.'

The stamina was undeniable – Cherry says he could actually reduce her to tears of boredom as, eagerly and interminably, he explored with her some new conundrum – but there is something about Willie's philosophical delvings that seemed to influence his life as well as his writing.

The idea of inauthenticity, of people becoming unable to distinguish between themselves and a socially imposed reality, is a theme in all his books from *Both the Ladies and the Gentlemen*, in which the social roles are played by policemen and judges, to *The Dictionary of National Celebrity*, where they are acted out by Jade Goody, Tony Blair and Natasha Kaplinsky. It had been there in *Letters to Emma Jane*. 'The idea of Emma Jane as a "real" ordinary call girl becoming a celebrity and receiving letters either from the general public or from real celebrities like Esther Rantzen was a fascinating idea in the making,' Geoffrey Strachan says. Willie would continue to be fascinated by 'the vibrant link between reality, real people, real celebrities who are seen and portrayed in a certain way and the unguarded truth between these outward shows'.

On the publication of the American edition of *The Henry Root Letters*, Willie attempted to explain to American readers the idea behind the letters, and why so many public figures fell for them.

'Sartre wrote somewhere … that, because we are always acting out social roles, we can none of us ever achieve a complete identification of the imaginary with the objectively real. A Canadian disc jockey or an English Prime Minister is not simply what he or she is by being assigned a social role but also by imagining himself as performing that role.

In the most obvious case of the Queen, her coronation was 'as much the social validation of a collective fantasy as the confirmation of a *de facto* role,' Willie argued.

> The letters of Henry Root succeeded just because I was sensible enough to write only to people who, in my judgement, could no longer distinguish between themselves and the bloated fictions validated by an undiscerning public.

In this context, Willie's enduring fascination with celebrity – 'a mask that eats into the face', as John Updike put it – becomes more understandable. He lived in the age of the inauthentic, where bad faith confronted him every time he opened a newspaper or switched on the TV.

But the idea of people acting out roles recurs closer to home. A dislocation between the imagined and the real world runs like a fault line through Willie's life.

Looking back during the 1980s on his career as a producer, he would explain that it was 'the wrong fantasy, it didn't fit – hence loss of morals. In my experience, loss of morals is invariably a result of trying out the wrong fantasy. The wrong fantasy leads to panic, and bad behaviour is usually a consequence of fear. Most people behave badly if they're frightened enough.'

And who plays out a fantasy, indeed a social role, more perfectly than a prostitute? In 1975, Willie told Julian Mitchell that it was only when he saw photographs of lesbians that he realised that it was what he really wanted and the idea of sex as another production, as an imagined escape from reality, soon took a hold of him. 'The satisfaction of mere lust should be theatrical – deeply imagined, with a whipcord narrative line, and carefully rehearsed. It should be discussable afterwards, like a great production. Without production values lust is pancake-thin and amateurish,' he wrote in *Is This Allowed?* His perfect other woman would 'satirise reality'.

It is almost as if his view of the world was an expression of a division within himself. Julian noticed this self-detachment – 'He corrects himself all the time, as though he's two people, one talking, the other listening and criticising,' he wrote in his diary. In interviews later, Willie would explain to journalists that it was sometimes as if someone else had been doing the misbehaving while the real Willie looked on, appalled.

With an uncompromising instinct for following his own morality, whatever the consequences, Willie could be said to have lived the life of an existential hero. Alternatively, he might simply have been trying to explain the damage within in his own personality, alienated from itself.

Willie and Anthony O'Hear shared a distaste for the new mood of anti-intellectualism and, working together at the Picasso Café on the King's Road, were to produce a book of which Willie would always be proud. He had an eye for hypocrisy and an ear for the trendy, vacuous cliché which, in *Henry Root's World of Knowledge*, established him as the great social satirist of the moment.

There were various media choruses in the early 1980s that enraged Willie. On TV, there was the chumminess, as fake as studio make-up, of presenters like Barry Norman, Michael Parkinson, Benny Green and Bill Grundy. On Fleet Street, a generation of opinionated, right-wing women – Jean Rook, Mary Kenny, Lynda Lee-Potter – were holding forth bossily while to their left, and equally strident, the journalistic voices of the women's movement were to be heard.

But it was the drawling, laconic, superior voice of a certain kind of English journalist, smugly authoritative in Thatcher's Britain, that provided the principal inspiration of Willie's and the Doctor's encyclopaedia. Everything about these men – their age, their casual snobbery, their all-encompassing boredom, their bloodlessness, their utterly predictable sets of opinions, their clubbishness, the bigotry and covert racism of their much-vaunted traditional values, their weary dismissal of anything that was new or original, their distrust of intelligence, their idle deployment of code-word adjectives (*'agreeable'*, *'congenial'*, *'amusing'*, *'felicitous'*, *'elegant'*, *'lamentable'*, *'tiresome'*) their unquestioning admiration for amateurism, the comfy position they held within their own little circle, their humourless determination only to be amused by each other, their nastiness when cornered – represented for Willie the worst of life in England.

What these groups had in common was that, within their circle, clichés of thought and language had replaced and impersonated genuine thought and ideas. Willie, says Anthony O'Hear, was, above all, a moralist. He sensed there was something fake about the positions and arguments of these people. Language was what gave them away.

Henry Root's World of Knowledge pointed up different varieties of lazy thinking, many of which have lived on. They might be from the world of showbusiness.

> MONROE, Marilyn (1926–61): She represented freedom to others but she wasn't free herself. Her life lacked a third act. We are all guilty.

Or from sport:

> COACHING: We are in danger of coaching the natural talent out of our most promising lads. We should not forget that Pele learned his skills heading a coconut against a wall and had never set eyes on a football before scoring a hat-trick at the age of seventeen in the World Cup Final in 1958.

Throughout the encyclopaedia, there is a useful system of cross-referencing:

> BRITISH, We: We British are a peculiar people. We're only at our best with our backs to the wall. See *Anglais, Le Vice.* 'Yet we can laugh at ourselves. One of our most agreeable characteristics.' See *Humour.*

There are recurrent themes. The entry for virtually every European capital is 'Be sure to visit its internationally famous vegetable market'. Most major actors are 'only four foot ten, you know' while an actress will invariably be 'looking more relaxed now that she's discovered who she really is' or 'like many people with a full address book, she found there were times when no one was in'.

As usual in Willie's works, there were some startling facts that had somehow eluded the *Readers Digest:*

CATS: Loyalty is not a word to be found in the average cat's vocabulary. If you took a cat from London to New York it would catch the first plane back to London unless you put butter on its paws.

Few of Willie's books divide his readers more definitely than *Henry Root's World of Knowledge*. In the *Sunday Express* Graham Lord, always a useful counter-indicator on these occasions (his review of Martin Amis's masterpiece *Money* consisted of three words, 'seedy and boring') found the book 'embarrassingly feeble, facetious and repetitive' but Craig Brown, reviewing it in the *Times Literary Supplement* welcomed a masterpiece and today remembers it as the book that helped change the way he saw the languid view of the world as seen from the *Spectator*. Will Self remembers coming across a copy in a rehabilitation clinic (what it was doing there is a mystery) and reading it regularly.

In the book trade magazine, Simon Bainbridge of the bookshop Hatchards praised 'the cleverest, funniest, truest, most carefully thought out, most original and best sustained work of humour since Stephen Potter's *Gamesmanship* series' but nonetheless listed it sorrowfully among his 'surprise duds' of the year so far as its sales were concerned. A book of clichés, a parody of anti-thinking, was never going to have the same effect as a collection of funny letters to celebrities. We are all guilty.

It was writing which introduced Willie to the novel idea that work can be pleasurable. From the early 1980s until he died, he would be involved in a book, television or journalistic project and, in the two years that followed his success with Henry Root, he advanced on several fronts. In addition to his columns and *Henry Root's World of Knowledge*, he established a foothold in the potentially profitable, if precarious world of what he liked to describe as 'toilet books'.

Ephemeral, journalistic, parodic, instant, these books of soundbite humour can be profitable and creatively interesting, but they are at the least dignified end of the literary market and are therefore often written under pseudonyms. The essence of them is somehow to capture and exploit the spirit of the moment in a way that is instantly recognisable and therefore easy to market. There is little room for subtlety or irony in the perfect toilet book. Britain under Margaret Thatcher badly needed to be amused and from the early 1980s onwards, the 'non-book' as it was more politely called became a staple of publishers' lists. Among the bestsellers of the time were Paul Manning's *How to be a Wally* (a spoof behavioural guide), *The Meaning of Life* (spoof definitions based on the names of towns) by John Lloyd and Douglas Adams and *Wicked Willie*, the adventures of a talking penis. It was not a time for subtlety.

The Henry Root Letters had helped pioneer the genre and now the idea of writing funny books, under different *personae* and perhaps in collaboration with another writer, appealed to Willie. With his unusual knack for becoming involved in the very thing which he mocked, he found himself writing a book of lists, where the central joke was class snobbery, and a collection of theatrical anecdotes.

The Complete Naff Guide, which would eventually be subtitled 'Where not to go, how not to speak, who not to be – a definitive guide for the socially aware', developed the idea of an etiquette guide into the form of outrageous lists, which ranged from 'Naff Lines of Poetry to Know if You Don't Know Any More' to 'Naff Causes of Death'. One entire chapter was devoted to 'Candidates for the All-Time Naffest Michael Parkinson Show' and was divided into 'Incoherent Sporting Egomaniacs', 'Actresses with Minds of Their Own (who then tell self-conscious and smutty jokes)', 'Utterly Mad Actors (to put Parky in a good light)' and so on.

Willie's collaborator on the book was Simon Carr, a young writer who had interviewed Willie for *Tatler*. Simey, as he became known to Willie, was a perfect co-writer for him. He was edgy and funny and laughed at the same things while caring rather a lot about them – sex, class, pomposity, public schools. The book, written under the vaguely familiar pseudonyms of Dr Kit Bryson, Selina Fitzherbert and Jean-Luc Leyris, was almost the last book to be commissioned by me, when I was editorial director at Arrow Books, the paperback imprint of the publishers Hutchinson.

Willie, I have to confess, made no particular impression on me when I first met him. There was something essentially quiet and correct about him, the innate respectability of a naval man. He dressed in the kind of clothes – John Lewis Partnership blazer, trousers with a crease – that would not have seemed out of place at the bar of a golf club or in a hotel of faded gentility in Kensington. He walked like an officer patrolling the upper deck, shoulders back, chest out, hands in his pockets. But there was something about him, an amused look behind the eyes, which suggested that none of this should be taken too seriously.

It was difficult at that time to lose money underestimating the innate snobbery of the English media and public and *The Complete Naff Guide* duly became a bestseller. Its publication was not, however, without problems. Promiscuously and wildly insulting to Willie's and Simon's favourite targets, the manuscript had been extensively and expensively read before publication, but on this occasion the publishers' caution had been in vain. Shortly after the book appeared, Arrow received a letter from the much-feared showbusiness lawyer Oscar Beuselinck, acting, he said, on behalf of the *Private Eye* journalist Paul Halloran. It was claimed that, in a manner that was hurtful and injurious to the reputation of Mr Halloran, the authors had included in the category 'Naff Inside Knowledge', the foul slur that 'Paul Halloran keeps his job on *Private Eye* because he's "got something" on Richard Ingrams'.

With surprising promptness, newspaper diarists reported on the case. Letters were exchanged between the two sets of lawyers. The publishers had been convinced by Willie that no one for *Private Eye* would dare sue but clearly their confidence in their author had been misplaced.

In fact, it hadn't been. Willie had been playing what had become one of his favourite games. 'He asked me to sue him,' Paul Halloran says now. It was all a set-up job. There was briefly a moment, as the legal costs began to rise, that Willie worried that a legal juggernaut was trundling away from him, out of control, but Halloran suggested that they settle out of court.

Remembering Willie's reputation as a producer, he suggested that a contribution should be made to Equity's Actors Fund.

Willie and Simon certainly shared that essential immaturity of comedy writers and made each other laugh. Simon's character – ambitious, subversive and reckless – amused and appealed to him. He admired Simon's writing, which was and is savagely witty, in love with language and jokes, always about to go that bit too far. Simon's effect on Willie was to push his jokes further, to be ruder, more outrageous and graphic. There would be other collaborations during the 1980s and at one point Simon even wrote a Henry Root novel – an odd idea, but one which seemed to please Willie, who agreed a sixty-forty split of all monies had the book ever been published.

Willie's relationships with younger writers, whose work he admired and whose character fascinated him, tended to be as complex and tempestuous as a love affair, but Simon remained an important presence in his life until the end.

In his obituary of Willie for the *Independent,* Simon looked back rather bleakly on the *Naff* years.

> Once, he looked around his small flat, at the yellowing books, the sofa ripped by cats, the male decay of loneliness. It was larger than Quentin Crisp's quarters (he had lived round the corner) but more depressing. 'You cannot live as I have lived and not end up like this,' he said. I remember a line he'd put into one of our collaborations twenty years before. 'Promiscuity is the M1 to loneliness!' He had been quoting one of the agony aunts. We laughed at the time.

There were other experiments, several of which either came to nothing or were commercial flops. His publisher, Weidenfeld & Nicolson, approached the singer Marianne Faithfull with the suggestion that Willie might ghost-write her memoirs. *Mrs Root's Diary* was signed up but never written. In 1984, a book of anecdotes, *Great Disasters of the Stage,* appeared. There was a collaboration between Willie, Anthony O'Hear and myself called *Bitov's Britain* which was enjoyed by Auberon Waugh but by few others, apart from the authors.

Responding to his publisher's plea for another work from Henry Root, Willie began to work on an eccentric mixture of fiction and letters which was narrated, to add to the oddity of the whole project, by Charlie's friend Kim Kindersley.

In *Henry Root's A – Z of Women*, the fictional Kim reveals that he has ambitions to be a writer. He goes to work for Root who, encouraged by the example of the newsreader Anna Ford, recently commissioned to write a book on men, had decided to research the subject of women. Unfortunately his experience is limited:

> What is there to say about women? The bedroom and the kitchen. The duvet and the blender. The corset and the rubber gloves. That covers it, does it not?

Researching women for an authoritative encyclopaedia, Kim and Henry Root never get beyond 'A' but by the end of the book they have experimented with bondage (Root going under the *nom de fouet* of 'Richard Ingrams'), dealt with some dodgy policemen from the Chelsea nick, made rude (and it later turned out libellous) remarks about the Duchess of Argyll, told the cluck! cluck! joke about the English women in a Spanish supermarket and sent off a number of letters. Since Henry Root's letters had been famous bestsellers, there were few recipients gullible enough to reply although one of them, perhaps surprisingly, was a bookshop, Foyles of Charing Cross Road. But the name of Root was no longer shifting units in the bookshops. Most of the publicity which accompanied publication concerned a threat of libel from the embattled old dragon and former sex siren, the Duchess of Argyll, which Weidenfeld settled with one £500 cheque to the Duchess and one of £3,210.90 to her lawyers for their costs.

There was more good news for m'learned friends in another of Willie's projects. Having used a number of aliases – Henry Root, Dr Kit Bryson, Selina Fitzherbert, Jean-Luc Leyris, Oleg Bitov – Willie realised that he had to establish his own name as an author.

He knew what subjects he was best writing about – tarts (scatty or perceptive), policemen (bent or stupid) and politicians (right-wing and sexually peculiar) – and he had a useful starting point with a comic play that had been written in 1978, based on the characters of *Both the Ladies and the Gentlemen*.

Even the title was there. It was called *The English Way of Doing Things*.

25
Bust-up at the Sheffield Club

'This is an unhappy dispute,' said Mr Justice Whitford in the High Court of Justice on May 23, 1985, adjudicating on the case of Philip Wiseman v. George Weidenfeld & Nicolson Limited and William Donaldson (also known as Henry Root). It was unhappy, the judge continued, because Mr Wiseman and Mr Donaldson had once been friends.

Indeed they had. Philip Wiseman, an American director living and working in London, had been the director of JP Donleavy's *The Ginger Man*, which Willie had produced. They had been something of a team, Donleavy, Donaldson, Dynevor and Wiseman, during the 1960s. Later, when Richard and Donleavy (known to his friends as 'Mike') had set up the Sheffield Club, an occasional dining group which would meet at Dynevor's flat on Sheffield Terrace for a roast meal, accompanied by expensive wines, Willie and Wiseman would be regular visitors.

The Sheffield Club had its own set of rules, which Donleavy had compiled. The guest list for their dinners was carefully chosen. On one occasion, it had been agreed that female guests had either to be titled or to be on the game. ('In the end, it was clear that the ladies on the game were just that bit more polite,' says JP Donleavy.) On another, a hapless American agent who had failed to pay a working girl having availed himself of her services was invited to dinner and found himself sitting opposite the girl herself. A full confession and the money was extracted.

During the 1970s, the Sheffield Club met less frequently

as the fortunes of those who had attended the dinners varied. JP Donleavy was a literary star, Willie was making his way as an author, but Philip Wiseman was doing less well. His marriage was over and he was short of work. All the same, the letters from Donleavy to Willie are full of affectionate, amused references to Dr Wizzam, The Wizzim, or Viscount Wiseman as he was variously called.

He had been disappointed not to be mentioned somewhere in *Both the Ladies and the Gentlemen*, JP Donleavy told Willie. 'Holy Jeese, it was the least he could have done after all he had previously done to me,' he had said.

The trouble that ended up in the High Court dated back to a cooperative venture between Willie and Wiseman that had taken place in 1978. Neither Wiseman's career as a director nor his private life was in good shape at that time, and Willie suggested that he should camp for a while in Mike Franklin's flat in Nevern Square, where Willie would work occasionally. At some point, it was agreed that, with Willie, he would develop a play, entitled either *One Good Apple* or *The Name of the Game*, from the characters of *Both the Ladies and the Gentlemen*.

There were differences of opinion, later expensively explored by lawyers, as to how the collaboration worked but Philip Wiseman, a neat, friendly man with an air of nervous wariness about him, has no doubt to this day of the way it worked.

It had been his idea to work together on a play. He had been surprised, once they started collaborating, to discover that Willie was utterly incapable of telling a story. 'In that way we complemented one another. He had a talent essentially with words and characters and a comic sense but he simply could not tell a story. I couldn't understand this. It was like a physicist not being able to add one and one.' The project took four months to write.

Wiseman believed – and believes – that he structured the play, added a character and that, without him, Willie had no idea how to tell a story. Willie said that he had felt sorry for Wiseman, that he had let him doze in the background while he, Willie, did the work. Nonetheless, he signed a handwritten document drawn up on September 24, 1978 at JP Donleavy's suggestion, agreeing that the play was a collaboration, that any moneys accruing from it would be split sixty-forty in Willie's favour and that Wiseman would direct any stage production.

The play, which was eventually retitled *The English Way of Doing Things*, was sent to Willie's agent Jonathan Clowes who submitted it to theatre managements under the names of the two authors. No one was interested.

The success of Henry Root in 1979 and 1980 both enthralled and frustrated Wiseman.

When JP Donleavy suggested on one occasion that literary collaborations rarely worked, he had protested. 'Holy fuck, that's wrong, Mike,' he said. 'Look what I've done for Willie.' Noting that Donleavy had not had a bestseller for a while, Wiseman suggested that he might be able to use some collaboration, too.

Such was Wiseman's conviction that Willie was somehow in his debt that JP Donleavy, aware that there might be problems ahead, drew up a further two-page contract which opened with the words:

> An agreement entered into as of this May 1980 day by and between William 'Will' Donaldson, intending future plaintiff and Philip 'The Doctor Wizzim' Wiseman, very likely if he doesn't mend his ways, future defendant and his co-defendant JP 'Guts' Donleavy.

The document, for all its jokiness, contained a sort of agreement. The plaintiff, Willie, was 'desirous to avoid taking legal proceedings as a result of having suffered severely, chronic and acute depredations to his peace of mind at the hands, voice and presence of the said defendant'. The defendant Wiseman would leave 'the said "Will" Donaldson hereinafter free at all times to pursue his now achieved comfortable and agreeable habits at Park Walk or at any other of his future country or town house addresses, or penthouse flats in Monte Carlo or elsewhere, without the screeching, implorements, incoherent pleadings, rabid protestations, salty language and hysterical rantings of the defendant.'

To that end, the agreement confirmed that any previous agreements between Willie and Wiseman had been signed under 'rapidly mounting harassment' and that 'said agreements procured under such duress are null, void and without effect'. This document was signed by Willie, Wiseman and Mr Donleavy and witnessed by Richard Dynevor.

As a writer, Willie was a great believer in the virtues of recycling. When, following the huge success of the Henry Root books, his publishers Weidenfeld & Nicolson suggested that he should write a novel, it occurred to him that his play *The English Way of Doing Things* could form the basis of one.

In January 1984, Wiseman saw an *Observer* review of Willie Donaldson's new book and went berserk. Willie had turned their play into his novel! As if to rub salt into the wound, the critic had commented that *The English Way of Doing Things* would make a tremendous play. Incensed, Wiseman consulted Rubinstein Callingham. Soon another great Donaldson-inspired lawyer's benefit was under way.

Wiseman was a scarily implacable litigant. He demanded £10,000 compensation (£5,000 more than the advance Willie had been paid for the book), plus his legal costs, joint credit in future editions and a share of future royalties.

Willie had been deeply worried by the case against him. Many of his misadventures had a comic craziness to them but there was nothing funny about the Wiseman case. If Willie had lost, which seemed likely at various stages, he would not only have been bankrupted but, far more seriously, his reputation and confidence as a writer would be destroyed. There is no more devastating charge that can be levelled against a writer than the accusation of plagiarism, which was what the case implied. To those of us looking on, it was a kind of madness, this claim of co-authorship rights on a book which was quintessentially and unmistakeably the work of our friend Willie. Even he, who rather liked the feeling of being in trouble, was frightened by what Wiseman and his lawyers were doing to him in 1985.

Several of Willie's friends, including Richard Dynevor and Mike Donleavy, were in the gallery of the court. We were gloomy when the Donleavy contract was deemed not to be relevant, aghast that Willie's barrister failed to ask Wiseman the killer question: Mr Donaldson's work can be read in any number of books; where, Mr Co-Author, is yours? Giving evidence, Willie, though nervous, was the epitome of logic and respectability. He only had one joke in his books, he said, and it was there in *The English Way of Doing Things*. The judge, Mr Justice Whitford, was amused by this idea and now and then would ask throughout the case, 'Is that the joke. Have we reached the joke?'

Overnight, before reaching his verdict, the judge seems to have done something which none of the well-paid lawyers on either side seemed to have done – or if they had, they failed to make it obvious – he read the play and he read the book that was supposedly based on it. There is certainly an overlap in some of the dialogue but both, clearly and patently, are the work of Willie Donaldson.

Whitford's summing up was almost embarrassingly brutal. 'I found Mr Donaldson a thoroughly reliable witness, very careful, very fair, and in complete contrast to Mr Wiseman, who was neither careful nor fair, but quite prepared to make very extravagant and unjustified claims,' the judge said. Wiseman, on the other hand, 'had not had any great success as an author; his promise in the field of directional activity has not apparently been realised – at least in recent years – so far.' The case against Weidenfeld & Nicolson and William Donaldson was dismissed.

It was an absurd case to bring, and at several points Philip Wiseman could have extricated himself by accepting a settlement out of court. Instead he had been humiliated, had lost money, and, more importantly, three close friendships.

Yet it is not difficult to see how he came to believe he had co-created *The English Way of Doing Things*. Willie was a generous and modest collaborator. Working with him, a writer really did begin to feel every bit as brilliant as he was; if anyone was hanging on the coat-tails of his co-writer's talent, it was, one soon thought, Willie. When another literary collaborator, Simon Carr, wrote in his obituary, 'He provided the strategic direction, the critical theory, the discipline, and the collaborator would provide the jokes,' Simon clearly believed what he wrote, but the work suggests otherwise. In the books Willie wrote with Simon, Anthony O'Hear, Craig Brown, Hermione Eyre and me, there is a remarkable consistency of tone and wit – and it is Willie's. Craig compared him to a Renaissance painter whose work was represented by that of his pupils. Those collaborations were the product of the school of Willie Donaldson.

In the early 1980s, Philip Wiseman thought that, like his friends Mike Donleavy and Will Donaldson, he too was going to be a successful writer. He had just written a six-part TV series based on Freud's *Interpretation of Dreams*. 'I felt that having my name over a successful play would set me up,' he says now with the frustration and disappointment of the would-be writer.

But Wiseman is tough. Twelve years later, in 1997, he contacted Willie once more with the idea that *The English Way of Doing Things*, suitably revised, might be staged. The part of Ken, the Australian Horse-Player, might be played by Simon Day of *The Fast Show*. Willie had a weakness for going back over projects of the past – in the early Nineties, he had actually approached Donald Langdon with the idea that they should adapt *The Council of Love*, that theatrical debacle of 1970, for film.

Now, because he had an instinctive sympathy for those who hang on to their dream in the face of impossible odds, he agreed to work with the man whose accusation of plagiarism had once almost destroyed his career. Sensibly, he kept the reunion a secret from those of us who had supported him in 1985.

They met at Wiseman's house in Battersea. Wiseman took to dropping off new drafts at Elm Park Mansions. Then, after two or three months, it was all over again. 'All of a sudden, I heard that someone wanted to publish the novel of *The English Way of Doing Things*,' Wiseman told me. 'I was once again furious. It was an insult beyond insults. So for us it was over, so far as I was concerned.'

There was not, in fact, a proposal to re-issue the novel in 1997, a moment when Willie could hardly get new books published, let alone an old one reissued, and how Wiseman became convinced of what he regarded as a second betrayal is a mystery. It may well be that Willie, sensing that the project was a dead duck, had found a way of bringing it to a close which would spare Wiseman's professional feelings. The two remained friends.

'You couldn't resist Willie after a certain point,' Philip Wiseman says today. 'I adored him – everyone did. He was a good gas.'

26
Ibiza's just the place for women with hurt eyes

Now back in the money, Willie was spending more time visiting his spiritual home, Ibiza. He would go there at regular intervals with Cherry, invite co-writers to work with him there. There would be secret and unofficial sponsored visits from working girls like Pretty Marie. Then, on one occasion, his former employee Angela Bodell visited for a family holiday with her husband and three children, with all expenses paid by Willie, including the cost of a nanny while the adults went out during the evening.

Angie played an odd and contradictory part in Willie's life. Italian-born and very pretty, she had, at the age of seventeen and then called Miss Picano, been working for the Jean Bell Agency when Willie acquired it. 'I once thought Angie was the most beautiful thing I'd ever seen,' he later wrote. 'One boring afternoon, I wandered out and bought a model agency – quite an expensive one at that – because Angie was the receptionist and I couldn't think of any other way of looking at her every day.'

He had flirted with her in a hopeful but self-mocking way. He told her that he wanted to see her in white thigh-length boots; she told him that, in the time-honoured phrase which happened to be true, she was 'not that sort of girl'. Willie, naturally enough, did his best to turn her into that sort of girl. He set up a photo session with the glamour model Stephanie Marrian and another girl at his wife Claire Gordon's flat and photographed her wearing Claire's clothes. At the end of the session, he paid her £100.

After Miss Picano left the Jean Bell Agency and had gone to work for an advertising firm, Willie kept in touch, taking her out to lunch occasionally. 'He was always trying to impress me,' she says now. 'What he loved, and what he hated, was that I wasn't going to be impressed.'

Although she was already going out with the man who would become her husband, John Bodell, Willie invited her (at a time when his finances were in meltdown) to fly to Paris with him and dine at the Ritz. In the taxi home, in London, Willie took her hand. She said, rather tactlessly under the circumstances, 'I wish you were my dad.'

Although he continued to insist that, with her looks, Miss Picano should be a model ('I might ring you next week to tell you in person how *naughty* you are not to be a STAR,' he wrote to her after she had married Bodell and had had the first of her three daughters), his relationship to Miss Picano changed during the 1970s.

Spiritually allergic to any kind of domestic life, he made an exception with Mrs Bodell. When her children went to school, he would travel out to Chingford, take her out to lunch, then accompany her to pick up the children from school. There is a brief, unexplained reference to her in *The Balloons in the Black Bag*. When, about to sell film rights to Clyde Packer for £7,500, he lists in his mind the possibilities of what he could do with the money, the first option, and the only innocent one, was: 'Give it all to Miss Picano'.

She visited Willie twice in Ibiza – once with a friend and the second time with her entire family. In 1985, John Bodell's model agency business was in trouble and he was facing bankruptcy. Willie, by that time no longer flush with funds, gave them £3,000.

He continued to see Angie throughout the 1980s, involving her in some of his projects. On one occasion, she was required to impersonate Selina Sidey, a casting director, over lunch with the *Daily Mail* columnist Lynda Lee-Potter, for which she was paid £150. 'It made it legitimate,' she says.

In the second half of the 1980s, when Willie's private life began to spiral downwards, Angie would be a sort of walker for him, attending dinner parties held by Willie's publisher or accompanying him to a Chas'n'Dave night in Chingford where she amazed and delighted Willie by getting up on stage and singing 'I've Got a Lovely Bunch of Coconuts'.

In 1994, standing in her kitchen, he had confessed that he had been in love with her for twenty-five years but said he was proud of what she had made of her life. 'Look at you,' he once said. 'A house and a husband and children, and here's me wanting to corrupt you. So who's the one who's laughing?'

It is a surprising story, even for those who thought they knew Willie. He rarely mentioned Miss Picano and never with a hint of romantic longing. In his writing, she appears regularly but playing a straight, caricature-free role. But, just as there were a small number of important women who, from 1966 onwards, were to play the perfect other woman in his turbulent sex life, so, now and then, he met someone for whom he longed in vain – pretty, worldly but with a moral centre that put them beyond corruption. There was something of a teenage crush in his attitude to these women, but they brought out the best in him. He was loyal down the years, concerned about their lives, generous to them.

Miranda Skillman, his secretary in 1961, had been one of these idealised women. 'What was particularly lovely,' Willie wrote in 1989, 'was to find that you are as beautiful as ever and happy and clever and all that too. You have done well, Miranda, and I rather wish Lord D and I had managed to emulate your good life.' Towards the end of the 1980s, he was to fall for Jo Drinkwater, a funny and charming journalist on *Tatler*, and around that time he began to see less of Miss Picano.

But they remained in touch, had the occasional lunch together. Once, around the year 2000, Angie received an odd call from Willie, asking her for money. 'It was literally for £20.' They met for the last time over lunch a couple of years before he died.

She was devastated, though, when she heard about his death. Willie was, she says, like a godfather to her, a guardian angel.

Although he referred to Cherry as 'Mrs Root' in his letters to Claudia Fitzherbert and even, rather to his confusion, to his accountant, she was some way from the billowing, fruity, former cocktail waitress who had appeared in *Henry Root's A–Z of Women*.

Stores toilet rolls and walks around all day in rubber gloves. Not much of a life on the face of it. The mail-order catalogues. The special offers through the post. The brochures. The problems with the washing-machine. Women's lot. Easily satisfied. And yet ... And yet.

Like Root, Willie was restless. He sensed, in his arrangements at Elm Park Mansions, that his life was becoming dangerously settled. It was harsh on Cherry, this, since she was no more domesticated or house-proud than he was. She had been with him for over a decade, longer than anyone else had managed, and had tactfully encouraged him to be slightly more orderly in his affairs – paying tax now and then, for example – without crowding him. She shared his sense of humour and approach to life. She was proud of his successes and kept scrapbooks of his reviews and cuttings. It should have been fine. They shared a bachelorish life, rarely went out, and enjoyed bad TV shows with the Doctor ('Are we sure there isn't something worse on the other side?' he would ask).

But Willie had perhaps never been entirely comfortable sharing his life – 'He doesn't like, or need, an emotional base,' Julian Mitchell had written after seeing him in 1973 – and a note of domestic discontentment was beginning to appear in his work. 'Homes are so sad,' he would soon be writing. 'They reflect intentions, hopes, disappointments. Here is real life, they say; here is a real person with a past.' Cherry, he believed, 'makes this mistake. She's kept every little note I've ever sent her and eventually they'll break her heart.'

There was no obvious sign of discontentment at Elm Park Mansions, Cherry says now. If Willie was unfaithful, she assumed that he was paying for it. She didn't like the idea but had decided to put up with it. There was no question of some great affair taking place.

She was right about Willie paying for it, but wrong about the great affair.

The girls don't talk. Researching into the life of Willie Donaldson, this basic fact of research had emerged. With very few exceptions, the men who had dealings with Willie, even his enemies, were happy to share their memories. The women who saw his civil, civilian side – Sonia Hobbs, Sarah Miles, Carly Simon, Cherry Donaldson, Angie Bodell – have provided their own versions. But the girls – those who have seen what one has to describe as the darker side of his sexuality – have tended to stay clear of me.

For many of them, it was not that they disliked Willie – 'He was a funny, intelligent man,' said the former madam Janie Jones before hanging up on me – more that he reminded them of things from their past that, unsurprisingly, they would prefer to remain undiscussed. Who, after all, would actually choose to chat about ancient tricks and bunk-ups and sexual adventures from two or three decades ago for the purpose of a book? Even Willie drew the line there.

I was sorry not to talk more to Stephanie Marrian, the Page Three girl who was a bit-player in Willie's life from the late Sixties until the very end. It was not that Stephanie had been a girlfriend or had been even remotely interested in seediness of any kind but Willie confided in her on a regular basis. She understood him. It was Stephanie who had first mentioned Melanie Soszynski, the woman who would change his life, to him. But when I rang Stephanie the mere mention of Willie's name seemed to enrage her. 'I don't really have much to say, frankly,' she mumbled. 'Goodbye.'

Melanie had another close friend who, in Willie's account of the affair in *Is This Allowed?* goes by the name of Candy. It was Candy who offered Willie advice when Melanie sank into addiction. After some sleuthing on the internet, I tracked Candy down. The name Willie Donaldson meant nothing to her, she said. She had hardly known Melanie, who had been a friend of a friend. She had been shocked to hear Melanie was on the game. She had spoken to her once when she was in her drugs clinic and had never heard of her again. When I mentioned that I had before me a chatty letter from her to Willie, thanking him for the book he had written about Melanie, Candy's memory improved. She did remember a Willie Donaldson now. It had all been a long time ago.

Willie's account of the end of what happened between him and Melanie Soszynski, a 'novel' called *Is this Allowed?*, is pitiless and forensic in its emotional detail yet also both more romantic and more squalid than what actually happened.

Willie had been seeing business girls, most of whom were on the books of a nearby escort agency, for some time. Now and then he would ask a girl out to Ibiza, to stay in the rented flat. He had met Melanie this way and, after a few months, he invited her to stay with him in the spring of 1985.

She was blonde and pretty in a hard-faced way, but she had a certain quality that excited Willie. She had, I was told by Candy, first been introduced to the idea that there was good money to be made from selling her body while working as a cocktail waitress. Several of the girls there were offered the chance to 'go case' as the technical phrase has it. In the opening pages of *Is This Allowed?*, as good and sad a piece of writing as he ever achieved, Willie described waiting for Melanie at the airport:

> I continue to pace, trying to remember what she's like. I met her twice, I think, after Tiffs introduced us. I know she wasn't beautiful, and she no more looked like Catherine Deneuve than I do. She must have been all right, though. If she hadn't been more or less all right I wouldn't have asked her to Ibiza. She'd been quite classy, I think, but whether going up or coming down I couldn't tell. It is hard to tell with these performing girls, they hide their origins quite expertly. On the one hand she could have been someone's daughter off the rails, on the other a resourceful girl from Stratford-atte-Bow. She hadn't been trying very hard, I do remember that – a minimum of make-up, hair not recently attended to, scuffed boots and jeans – all of which suggested confidence, or apathy. I think she quite amused me, though, and she had a quality – a kind of relaxed assurance in the way she came on stage – which seemed to be a guarantee that she was expert where it mattered, that in spite of the scuffed and casual clothes everything was lovely underneath. Her body was a delight, in fact, satiny, unflagging, softly inflated everywhere – the sort of

body which looks at its best on a beach, which should be sold in beach shops with other inflatable things. Tiffs had said she'd got it made, but I didn't think she'd got it made at all. She was rather pale and easily startled, running around to not much purpose, eager and regretful, with huge hurt eyes. I thought she was adrift and a little bit afraid, but I'd been pleased about the eyes. There's nothing less boring than a woman with hurt eyes, she'll do anything just in case, she'll believe what you tell her just in case it might be true. It was probably the hurt eyes that had made me ask her to Ibiza. Ibiza's just the place for women with hurt eyes, who want to think there's still a chance.

There is, as it happens, another view of Melanie, who was cunningly disguised in the book as 'Melissa'. On one of her first visits to Ibiza, Willie was in the company of Mike O'Mara, an American friend who lived in London and who was his new publisher. O'Mara saw a different performing girl. 'She was a real bimbo – very short with enhanced boobs,' he says. 'She sunbathed all day and then in the evening would say daft things like "What do you think of my new boobs?" It seemed to me that Willie filed her away during the day and took her out in the evening. He insisted that first night on taking us to this sleazy club and that I dance with Melanie, which he found very amusing.'

In their different versions, Willie and Mike agreed on one thing: Melanie was using coke a lot. When Mike flew home with her a few days later, he says 'she was in terrible shape – she was so gone, she would never have made it home if I hadn't been there'. At London airport, she was met by a stretch limo.

But Willie was enchanted. He had an almost visceral horror of the vulgar cliché and was delighted to find that, unlike the other professional women he had brought to Ibiza, she avoided the clunkingly obvious, tarty phrase. High, she was a performer and turned heads with her little white boots, short shirt and unself-conscious flirtiness. He invented a mildly self-mocking term for her, which was both affectionate and recognised the absurdity of their situation. She was his Princess; he was her prince. Willie had been warned that Melanie was a ruthless whore, but he liked that in a girl, particularly if she had those all-important hurt eyes. Quite quickly, he fell for her.

There is the Melanie story, and then there is the Melissa story of *Is This Allowed?*, but the sad little sequence of real events and their retelling in semi-fictional form share the same basic facts.

Melanie set up a fever in Willie's brain and made him realise the full extent of his dissatisfaction with his life with Cherry. Returning to England, he found himself caught up in domestic and professional turbulence which merely made his longing for what he had discovered with Melanie burn stronger. Cherry's mother had been diagnosed with liver cancer and given a year to live. The idiotic, mad drama of the copyright case surrounding *The English Way of Doing Things* was heading inexorably towards the High Court.

Melanie was Willie's drug of choice. She sensed that what really excited him was sexual jealousy and, helped by her drug of choice, she was prepared to go as far as he wanted, taunting him, betraying him with other men and then returning to face his ecstatic rage.

They returned to Ibiza, where these games were played out. 'I keep thinking of a night in Ibiza when I let her go to Ku with a Chilean beach boy she picked up on Salinas,' Willie would write.

I went to bed, but I couldn't sleep; I was tormented by the hot dazzling image of brown, leathery hands touching her soft body, of the look of defiant acquiescence in her eyes for someone else – and I couldn't take it. I got up in the middle of the night and I rang her at Ku, screamed at her and told her to come home at once. She did, immediately, quite meekly – and now I wish she hadn't. I wish she'd defied me, hadn't come home at all. I don't want to be hurt: I want to hurt her and win her back, to punish and repossess her.

Back in London, he confessed to Cherry and months of pain and indecision, of moving in and out of Elm Park Mansions, followed. Willie was later to write of the anguished, increasingly perverse affair with Melanie.

One night – through no fault of my own, I think – an innocent little game of ours gets slightly out of hand. I look at
her, and suddenly I don't want her – or rather I want more,
I want to endanger us. I want to wound and repossess her,
to prove the strength of my awful need by inflicting damage
and then repairing it. I want to go to the very edge and see
what hell is. I want her to do the inconceivable, and I dread
her doing it.

The lived, as opposed to the written, version is more complex
and emotionally muddled. Willie may have been obsessed by
Melanie but he was also begging Cherry not to allow what he
called his 'squalid cavortings' to destroy their relationship. 'I
want to marry you and live with you forever – it's my only
chance,' he wrote to Cherry. In another note, he referred to his
'sick shame and great love for you' and begged her: 'Please
don't be hurt by something so cheap and fatuous.' It is startlingly different and more complicated from the story he would
soon be writing.

Melanie was on her way down. She became involved with a
group of crackheads, including the Marquess of Blandford, in the
flat upstairs from hers. She was introduced to the crack pipe and,
by the time Willie could do anything, was hopelessly addicted. In
order to reach her, to help her – or perhaps to make her more like
the Melanie he liked – Willie took crack with her. Eventually, she
was arrested, with the Marquess of Blandford and others. Having
blown what was left of his money, Willie and Melanie's mother
took her to a drug rehabilitation clinic, Broadway Lodge at
Weston-super-Mare, Willie paying the £1,300 required for the
first two weeks there.

It is here that Melanie vanishes. Willie rang her occasionally
but found that the treatment at Broadway Lodge involved eras-
ing her past, a cure which would instil in him a lifelong loathing
of the 'mad Christians' and their manner of dealing with addiction. Candy says she called too, but Melanie was no longer the
person she knew and was anxious to get off the telephone.

In May 1986 Princess Diana visited Broadway Lodge and

met Willie's ex-Princess – described, bizarrely, as 'poor little rich girl Melanie' in the *Daily Express*.

> 'Using cocaine was just the natural thing to do in my set,' said Melanie. 'If I couldn't get coke, I would turn to alcohol. Slowly everything collapsed around me. I couldn't get work, friends deserted me, morals declined ... I was always the little girl lost, feigning innocence if I was in trouble. But that's being drummed out of me.'

It was the last sighting of Melanie, and Willie was genuinely heartbroken. Back with Cherry – he had stayed for a few weeks with me and my family – he tried to repair the damage, all the while writing *Is This Allowed?* On one occasion, he went with Angela Picano to see Melanie's mother in Harlow, Essex.

In August, he and Cherry were married but too much damage had been done. 'It was just something I couldn't recover from,' Cherry says now. 'And the fact that he was writing the book didn't help.' In the spring of 1987, after nine months of marriage, Cherry moved out of 139 Elm Park Mansions, never to return.

Later that year, after *Is This Allowed?* had been published, Willie made one last attempt to track Melanie down. He sent out letters to various journalists on his old Film and Television Copyright headed paper and under the name of Angela Picano. FTC Ltd had bought film rights in Donaldson's novel, the letter revealed, and the producer was looking for a Miss Melanie Soszynski about whom the book was written but who had since disappeared. 'We are extremely eager to find her because we think she might play the lead in the film. She used to be an actress. Might this be a story for you?'

If any of the journalists took the bait, Melanie did not and this last desperate effort to flush her out failed.

Interviewed about *Is This Allowed?* on its publication, Willie explained: 'You are meant to think, what will a writer stop short of? There was certainly a point when I realised I was writing about evil and actually indulging in it at the same time. I wrote it in a sort of flood of embarrassment. I wrote it when I was still in love with her.' But it was a later plot summary – 'Older man is hooked on a hooker who's hooked on drugs. Oh dear' – that was closer in tone to the critical reaction it received.

This discomfiting book, neither fact nor entirely fiction, the theme of which is the sexual obsession of a middle-aged Old Wykehamist for a young prostitute, was never going to have an easy ride among reviewers. What reputation Willie had was as a humorist and literary prankster. The novel (as it was billed) did not cause much of a stir on the books pages. Willie's supporter Auberon Waugh writing in the *Independent* saw it as a warning to parents not to send their children to Winchester, adding that it was 'brilliant in describing the twisted arguments of a psychopath'. Donaldson was not, Waugh pointed out, describing himself but 'castigating the darker side of a character which he imagines to have been shaped by its schooldays'.

Waugh's review contains a wonderful compliment to Willie which was only slightly spoilt by its qualifier: 'For the skill and wit of his writing he deserves to be hailed as an English Nabokov … among a small section of the upper class in a brief period of our national history.'

At the end of the decade, David Sexton, literary editor of the now-defunct *Sunday Correspondent*, listed it in a section called 'Funnies', which also included stories by Alan Bennett and novels by Martin Amis and Julian Barnes.

Auberon Waugh's mention of Nabokov was astute. *Is This Allowed?* was more than a confession which happened to have been disguised as a novel, mainly for legal reasons. The narrator was colder, nastier and more self-deceptive than the real Willie, and his attitude to his Princess had the suave intellectual dishonesty of a public-school educated Humbert Humbert. 'And yet in some way I can't help blaming myself,' the fictional Willie reflects. 'I knew from the start what sort of person she was – a pretty gangster, vicious and cheerful, ruthless and sentimental – and yet I let her use me, even let her take me down to her crude level from time to time.'

It is a chilling and unforgiving variation on the theme of a writer's exploitation of real, breathing, bleeding material that adds potency and depth to a story of sexual power-play.

In *Is This Allowed?*, Willie proved that, when he lowered the dazzling shield of his comedy, he could write with the clear eye of a novelist. Here he is introducing his Princess to the Ibizan social scene:

> We join the enemy – the happy crush of young people pulled by the weight of music in the distance, pushing, laughing, celebrating this once-off, unexclusive triumph – being young – hurrying towards the wall of music coming from the Bar Zoo as if afraid they may grow old before they get there. We leave them here and head towards Ponce Corner, where, dazed with flirty self-regard, the island's hotshots lounge outside the Bar Chic and the Bar Tango, where everyone under eighty deals in drugs, not least Tanit, the heavy centre of the in-set, a massively composed half-naked negro, who came out of the sea ten years ago proclaiming himself to the island God of Ibiza. In spite of his divine power Tanit the island God carries cocaine in his cache-sexe in case chemistry's required. With him as usual is his pal El Pimpo, an enormous Italian with a tiny head, not bigger than a lemon. Tanit and El Pimpo never go to bed, but spend their nights gazing into one another's eyes, as if the other is a mirror reflecting the only company worth keeping. With them is their exotic retinue of twerps.

The shared madness of two people, each of whose self-destructiveness ignites that of the other, is conveyed with an icy passion and there is a sense of generalised revulsion which, were the writing any less brilliant, would be almost unbearable to read.

In his everyday life, Willie kept a lid on his emotion. Sleeping in my office at the worst of times, his final fall-out with Cherry, he was distracted and unhappy but he was in no way falling apart. Only in his writing was the full crisis of his life exposed.

He was suffering from a crushing, inescapable sense of boredom. What he calls 'the real world ... of fear and rate demands and veins', gave him the horrors. He was bored of the toilet books he was writing, 'books in which one makes jokes about imaginary social groups, books with inferior cartoons'. At work with Simon Carr, on another borrowed idea, *You Want, You'd Settle For, You Get,* he provides heartless examples through the text:

> You want the girl and the money at twenty-five. You'd settle for the girl and money at thirty-five. You get the girl and the money at fifty-five and it's too late and your legs have turned blue.

Willie had been promising himself and various publishers that he would soon be writing his memoirs and incidents from the past, mainly from his days at Winchester, had drifted through the narrative of *Is This Allowed?* in an abstracted, interrupted way. The truth, Willie had discovered, was that, while unable to escape from his past and increasingly haunted by it, it also failed really to interest him. He disliked his young self, with all his hopes and failures, almost as much as the fifty-year-old he had become. 'I am bored by the past,' he wrote, 'and I'm making it all up anyway.'

The facts may be reordered, and some of the names changed but it was emotionally true. On to this wasteland of boredom and revulsion, there emerged someone who identified Willie's true sexual nature and (it seemed to him, anyway) shared his tastes.

'Since I never had fulfilling sex until the age of forty-nine, I used to fantasise – necessarily – about things that hadn't happened,' he wrote some fifteen years later. 'Once I had been educated by a damaged girl from Harlow New Town, I was able to fantasise about reality. The problem here is that reality has to get better and better, else what is there to fantasise about?'

The fantasy, a heady mix of voyeurism, masochism and brutality, involved being a part of the other person's infidelity and betrayal, getting a charge out of jealousy, and then exacting punishment. Melanie, at least in Willie's version of her, was excited by the same thing. She liked to be betrayed, and wanted to be punished: one of the most harrowing scenes in *Is This Allowed?* was when Willie does finally knock her about.

He hurts her; she hurts him. The process could only work by

becoming more extreme. In the book, Willie presents the violence as having exploded at the feverish end of the affair, by which time Melanie had become an addicted crackhead, but there is evidence that it was part of their actual relationship from an earlier stage.

Willie's old pal JP Donleavy met up with him in London around this time. 'He begged me to come across London to Sloane Square,' Donleavy told me. 'He said, "Please come, you will see a woman in all her glory – there will be a light shining on her. She will be a vision." He implored me for so long that eventually I agreed. We went to this block of flats off Sloane Square and down a long hall at the end of which there seemed to be a door ajar. He opened this door and there was exactly the scene Willie had described: the light, the woman, who was in a state of undress. She was most attractive. I was never expecting this scene but it was exactly as he had described. I finally excused myself after a bit of conversation in the hall. He told me later that, after I had gone off, she had commented to him: "That is the most impressive man I've met in all my life." Willie was infuriated and attacked her and gave her a beating.'

'Writers can *murder*,' the Melanie character, Melissa, tells Willie in *Is This Allowed?* 'You could kill me off – and no one would ever know. You could write a book and say that I was dead. I could run around saying, no – look, I'm alive, I'm OK, that's not what happened at all. But I couldn't tell everyone.'

Willie did in a sense kill off the Melanie that he had known. 'She's dead,' he would say with a dull certainty that precluded any further questions.

As it turned out, there has been no running around on Melanie's part to tell the world that she is alive, she is OK. Neither Stephanie nor Candy have heard from her since she emerged from the clinic. One prediction from *Is This Allowed?* turned out to be true. The book is all that people now know about Melanie Soszynski. She is, let us hope, living a new life under a new name.

sitting on the wrong end of a shooting stick

Even when his life was in turmoil, and his brain boiling with thoughts of revenge, Willie worked; indeed, the worse things were going at home, the more he threw himself into new projects.

Although he was dismissive about the business of churning out clever-dick spoofs and parodies for the toilet book market, he enjoyed it, too. These books provided him with an opportunity to tease, to goose his enemies. He genuinely loved making people laugh and the best of his toilet books allowed him to adopt different disguises and make silly jokes that were often sublimely funny. For *Is this Allowed?* he had to dig deep. The great advantage of the toilet book was that it allowed him to skitter over the surface of things.

It was also as social a process as writing can ever be. During the second half of the 1980s, Willie wrote with Simon Carr, with me and was in touch with several publishers. Most of his books were now published by Mike O'Mara, who was, in many ways, the perfect editor for Willie. Since he owned his own publishing house, he was not prey to the dead hand of corporative correctness that was settling upon the book industry at the time. Like Willie, he was something of an outsider and was happiest when his books, which would include Andrew Morton's famous unofficially authorised biography of Princess Diana, were causing scandal and fuss. He could discuss the complexities of American football, a new obsession of Willie's. He loved Willie's company and was a huge admirer of his writing. 'What we are talking about is a genius,' O'Mara says now. 'Although he was unfulfilled, he was a man of enormous talent. He was the wittiest man I have worked with including Peter Ustinov and Barry Humphries.'

Collaborating with Willie was an unmitigated delight. Writing can be tough but he enjoyed, more than anyone I know, the joy of getting the right, economically funny, phrase, the unexpected joke. Even the most apparently silly and ephemeral book, he would take seriously. There would be writers' conferences over coffee or lunch, lengthy discussions about strategy, structure, tone. Decisions would be made about who would write what. His own contributions – first handwritten, then typed, then corrected – would set the authorial tone and, although as a co-writer one was forever having to raise one's game to be even close to him, there was never any sense of his being the senior partner. Naturally, effortlessly, Willie provided the all-important lesson that the best kind of writing has something childish, playful and irresponsible about it. If you feel you are getting away with something – behaving like naughty teenagers, in the scolding phrase one of the more disapproving critics, Peter York, used to describe an earlier collaboration of Willie's – then you are probably on the right track.

When a grandee from the BBC discovered *The English Way of Doing Things* and commissioned a pilot for a sitcom, Willie involved me as co-writer, in spite of the fact that I had even less experience of writing for television than he did. The memoir that had become a play that had become a novel that had become a court case was given one more turn as a potential TV comedy. Nothing came of it.

In 1986, Willie invented a new character. Talbot Church was one of the new breed of court correspondents who, at a time when the public obsession with royalty was becoming increasingly absurd, offered his own brand of expertise as a palace-watcher. Church, whose press byline was 'The man the Royals trust', combined a plummy authoritative tone of voice with the leery curiosity of a foot-in-the-door journalist. When Prince Andrew and Sarah Ferguson announced their engagement, Talbot Church was on hand with a collection of facts presented under the title of *101 Things You Didn't Know About the Royal Lovebirds*.

Published by Michael O'Mara, it was, as the blurb put it, 'an unforgettable documentary and a book to cherish in years to come'.

Willie was adept at parodying the tabloid style of royal correspondents – clammy, confiding, simultaneously voyeuristic and cringingly respectful – and together we invented a series of facts that were either plonkingly banal or absurd. It was Church who revealed exclusively that the Sailor Prince was at one point thought to suffer from something called 'Smith's Condition'.

In November 1984, an unusual incident threw some light on the Prince's extraordinary courage and complete indifference to pain. One evening in Buckingham Palace, he wandered into Prince Charles's quarters, where he found the future king conducting some 'mind over matter' experiments with a group of orange-sheeted Indians – levitating, sitting on hot coals, putting needles through their noses and so forth.

Try-anything-once Andrew joined in and it was soon discovered that he could sit on a lighted gas-ring for longer than the fakirs could. A Harley Street neurophysiologist was consulted and he diagnosed Smith's Condition. In sufferers from Smith's Condition, signals from different parts of the body reach the brain more slowly than they do in normal people. If a sufferer pricks his finger, for instance, he may not feel anything for as long as five minutes, by which time he has forgotten the incident and he will carry on as if nothing has happened.

In a fit young man, the condition is trivial, manifesting itself in feats of extraordinary courage. In later life, when broken bones should be treated immediately, it is more serious, and it was thought at first that the daredevil Prince would have to cut out his more hair-raising escapades.

Fortunately, a leading neurophysiologist from Germany was brought in and after further, and much more rigorous tests, it was discovered that Andrew didn't suffer from Smith's Condition at all, but was simply quite exceptionally brave.

In one sense at least, the royal wedding tie-in was a success. In spite of containing stories about Prince Andrew levitating over gas-rings, and being categorised by its publisher as 'Humour/ reference', the work of Talbot Church was taken seriously in some quarters. Several of his stories found their way into the pages of a leading newspaper and were presented, without accreditation, as facts. Incensed, O'Mara rang the editor, who expressed regret that Mr Church had not been named as the source of the stories; the revelation that they were entirely fictional worried him less. Some things, Talbot Church proved, are beyond parody.

It had been some time now since Henry Root had bothered serious-minded people with his letters, and now Willie came up with a new Root project. *The Soap Letters*, again published by Michael O'Mara, was one of Willie's madder projects. Root, it turns out, is in trouble. He weighs twenty-two stone, Mrs Root has 'gone off with Bath's boy Weymouth' and now he finds himself watching *Terry and June* on his own while eating Cod Florentine cooked in a bag. He has decided to take a different approach and 'henceforth talk to women about themselves, about their operations, their intestinal gasses – that's what they like, is it not?'

Root has been sent a play called *The Westenders*, which had been written by a pensioner fan of the original *Henry Root Letters*. He sends the play out under his own name and gets sucked into the world of TV production.

There is, in fact, not much Root in *The Soap Letters*. Willie resolved the obvious problem that only the gullible (a bishop, a few casting directors) were going to reply to a Henry Root letter by inventing a new cast of fictional letter-writers. As the idea of a soap series based on scandal in public life and called *Crack-Up* is developed, he introduced a series of characters, writing from different firms, notably Film and Television Copyrights Ltd, which had a number of dodgy directors, some of them American, casting directors, secretaries and a publicist called Sandy McPeak. The name of two of his old friends, Julia Mortimer and Angela Picano, appear at the foot of several letters.

Interspersed with their correspondence with each other and with their various targets – Jeffrey Archer, Judge Pickles, Lynda

Lee-Potter and others – is the treatment and various scenes from *Crack-Up*. One involves the Marquis of Beauchamp and his circle of crack addicts. Another features participants in various scandals of the 1960s. Throughout there are commentaries from the thinkers Willie found most funny: Peregrine Worsthorne, AN Wilson, Richard West, Max Hastings, Anna Raeburn. Towards the end of what little story there is, one of the bathetic commentators, Geoffrey Wheatcroft, while delivering inanities during a scene involving Bob Geldof and Paula Yates, sees the casting director of Film and Television Copyrights, Selina Sidey, and gasps:

> She's the most beautiful girl I've ever seen! I'm tired of mooching around in books and sitting on the wrong end of a shooting stick! I must follow her wherever she goes.

Wheatcroft, hired by Sidey, is appointed Assistant Publicity Director (Turkeys) and starts sending out letters from FTC Ltd.

If *The Soap Letters* were less funny, one could almost present it as experimental, avant-garde fiction. The narrative is driven by letters from real people and mixes them with those from invented characters (among them, Talbot Church) with a feverish abandon. At one point in the juggling act, the *Sunday Times* solemnly reported that 'the moral standards of Britain's best and brightest are to be chronicled in an extraordinary television serial in which actors will play, among many others, Cecil Parkinson, Sarah Keays, Jeffrey Archer and John Profumo'.

At the time, *The Soap Letters* must have seemed like another successful, if rather shambolic Henry Root joke. Reading it now, though, it is impossible to ignore the sense of rage that emerges between, and within, the jokes. Partly a moral disgust, it was also personal.

From the early 1970s onwards, Willie was known to some of his closer friends as 'Button'. The nickname originated from his childhood, he said. His sister Jane and he used to read a book called *The Little Green Button Man,* in which the Button Man in question would occasionally get into such a rage that he would

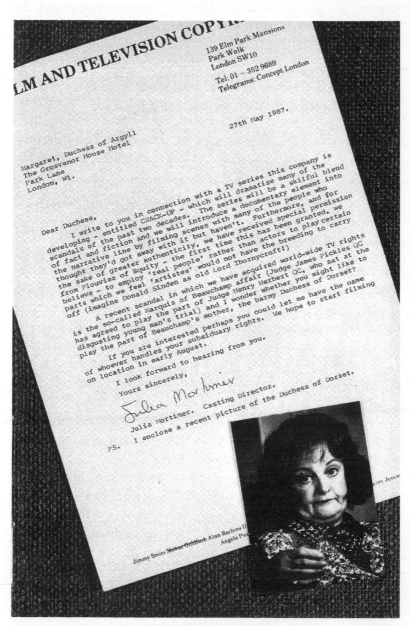

FILM AND TELEVISION COPYRI...

139 Elm Park Mansions
Park Walk
London SW10

Tel: 01 – 352 9689
Telegrams: Concept London

27th May 1987.

Margaret, Duchess of Argyll
The Grosvenor House Hotel
Park Lane
London, W1.

Dear Duchess,

I write to you in connection with a TV series this company is developing – entitled CRACK-UP – which will dramatise many of the scandals of the past two decades. The series will be a skilful blend of fact and fiction and we will introduce a documentary element into the narrative line by filming scenes with many of the people who thought they'd got away with it but haven't. Furthermore, and for the sake of greater authenticity, we have received special permission from Plouviez of Equity – the first time this has been granted, we believe – to employ 'real people' rather than actors to play certain parts which we feel 'artistes' would not have the breeding to carry off (imagine Donald Sinden as old Lord Thornycroft!)

A recent scandal in which we have acquired world-wide TV rights is the so-called Marquis of Beauchamp affair (Judge James Pickles QC has agreed to play the part of Judge Henry Herbert QC, who sat at the disgusting young man's trial) and I wonder whether you might like to play the part of Beauchamp's mother, the barmy Duchess of Dorset?.

If you are interested perhaps you could let me have the name of whoever handles your subsidiary rights. We hope to start filming on location in early August.

I look forward to hearing from you.

Yours sincerely,

Julia Mortimer

Julia Mortimer. Casting Director.

PS.   I enclose a recent picture of the Duchess of Dorset.

Jimmy Smits   Milton Oulofarb   Alan Rachins D... Angela Pic...   ...erry Jerem...

From *The Soap Letters* – The Duchess of Argyll
is offered a part in *Crack-Up*.

revolve on the spot, disappearing through the floorboards, like a circular saw through butter. At that age, Willie had such a terrible temper that Jane took to calling him 'Button'.

Whether or not the story is true (Jane has no recollection of it and there is no such book as *The Little Green Button Man*), Willie liked the nickname. When Claudia Fitzherbert wrote a 'Dear Button' letter, he replied that it 'made me gurgle and beam with pleasure'.

But there was little outward sign of the Button-like rage in Willie's adult life. He wrote about his red-hot sexual jealousy in *Is This Allowed?* but then that was part of the peculiar state of his intimate life. When a spark of bitterness or personal unkindness poked through his prose like a thorn, it was always a bit of a shock. It seemed so out of character.

In fact, as perhaps with a lot of funny writers, there was more anger behind his work that it seemed. As he grew older, the animus he felt towards himself, but also towards people he decided had done him harm, grew stronger.

In a conversation with Griff Rhys-Jones, published in *Ritz* magazine in 1982, Willie commented – complained perhaps – that 'laughter softens the blow. I have a theory that comedy isn't the medium if you want to hurt. Or really make people sit up and think.'

Increasingly, it became clear that Willie not only wanted to make people sit up and think but also, just now and then, wanted to draw blood.

The Soap Letters includes some distinctly personal targets. A Princess Soszynski, the crack-addict associate of the Marquis of Beauchamp, is to star in Root's soap opera. Described variously as 'a leather-clad sadist', a 'nasty little tart' and 'as tempting as a poisoned nectarine', she smokes crack, takes off her clothes at a party at her flat (the real address given) and is paid for sex. At the end of the scene, 'a fishy Christian counsellor from 'a drug addiction clinic practising the sinister Minnesota Method' appears and offers the princess a place at the clinic. 'That will be £800 a week plus VAT for a six-week course of group therapy. Defecating into a bucket on an open podium in front of a roomful of emotional cripples. Cure by humiliation – the Christian way. Two weeks in advance – sign here.'

In *The Soap Letters*, Willie discovered that he could get away with a lot under the guise of comedy. Famously averse to confrontation, and rarely one to show his anger in person, he had found a useful form of public therapy.

In 1988 and 1989, various Willie Donaldson projects seem to have been conceived, announced, put under contract, and not written. A British publisher signed up a mysterious project called HFB for a £12,000 advance (£3,000 put down on signature) which was never delivered.

More surprisingly, there were the *Henry Root – Robert Maxwell Letters*, which he advertised in the personal columns of *Private Eye*.

All that is to be found of this project in Willie's papers are some letters from hopeful fans, all of whom attached their £5.95 plus £2 postage. Of almost all of Willie's stunts, I find this the most surprising. He had never mentioned the idea to me or to any other friends, nor is there evidence of any work being done, let alone rejected by publishers. Was Willie really conning his readers? The return of this enterprise would be minimal and his home address was contained in the advertisement. Did he open a

bank account in the name of Henry Root? While the letters are in the file, the cheques have gone.

Another Root project, and one which Willie does seem to have intended to write, was *Henry Root and the House of Windsor*, which was signed up by the Australian publisher Morry Schwarz for a total advance of £15,000, a third of which was paid on signature of the contract in January 1988. It was a promising idea, with Root and a team of dodgy financial backers, casting directors, many of whom had featured in *Crack-Up*, setting up a ten-hour drama-documentary about the Royal Family, backed by Australian and Canadian money and entitled *The Professionals*.

Willie compiled a few biographical entries, as written by Root, some of which were old favourites: (the Duchess of Argyll was to the fore, naturally) while some of them were entirely new.

> *MOTHER, The Queen*
> ... She's a tough old trout, a country woman, still one of the best shots in the Highlands, can tell which way the wind's blowing by sniffing a guest's plus-fours, can discover the whereabouts of a covey by biting into a pheasant turd, at the Highland Games presides over demonstrations of a little mole being trapped by spikes flying into its brain ("completely painless!"), leads the applause as an otter is torn to pieces ("If you don't live in the country you wouldn't understand!") The Princess of Wales fainted when she was first made to witness this and the Queen Mum God bless her brought her round by having a fox's severed penis inserted in her ear, causing the Princess to faint again. ('The silly girl should be savaged by a badger. Then she'd know what living in the country means'.)

The Windsors were an excellent subject for Willie – a focus for snobbery and celebrity worship, not only stupid themselves but the cause of stupidity in others – but sadly this promising venture remained at the planning stage and Morry Schwartz never got his book.

28
A profound instinct to corrupt and destroy

The affair with Melanie had left a single, important legacy. From the mid-1980s until a couple of years before he died, Willie became a regular user of crack cocaine.

There are different stories about how Willie discovered crack. He would occasionally claim that it was he who put Melanie on the pipe but a more plausible account is contained in *Is This Allowed?*, where Melissa/Melanie had traded up from her cocaine habit when she was taken up by the Marquis of Beauchamp and his crowd at Bristol House. A skeletal crack-head after a six-week binge, she had persuaded Willie to freebase with her.

Either way, Melanie seems to have been ready for it – self-destructive and already a serious user of coke. Willie's enthusiasm for crack is more difficult to explain. He had loathed alcohol so much throughout his adult life that it coloured his judgement of character: much of his peculiarly hostile attitude towards Peter Cook (or at least Peter Cook's reputation) can be explained by the fact that, in the second half of his life, Cook was a serious boozer. As for drugs, he disapproved of them all except for pot, according to Cherry, and had been furious when she had once tried cocaine. Yet after six months or so with his Princess, he was smoking it in its purest, most lethal form.

Willie claimed that, at a session among the recovering addicts at Broadway Lodge, Melanie was told that she could be cured but that they could do nothing for Mr Donaldson. If that is true – and Willie did attend a 'family session' at Broadway Lodge –

then the 'mad Christians' to whom he referred so contemptu-
ously were probably right. Willie did not want to be cured.

'On crack, you know you're happy,' he wrote in an extraordinary article for the London *Evening Standard* in 2003.

> Nothing can go wrong. The real world, the world of dry-
> cleaning and money-off, of weddings in tents and pension
> plans, has, like a fat woman in a pantomime, sat on a chair
> that isn't there and is looking very silly indeed. For the
> moment, you're victorious, and that's quite a feeling to
> have; but equally, quite a feeling never to have again. Sooner
> or later, you can't recapture it. For months, years, you spend
> all your money chasing the all-conquering euphoria of that
> first 'high'.

The wooziness of booze, the unfocussed contentment of grass,
the all-too-focused intensity of coke: none of them was what
appealed to Willie. The big hit – 'an all-body orgasm', in the
words of writer and painter Sebastian Horsley, later to be Willie's
friend – was what he was after.

Although Willie was eventually to set much of the action of
his memoir *From Winchester to This* around the crack-pipe, he
never wrote about the physical experience it delivered. Will Self,
who once accompanied Willie to a crack den, has done so,
through his character Tembe in the short story 'The Rock of
Crack as Big as the Ritz':

> It was the strongest hit off a pipe that Tembe could ever
> remember taking. He felt this as the crack lifted him up and
> up. The drug seemed to be completing some open circuit in
> his brain, turning it into a humming, pulsating lattice-work
> of neurones. And the awareness of this fact, the giant nature
> of the hit, became part of the hit itself – in the same way that
> the realisation that crack was the desire for crack had
> become part of the hit as well.
>
> Up and up. Inside and outside – Tembe felt his bowels
> gurgle and loosen, the sweat break out on his forehead and
> begin to course down his chest, drip from his armpits. And

still the rocky high mounted ahead of him. Now he could sense the red-black thrumming of his heart, accelerating through its gearbox. The edges of his vision were fuzzing with black deathly, velvet pleasure. Tembe set the pipe down gently on the surface of the table. He was *all*-powerful.

Rachel Garley, who was later to see Willie freebasing, has a more homely description of what happened to him. Willie on the pipe, she says, was 'like a Japanese person having an orgasm'.

Willie started freebasing at a moment of crisis in his life. The battle in the High Court with Wiseman had been traumatic. He had loved and lost Melanie, the woman who had finally showed him what he wanted. He had been left by Cherry and was afflicted by feelings of guilt for what he had done to her, and perhaps not done for his son Charlie. *Is This Allowed?*, a breakthrough in creative terms, had brought him less satisfaction than it should have. It had been painful to write, and had sold badly.

He was vulnerable and, like his father, needed a prop when the pain of life became unbearable. 'There's this great psychological need, this emptiness,' says Simon Tyszko, one of his dealers at the time. 'It's as if there's this great hole in the centre of your being, a very cold brittle place and, when you're using, that hole is filled perfectly, like a piece fitting in a jigsaw.'

In many ways, crack was the perfect drug for Willie. Whereas gin, heroin or pot make you feel mellow, crack is hard, violent and dramatic; it exacerbates the pain, and even its high is about endlessly deferred satisfaction, what Will Self calls 'a great crashing breaker of pure want'. That will have appealed to Willie whose life was restlessly in the past or the future but rarely in the present. At those occasional moments when he had achieved what he wanted, when his life reached a moment of stability, there was something in his personality that would sabotage the achievement, destroy the stability.

Crack had the practical advantage of being an occasional treat for Willie, rather than an obvious addiction. Such was his ability to operate normally, to write as well as ever, to be his normal sweet and funny self, that for most of the years of our friendship,

I had the suspicion that his occasional remarks and columns on the subject of his drug-taking were one of his elaborate jokes. Even on the occasion when I walked into his flat and there were two girls with him, and a molehill of white powder on some scales, I thought he was pulling my leg.

When, in 1989, his main source of income became a column in the *Independent*, it provided him with a perfect routine. He would write the column on Wednesday, polish and file it on Thursday. From that afternoon onwards, sometimes until the end of the weekend, it was party time.

Crack and sex tend to go together, and the type of sex it led to – hard, objectified, perverse, commercial – suited Willie just fine. Even when he had established a little crack-taking social circle of young writers and film-makers, the pipe would only be a prelude to the real action that would be happening later when he received a visit from Abby, Isabelle, Tracy, Michelle or one of the other escort agency girls.

But it is possible to dig too deep into the mulch of character and sexuality to find a reason why crack thrilled Willie Donaldson. *Is This Allowed?* contains this passage when 'Melissa's' dealer is arrested and she and Willie have to visit other connections across London:

> I love all this – the excitement, the risk, the paranoia, driving back at top speed, laughing at our audacity, swerving all over the road with granules of coke on board. We park the car and run upstairs, close the curtains and examine the goods, like criminals who've robbed a bank.

It was the transgressive thrill of buying, dealing and smoking crack – the mad adventure of it all – which excited Willie. 'After deep thought I conclude that your addiction is gambling,' Willie's sister Jane had once written to him. 'You cannot value anything unless you are within a hair's breadth of losing it. And this is the fundamental difference between us. You are a risk taker and I am a terrified worm.' She was right. There was part of him that needed to be on the edge of catastrophe to feel alive. In the 1960s, it was the roller coaster of wealth and bankruptcy – one moment, the talk of the town, the next hiding in Sarah Miles's attic – that answered this need. Then he was moving with call girls and bent policemen. Henry Root, with his capacity for infuriating the powerful and the respected, played his part in the 1980s.

Now it was time for a bigger adventure, a new plot-line to the story of his life. The advantage of crack over cocaine is that, while one was acceptable, even expected, at dinner parties of media folk, crack had a rat-like inner-city bite to its reputation. It was, he wrote, 'the most perverse drug, the most subversive of the natural order, a drug not for professional people but for the unaspirational; for people who don't want the nice things: a home, a lawn, a wife, access to a place in Portugal'.

In interviews, Willie loved telling stories of visits to crack-dens or how, desperate for a hit, he would meet armed Yardies on a street corner in the early hours of the morning at a cashpoint; invariably and typically for one of his stories, the Yardies turn out to be pillars of decency and morality.

That story may or may not have been true but the evidence suggests that Willie was rather less comfortable on the front line than he would have us believe. In around 1988, his new agent Cat Ledger introduced him to Will Self, then making a name for himself, with a view to their working together on what Willie called 'toilet books' and Will refers to as '*bricolage* projects'.

They discovered that they had friends – dealers, rather – in common as well as an enthusiasm for the pipe. On one occasion, Will invited Willie to dinner. 'To be frank, I was rather savage to him,' Will Self says now. 'At one point, I said to him, "Come on then, if you're such a druggie, let's go and score." It was mean of me, out-macho-ing him like that. It was all rather shameful.' They got into Will's car and drove to a notorious tower block off the Harrow Road. 'We got to first a urine-soaked vestibule and he turned tail and fled. I'm not sure who this redounds worse on: him or me.'

Nothing came of the *bricolage* project. Will moved on to writing fiction and rarely saw Willie after that. 'It was,' says Will, 'a combination of my domestic life and paradoxically my wildness which put him off.'

Although Willie kept in touch with a small number of his old friends, his social life had changed. Roy Stevens, known as 'Honest John' in his writing, had become a close friend and useful contact. He was intelligent and as curious about Willie's world as Willie was about his. A new enterprise involved writing to drugs companies as a pharmacological researcher, asking for samples of their products. Although he never, as Willie used to claim, acquired so many drugs that he was able to open a warehouse off the A4, he was certainly a ready supplier of tranks and sleeping-pills, must-have accessories for the crack-user, providing a way down, a 'parachute', from the jangling panic and paranoia that soon sets in.

On many of Willie's answer-machine tapes, it is the plummy tones of Honest John – 'Hi Willie, HJ Pharmaceuticals Ltd here' – which are to be heard more frequently than any other caller.

At around the time when Honest John was enjoying his freedom, another old friend was being sentenced to seven years in prison for dealing. Willie had first met Andy Dempsey, a former actor and stuntman, when Andy was seeing Dawn Upstairs in the early Seventies.

Andy, a good-looking South Londoner who speaks in the quiet, well-mannered tones of someone who is used to being listened to, had become a supplier of substances to the quality. He was outraged, probably with justification, that his sentence was incomparably harsher than those inflicted on other, better connected dealers.

Willie had always loved the low life. 'I'm more at ease among thieves and prostitutes than among literary people – one doesn't have to try so hard,' he once said, but it went deeper than that. He had been thrilled by villainy since the late 1950s and throughout the following decades had moved, to borrow his own phrase from *Brewer's Rogues, Villains and Eccentrics,* in 'the shadowy milieu, where well-born idlers meet the criminal class'. In 1971, Julian Mitchell was commenting in his diary that Willie was 'very involved in the cops and robbers myth and has fantasies about the "heavy mob".'

By the time his social and literary standing had gone into decline in the late 1980s, Willie was in the shadows himself. The Root boom years were over, he had frittered away what little capital he had during his feverish affair with Melanie, and he had a crack habit to support. An average session with the pipe would set him back around £400. A weekend's entertainment would cost him £2,000.

Like many users, Willie supplemented his income by dealing. 'I'll kill them – slowly, happily, torturing them first,' his narrator had written after discovering that Melissa/Melanie had fallen in with a drugs crowd. 'And to think I've always sneered at mad mothers on TV saying death's too good for dealers!' Now he would occasionally cash cheques for £500 to £700, with which he would fund his dealer Simon Tyszko's enterprises. Tyszko says Willie was as incompetent at dealing drugs as he was.

The tabloid press was another source of income. Andy Dempsey's story was written up by Willie and sold to the *News of the World*. When a woman who had briefly been a tabloid star after she had an affair with a cabinet minister wanted to earn some money by 'confessing' to a lesbian affair, it was Willie who effected an introduction to the working girl who would pose as her lover. The story duly appeared in a Sunday tabloid.

An old friend from the 1970s, Simone Washington, found herself in the happy position of having billets-doux and a compromising answerphone message from a lover, the MP Sir Anthony Meyer, who had just announced that he would stand against Mrs Thatcher in a leadership contest. Over an exciting weekend, during which Simone stayed at Elm Park Mansions, the pair negotiated with one tabloid after the other. Their joint efforts earned them £2,000 but what was to have been a great political scandal turned out to be a damp squib. Meyer, a game old gent, seems to have had a Donaldsonesque poise on these matters, and was unmoved by the revelation, as his wife knew about the arrangement. When a journalist rang Meyer at home, he called out: 'Darling, it's someone from the Daily Sleaze asking about Simone.'

I was seeing quite a lot of Willie at this point, spoke to him most days on the telephone, and thought, wrongly, that I knew him perfectly well. He was a superb conversationalist – one would put down the phone after talking to Willie feeling energised and better about the world and oneself. He was a master of the art of higher gossip, revealing various intimacies about mutual friends without ever seeming sour or unkind. (Only when researching this book have I discovered that, of course, he was sharing my intimacies around, too.) He invariably took a harsh and self-abasing view of his own behaviour.

I could never quite understand why such a sweet and generous man could be quite so riven by feelings of guilt.

Two bright and promising young men, Kim Kindersley and Peter Morgan, were making their way in the film business at this time. Kim had lost touch with Charlie but was back in contact with Willie. One evening when Peter and Kim were out chasing women and having fun, Kim had an idea. 'Let's go and get some drugs from Uncle Willie,' he said.

When they arrived at Elm Park Mansions, Willie had a suggestion to make. 'Have you ever tried cocaine washed up?' he asked.

Seeing Willie, as he went through the complexities of cooking the cocaine and preparing the crack pipe, was, says Kim, funny and endearing. 'Cooking's half the fun,' Willie would write later. 'Measuring, mixing, stirring, getting the balance of ingredients exactly right, warming the promising soup over a gentle flame – anxiously waiting for the lumps to form.' This vision of culinary order – Willie as a Jamie Oliver of narcotics – is not borne out by those who saw him at work and were scandalised by the general sloppiness and wastage.

It was Kim's and Peter's first experience of crack and, for Kim, 139 Elm Park Mansions became his occasional crack den. He admits that the whole thing was 'a bit pied-piperish' and discovered, perhaps fortunately, that Willie's drug of choice was not for him – in fact, it was 'a nightmare'. Quite soon Kim decided that Willie was heading in a strange direction and that spending too much time with him was a bad idea.

Willie was now at the centre of quite a hip little scene. Another young writer, Amy Jenkins, later to create the TV series *This Life* and to be one of the highest-paid first novelists of the 1990s, was going through what she now calls her 'party phase' and was going out with Simon Tyszko. Although she saw a lot of Willie during that time, she only once took crack with him.

'It was seven in the evening and I went round to the flat,' she says. 'He was there with Peter Morgan and it wasn't exactly a wild evening. They had a pathetic little rock and it was all kind of a damp squib. They improvised with a little piece of tin foil on a teapot. The foil had holes in it and they melted the crack with a lighter and then smoked it through the teapot spout. I only took one little puff because I was going out to dinner with my parents that night.'

Perhaps because he had never quite managed to grow up himself, Willie liked nothing better than being with people in their twenties and thirties. Now he managed, mysteriously, to be avuncular and concerned even while giving his young friends crack. When Kim brought along half a bottle of vodka to the flat to help him come down from the crack, Willie was genuinely disapproving, muttering: 'You know you really shouldn't touch that stuff.' Before Amy's only experience with the pipe, he had warned her gloomily: 'You'll be wanting to take your clothes off. Please don't take your clothes off – all the girls do that.' He was right. She did want to, but managed to resist the impulse. Like Kim, Amy looks back on those times with a surprising fondness.

Encouraging Amy with her writing, he gave her a copy of *Is This Allowed?* and, while she worked on a screenplay, they would meet for what he called 'writers' workshops' at a local café. He naturally assumed a great intimacy, she says, and the result was that their conversations were 'a warm and cosy place to be'. 'Willie', she says, 'made me racier, funnier than I was'.

It is odd, this. Sometimes it seems as if it was precisely when Willie had established a relationship of ease that he needed to push it beyond the acceptable. It happened with Melanie and now it happened with his new friends. Amy, like Kim, realised that she had to get away. Willie, she believed, was a serious addict. She went into a rehabilitation clinic. Once they were off drugs, she and her friends viewed Uncle Willie rather differently. 'We had thought he was so funny but, now we were straight, we worried about him. We stopped seeing him as charming and eccentric and saw him more as alarming and sad.'

When I went to see Peter Morgan, he was slightly preoccupied with various projects. Filming on *The Queen*, which would be one of the hits of the 2006 autumn, was just being completed under the directorship of Stephen Frears. Rehearsals for *Frost/Nixon*, a play whose Donmar Warehouse production would win ecstatic reviews, would be starting shortly. Then there was work to be done on the major Channel 4 documentary *Longford*. With hits on film, in the theatre and on TV, all in the same season, he would soon be described in one newspaper profile as 'Britain's most talented scriptwriter'.

I had met Peter at Willie's funeral and felt I knew him well in the form of Pete the Schnoz, a blazing star and dangerous intimate in Willie's memoir *From Winchester to This*. The Schnoz, I knew from that book, would frequently 'horrify himself at the nearest place of danger'. He was ambitious, with 'a steely, manipulative, rather unattractive feminine side which may save him in the end', according to Willie.

> Or will it? There have been times when I have seen my Schnoz utterly reduced, slumped on the floor, eyes wide with terror, screaming silently for help. I've been quite alarmed – compelled momentarily to imagine him broken in a seaside clinic, without dignity or self-respect, holding hands in a group and putting his trust in Him up there. Happily, this vision quickly passes. They won't take my Schnoz away from me, like they took Melanie away, put him on a programme for life and tell him, as they told Melanie, never to speak to me again.

By the looks of things, that 'rather unattractive feminine side' had won out. Peter Morgan did indeed go to the seaside clinic and as he talked to me in his office – Baftas on the mantelpiece, framed posters of his hits on the wall – he was the very picture of a successful young writer. Leg hitched over the arm of his armchair, bearishly confident, he spoke of Willie with passion.

'I've not met many more brilliant people,' he says. 'My relationship with him goes beyond anything that has gone before or since. I was completely delighted by him. I absolutely loved him. Willie got an "access all areas" to my life.' It was to Willie that Peter always turned for advice as a writer and it was Willie who gave him the confidence to aim high, encouraged him to take difficult options. 'For Willie, I straddled two things: bookish friend and sluttish friend,' Peter says.

All the same, the rock on which this intimacy was built was crack. 'There is no doubt that an interaction of the Bonnie and Clyde type happens when drugs are involved. It locks you into a partnership of druggie exhilaration. There is nothing more intoxicating. You are strapped together as if to a rocket.'

Peter seems to have quite happy memories of the early days of their friendship, during what he calls 'the rosiest stage of Willie's crack use'. Willie had started to earn money again and was being supplied principally by Gilly, a smart and well-spoken girl at the top end of the dealing spectrum. Later, when Peter and Willie were working together on a TV project, they did visit a crack house, but Willie was uncomfortable there, the clientele of hookers and criminals being too rough even for his taste.

What Willie loved, Peter says, was to talk about sex with intelligent people. The drugs were intimately connected to sex although Willie's particular taste, which Peter describes as 'that whole British, The Perverts of Penzance, tie-me-to-a-radiator-and-put-a-chilli-up-my-arse thing', had never remotely connected with him. Willie's ultimate fantasy was 'to find someone really prim, as it were, and watch her fall into his narcotic embrace'.

Peter parted company with drugs in 1994 and although he went on seeing Willie, whose advice about work he valued above that of virtually any other friend, his memory of Willie now has the swollen bitterness of a lover. 'The Willie of that time was unbelievably damaging personally,' Peter says. 'He spoke with savagery about people. He was vicious in his put-downs, there was a real record of him having associated with people whom he would essentially destroy. There was nothing he liked more than seeing a brilliant young person and then watching them explode. There was an extraordinary malevolence and irresponsibility about doing that to younger people. Willie had a profound instinct to corrupt and destroy. There was an extremely large Dionysian streak to him. He was quite diabolical.'

I was shaken by this view of Willie from someone who had apparently known him so well and felt a stab of retrospective sympathy for him. As, one by one, his smart young crack buddies left his narcotic embrace, I'm sure that there was a side of him, the generous part that he kept so carefully hidden, which was pleased by their subsequent success.

The rosiest stage of his crack use was over and some rough times lay ahead but the adventure, the dangerous anticipation, the sheer, thrilling inappropriateness of what he was doing, remained. Those who were with him on these occasions remember him preparing the flat, setting up the deal, ringing every ten minutes or so to hurry up the delivery, leaning out of the window to see if the dealer was approaching.

It is the side of Willie the crackhead which his straight friends rarely saw – excited, childlike, happy.

29
I am the Fat Man

There has never been a newspaper column quite like William Donaldson's Week, which the *Independent* began publishing from April 1989. In its 900-word form, Willie found a perfect framework to present a version of his world. There was no space for fleshing out, for filling in the complexities of a story, for any obvious seriousness. The past and the present, fact and fiction, were there in brilliant sketches, in which it was impossible for the reader to tell where the crazed comic fantasy ended and the more painful reality began.

It was funny, but dangerous. The man writing seemed to be recklessly prepared to betray all around him, above all himself. 'As I've grown older I've become a little unset in my ways,' he wrote.

> It's all over, more or less, and luckily there isn't time to put things right; small victories have been fortuitous, one's better schemes have ended in bizarre confusion; one has comforted those who wished one ill and frightened the life out of the few people one wanted to protect; nothing's at stake, nothing matters any more – so one can afford to experiment, to live more dangerously than one would have thought prudent hitherto.

If Willie had given up on himself, there was no sign of it in his writing. In the best of the columns, a scary tension exists between the tight, controlled funny prose and the shambles it describes.

He had used his life before, first in the semi-memoirs of the mid-1970s and later in *Is This Allowed?*, but books demanded a shape, a cooling distance from the material being described. A weekly column, entirely autobiographical in its tone, required him not only to be an archaeologist in the ruins of his past, but to reflect what was happening to him at the time. Virtually everything in his life was potential material.

The column has been compared in its honesty and elegant despair to what Jeffrey Bernard was spilling out every week for Low Life in the *Spectator*, but there's a care to the writing, a controlling intelligence and curiosity, that puts it in a different league. Bernard, in fact, exemplified many of the things Willie loathed – the languid English amateurism, the indolent egotism, the name-dropping, the boozed-up lack of focus that characterised what he called the *'delirium tremens* school of columnists'. At one point, he wrote a very sharp parody of Low Life in his *Independent* column.

> It's the little coincidences that get you in the end, isn't it? I went into a boozer the other day and there was this bloke I hadn't seen for twenty-five years. We were both a bit taken aback but we had a couple and then he said if he didn't see me for another twenty-five years it would be too soon for him. And I thought twenty-five years, that's a laugh. If either of us lives for another twenty-five weeks it will be a miracle. And talking about miracles, what chance do you give us in the West Indies this winter?
>
> Which reminds me. I spent yesterday in the Coach and Horses with Jeffrey Bernard, which is another coincidence, come to think...

On it goes, from saloon-bar cliché – 'Which reminds me', 'Mind you' – to sloppy cultural name-dropping (Graham Greene, 'the guvnor in my opinion', turned to his column first which 'makes it all worthwhile somehow'), seasoned with a drizzling self-pity.

By now he was limbering up for his much-promised and frequently delayed memoirs, which he had been commissioned to write by Paul Sidey of Hutchinson. So, beside stories taken from the present – tales of crack, of the new love of his life, of a TV series and writing projects – he began to dive back into the past.

Some of the stories from the 1960s came out. Mrs Mouse had several walk-on parts, as did the subsequent brothel years with Emma Jane Crampton. The story from 1976 about the Major and his unsuccessful drugs run was given another outing, and a contemporary setting. But what was increasingly on Willie's mind as he grew older was his childhood and his family.

Something odd happened when he returned to Sunningdale in his writing. The scenes and characters to which he had previously made brief and generally neutral reference in his writings now emerged in the bold, comical strokes of strip-cartoon characters. His father was a tragic figure, remote from his children and the victim of both family expectations and – this was to become something of an obsession of Willie's – of the harsh and brutal snobbery of his mother.

Mrs Donaldson, who had written a war diary for him, who had taken him to see matinées in London, who had consulted with the headmaster's wife as to whether he was big enough to play in the school football team, who was admired and liked by his friends at Winchester, had now mysteriously become the villain of the piece. The stories that Willie told about his childhood revealed him as a spoilt brat, over-indulged by his parents, Mr Donaldson as a miserable, boozed-up loser and his mother as an iron-willed suburbanite snob.

In an early column, he admits that his mother was a good egg, but then went on to describe her as being commoner than his sister and himself, and 'definitely a criminal. During the war she buried enough black-market petrol in her orchard to take the Eighth Army from here to Tobruk'. He lifted from his mother's diary the account of the gardener offering to stand guard outside the house against the Germans, gave the lead role to the chauffeur and claimed that after the war Mrs Donaldson fired the chauffeur for voting socialist.

That story, and others, upset and bewildered his sister Jane, and enraged Willie's childhood friend Ray Salter. 'Betty Donaldson had always been so kind and generous,' Ray says. 'When Willie started writing about her in his column, it absolutely drove me to distraction. It was a betrayal – monstrous. I didn't have anything to do with him for a year or so but then one day I saw him coming out of a butcher on the King's Road, carrying a plastic bag with two sausages in it. I said, "You were just so wrong about Betty." And he agreed and said, "I know. I'm extremely sorry about that and I know I was wrong".'

That, it has to be said, was Willie's way: apologise, express grovelling regret – and then do it all over again.

Later, in his memoirs, Willie would explain that 'literary strategy' lay behind this retrospective myth-making. He wanted to show 'that the present affects one's perception of the past – indeed, that it radically alters it – as much as the past determines the present,' he wrote.

> Not only would this version be easier to write and more dramatic (my father at the grand piano, awash with alcohol and disappointment; my mother, disgusted by his weakness, excluding him from his children's good opinion), it would reflect better on me, I think; would suggest that I feel remorse for the way I treated my father; that in this regard I have grown kinder than my sister Bobo.

There is a sort of truth here. Willie did indeed feel guilty about the way he treated his father, who had died probably when his son's relationship with him was at its worst, making the repair of adulthood impossible, freezing the misery in time. On the other hand, it is difficult to see quite what there was in his present life that made him turn on his mother with such venom.

But the key phrase in this confessional insight is 'more dramatic'. He was a storyteller whose only story was his own. The extraordinary events of his adult life had provided ample material but now he was turning to a childhood that was only extraordinary in its order, security and contentment. So he had to goose it up a bit.

'A writer's autobiography is a lived fiction, a literary act,' Jeremy Adler has commented in the context of Elias Canetti, one of Willie's literary idols. 'Canetti is interested in a symbolic representation of his life, not in historical exactitude, let alone life as it is lived.'

Willie would have liked that idea of a lived fiction, but the attitude towards his mother spilled into his life. While several of those close to him in the last fifteen years of his life remember Willie talking of his father with some fondness, none recalls any serious mention of Mrs Donaldson. The few references he made to her were comical and caricatured.

Yet clearly his relationship with his mother had been unusually close and the effect of her death had been devastating. The psychotherapist Phillip Hodson, who knew Willie from the mid-1970s, suggests that 'maybe the loss of his mother becomes *harder* to bear with time. Consider – she was the first, or at least the most important, woman ever to "let him down" (by dying). The effect of this is to some extent masked by youthful optimism but as the story of his life unfolds into the middle years, and he begins to consider his life as a narrative, he realises that she deprived him of some inner sense of security which – had this been supplied – would have made the disappointments of middle age easier to bear'.

To ignore for a moment Willie's warning to biographers about trying to give a contradictory life fictional coherence, it is noticeable that so much in his adult life can be traced back to the years before his mother died. His fascination with old-fashioned comedy and cabaret dates back to his trips with Mrs Donaldson to London. There is the oddness of his sex life which, he claimed, had been shaped by seeing the performing women of the Folies Bergères at the age of fifteen; in 1971, he told Julian Mitchell that he 'never got beyond the sexual stage we were at when we went to Paris together and read pornography all day and finally went out and got ourselves picked up by tarts'. His housemaster at Winchester had loved philosophy, his lifelong passion for Philip Larkin was inculcated by Mitchell when they were both in the navy.

In this context, some of the oddities of his adult life make more sense: the exaggerated respect he had for grown-ups like FR Leavis, Jonathan Miller, Donald Albery, the hopeless, romantic crushes on idealised women, the preference for being among young people, the dislike of being rebuked. And what, after all, could be more childish than the habit of sending spoof letters to famous people?

Something had changed in his view of others, or perhaps it had always been there, but concealed. As he wrote, nothing was at stake, nothing mattered any more. He was liberated to use lovers and friends, the past and the present, as the material for William Donaldson's Week.

The most frequently mentioned character in the column, first as an object of silly-old-man adoration but eventually of rage and mockery, was the woman described in his column as 'Alison', 'my beloved' ('who I love with all my wallet', he would occasionally add), 'my baby', 'my part-time literary agent' and, finally, when she had left him, under her real name, Penny.

Another escort-agency visitor, Penny was one of the great loves of Willie's later life. She saw him, usually once a week, for six years and was to play in his memoirs the all-important part of romantic, self-destructive bad girl that Melanie/Melissa had occupied in *Is This Allowed?* This time, though, the fantasy was different. Penny was not an exhibitionist dancer on tables – indeed, the description of her in *From Winchester to This*, 'a crisp girl who you encounter from time to time in Kall Kwik and after six months you realise you want to fuck her', gets her pretty well. Respectable to the point of dullness, she was a quiet, rather mousey-looking girl who was respectable in almost every sense and was studying to be a garden designer. She was also on the game, a user of crack and prepared to go every bit as far as Willie wanted her to go and further. 'I am easily disturbed by women who are demure masochists,' he was later to say in an unpublished interview.

Penny was perfect for Willie. He could take her to functions, confident that she would not be vulgar or embarrass him. She had come from that all-important damaged background which he found so attractive. She was, like Melanie, someone to be unfaithful with. If Willie wanted Fat Tracey from the escort agency to take Penny to an Ann Summers sex shop, get her dressed up in the most provocative gear, bring her back to Willie to show her off and then take her away to be fucked by a black man, Penny was quite prepared to play the game. Betrayal was part of the excitement.

Then, after six years, she really did betray him. Among her

other clients was the owner of a computer firm, whom Willie called in his column 'the Fat Man'. Like Willie, he fell for Penny and offered to take her away from the world of working girls, drugs and clever-dick writers of dubious morals. Without warning, she left London to set up home in Cornwall with the Fat Man.

Abandoned for domestic contentment and a man in trade: it was not the way it was supposed to end. In its way, Penny's desertion was more unbearable than Melanie falling into the hands of mad Christians in a clinic.

Over the summer of 1995 and beyond, Willie pummelled the readers of the *Independent* with jokes and routines about his collapsing private life. When it became clear that 'Alison' was not coming back, he wrote a clever piece about his cat Penny, who was spoilt, wilful, indulged and adorable.

OK, you're utterly captivated, I can tell, as hooked as I was. And I was so hooked, so terrified of losing her, that I searched around in reference books for something – anything – to which cats were vulnerable, shortly discovering that there is a magic mushroom, native to South America, but obtainable here, on which snow leopards become euphorically intoxicated, rolling on their backs and inviting chance passers-by to rub their stomachs.

I know what you think; you think that I acquired some of these magic mushrooms, that I fed them to Penny, my Burmese cat, and that she instantly became as infatuated as I was. You're right about that, as it happens, but wrong in what you're thinking now. You think that, wishing to lift our relationship to new and even more ecstatic heights of co-dependency, I stepped up the dose, and thereby killed her.

That's not what happened. My cat Penny didn't die. Saying she did was an attempt to control her at the end ....

On Thursday she and I got high and then she suddenly said (cat lovers – and who else will have got this far? – know that cats can talk) that she wanted to be a dog, if you please, and that she was leaving now – wanting only (what I'd never guessed) to fetch a fat man his slippers and slobber over him.

From then on, the gloves were off. In subsequent columns, Penny was called by her real name. Her professional past was exposed. Willie pretended in his writing to have paid a visit to Penny in Cornwall, naming the road in which she lived and providing the Fat Man's initials. 'At that moment Penny, my beloved, and her fat man went into the bedroom and, within seconds, a deafening simulated climax echoed like thunder through the house. Then Penny, my beloved, ran from the bedroom, opened a wall safe, threw a wedge of cash inside, closed the safe and returned to the bedroom before the last echo of that fraudulent climax had died away.'

To ensure that the community where the couple were now living knew of Penny's past, Willie leaked the story of his campaign to the *Cornish Guardian* which ran a story, headlined 'COLUM-NIST'S "FAT MAN" VENDETTA', naming the couple.

Eventually the *Independent* received a letter of complaint: 'I am the "fat man" named virtually every week in this column,' the Fat Man wrote, with some desperation. On December 14, Willie gave an undertaking to make no more mention of the former beloved. Within two weeks, he had included full particulars of the Fat Man's house, which he was selling after the break-up of his marriage. In February and March, he replaced the phrase 'the Fat Man' with the word 'bleep'. He was reported to the Press Council. After careful assessment, the council decided that there had been no breach of the code of practice since no real names had been used.

Off the page, Willie was busy, too. He discovered that the Fat Man's firm had gone bankrupt and, with the help of Roy Stevens, made plans to go down to Cornwall and confront them at his public examination. He pursued a lawsuit against Penny, claim-ing that she owed him £12,000. He then wrote to the Inland Revenue claiming that she had failed to declare earnings of £50,000 a year for the previous five years.

If you were his princess, his baby or his beloved, it didn't pay to fall out with Willie Donaldson.

Where do they go, the business girls? Like Melanie, Penny has disappeared from circulation. I did some asking around among her friends and some light sleuthing. I wrote to the Fat Man. Silence. No one knew where Penny was, whether she was still together with the Fat Man, if she was a happy, domestic mum who remembers her days of sex and crack-taking at Elm Park Mansions only occasionally – perhaps when she reaches for a teapot or wraps a roast chicken in tinfoil.

I decided to pay a visit on the business which, down the years, had provided Willie with so much excitement. I knew where the agency was situated – I used to play the guitar at a restaurant downstairs and now and then Penny would scurry by, head down, on her way to work while I was taking a break. Now, early one evening, I climbed the stairs and knocked on the unprepossessing plywood door.

The door was opened immediately by a smooth-looking man, impeccably dressed in a slightly old-fashioned style, like a crooner appearing at a farewell concert in Las Vegas.

'You're early,' he said.

I explained, haltingly, that I wasn't there as a customer but trying to find some information about a couple of girls. I mentioned Melanie and Penny by their full names.

'Ah,' the man smiled. 'That will be to do with Mr Donaldson.'

It was. I asked if they knew him well there.

A look, almost of fondness, crossed his face. 'I'll never forget the time when he came up here with a rocking-horse. It was for Penny. Gosh, that must be years ago now.'

He did not, of course, have the slightest idea what had happened to Penny, or indeed to Melanie, but he suggested I returned a bit later, after eight o'clock, and ask for Tilly.

After a couple of hours I returned, following a couple of elegant, long-legged, skimpily dressed girls, chatting in foreign accents, up the stairs, then knocking once more at the door. Another girl, but, unlike the others, in normal civilian clothes, opened it. I asked for Tilly and she let me in.

The reception of the agency is not what one might expect.

There are no *chaises longues* or velvet curtains. The lighting was bright. There were chairs around the plain small room with a counter in one corner. A single-bar electric fire was in the middle of the room. It was like the reception of a small downmarket hotel.

Tilly emerged from a door behind the counter, a woman in her sixties who, if it were not for her low-cut dress, might have been a matron from a 1950s film. I explained my quest.

Tilly remembered Penny. 'She went off with the large gentleman,' she said. We agreed that it had all been a long time ago. She wondered what Penny was up to these days.

I asked whether some of the other girls might be able to talk to me. Isabelle, Willie used to talk about and Tracey, and Abby.

'Abby doesn't want to know these days,' said Tilly, with a hint of disapproval in her voice. She had no idea where the others were either. 'It was all a long time ago,' she said.

Now that Willie was writing ruthlessly from his daily life, his attitude to friendship was brought into sharper focus. Some, finding themselves being brought on to the stage in clownish garb, for the amusement of readers of the *Independent*, were hurt and annoyed. One former colleague went so far as to write a letter to the editor, demanding an apology and threatening 'the strongest possible action'.

An impression that I gained during the years that I knew him has been confirmed during the research of this book: Willie's idea of male friendships were passionate, important and highly unusual.

Long before the days of Melanie and Penny, Peter and Kim, he had a reputation for corrupting those who knew him. Only after his death, talking to different friends, have I begun to understand how that worked.

Willie was curious, like any writer. He was also intrigued by sex. He presented himself as a pervert – 'I'm a complete lunatic, sexually,' he would say – but he was also fascinated by what excited his men friends.

On the whole, people do not like discussing seedy incidents from their past. Just as the women involved in Willie's darker moments have mostly made themselves scarce as I researched, so the men have become suddenly rather vague about the precise circumstances of some dubious adventure in which they became embroiled during their friendship with Willie.

One old friend recalled, while staying at Elm Park Mansions, how Willie had confessed that he was only interested now in seeing black girls, but when a Nigerian girl, young, awkward and with bad English, appeared, he was so sorry for her that he paid her off.

Another friend remembers that, when they were together, he would insist on getting a blonde girl. He had become obsessed by the idea of women doing strange and experimental things, liberated by the fact that they were under someone else's control.

Another 'found himself' in a room with Willie where two half-naked girls were beating each other up. Then there was Donleavy's odd story about being invited to see Melanie at her flat 'in a state of undress'.

It began to seem as if, while appearing to pursue his own desires, Willie was in fact attempting to realise the fantasies of his friends. It seemed a strange idea and at odds with the Willie I knew until I remembered that, back in the 1980s, he had arranged for me to have lunch with the girl he called Pretty Marie. She was indeed pretty – I had seen the photographs – Willie had told me that she was eager to meet me.

There are several reasons why Pretty Marie's interest now seems unlikely, among them the fact that she was a busy full-time working girl and, in her private life, was married. Unsurprisingly, she was bored by me, I was bored by her, and nothing happened beyond a dreary lunch.

'The world is divided into tarts and punters,' he would tell his friend, the writer Christopher Matthew. 'I'm a punter. You're a tart.' All the same, he talked to Christopher about making his home videos (a couple of girls larking about, naked, at Elm Park Mansions) and once, when they were lunching at Searcy's, a couple of attractive call-girl friends of Willie's happened to be passing by and joined them for coffee. In front of Christopher, they talked casually about their way of life.

Just as the women to whom he was attracted, but who had declined to fall in love with him, retained his respect, so the men who showed no sign of being sexual lunatics tended to avoid becoming comic foils in his writing. His close friend Craig Brown recalls how Willie would make some kind of intimate confession and then wait for Craig to contribute something of the same. 'I would just look at him, bemused,' Craig says. 'I think I kept a distance from that side of things. When he mentioned these girls, I was quite priggish, but also rather confused. I could never remember which was which.'

Craig belongs to the select band of men who are not joke figures in Willie's writings. Willie was an admirer of his effortless comic inventiveness, but I suspect also that Craig's distance and 'priggishness' caused Willie to respect him more than others of his friends.

Once his everyday life became material for his Saturday column, being a friend of Willie's meant knowing that one was required to accept the role of occasional clown for readers of the *Independent*. This was not always easy.

The problem was that the spoofed-up, written version of a friendship, Canetti's 'lived fiction', can sometimes take over from the real thing. 'I felt that suddenly I was on the outside, amusing him as a faintly comic character,' Christopher Matthew says now, with something approaching bitterness in his voice. They had been friends and lunch partners during the 1980s but, once Willie's column started, Christopher became part of a humorous *galère* of characters who would appear in the weekend's *Independent*. 'In the end I started playing up to it. Instead of being myself, I found myself playing the part expected of me. He used to say, "Oh, you funny little chap" during our conversations. I wondered at the end whether I was really a friend or simply the funny little chap.'

Casting a friend in the fall-guy role in his writing could be affectionate. His best friend Richard Dynevor, who had put up with it for years, would occasionally remonstrate with Willie. 'But it's so funny,' would be Willie's reply. He had always managed to separate his true self from his written one – 'Myself a fictional character as much as anyone else,' he had scrawled in the margin of a draft letter in his defence from Andreas Whittam Smith, then editor of the *Independent* to the Press Council – and was genuinely bemused when others failed to take the same attitude.

But sometimes it was difficult being one of Willie's fictional characters. I remember being occasionally startled by my appearances in his column and wondering whether behind the comedy was the way Willie really viewed me – conceited, ambitious, distinctly hypocritical in my moral attitudes. I must have stopped reading it at some point because, looking at the later columns now, I am startled by the malevolence of the humour.

'I don't like Blacker, never have,' he wrote early on. Soon I was being swiped whenever a joke offered itself. Describing the idea behind *You Want, You Settle For, You Get*, Willie explained that you want to write a toilet book with Peter Morgan, you'd settle for Simon Carr, you get 'a stooped contemporary who has just been fired from Pizza Pomodoro for not knowing who Guns 'n' Roses are', later identified as me. At the time I was trying to be taken seriously as a novelist, and so Willie was careful to mention a silly pseudonymous book I had written ten years previously. In one column I was a pompous ass, the next I had been recruited as the 'old party to play stooge or straight man' for Willie's anecdotes in his memoirs. One week, bizarrely, he took to referring to me as 'Terence Blackler'. I was 'notoriously vain', balding and eventually older than him.

Willie was cross with me but, rather than risk any confrontation, he preferred to jab at me with jokes. One of the reasons for his anger, I now realise, was that I had expressed my disapproval of his hounding Penny through his column – it seemed, and seems, to me like a writer bullying someone who had no right to reply.

But there was another problem. I was behaving badly in my marriage at the time and I would talk to Willie, telling him things about my life that I would tell virtually no one else. One day, I discovered that he was betraying confidences, and to disastrous effect. I was enraged, and we had a row. Soon afterwards the references to me in his column became ruder.

Quite how annoyed he was with me I had never realised until I read the first draft of his memoirs, the contract for which was cancelled by the publishers on legal grounds, one of the main potential litigants being me. The story of our row is treated at some length in *From Sunningdale to This*, as it was then called, but is distorted and given an additional twist: at the same time as complaining about his behaviour, he claimed that I was asking him to set me up with his friend Stefs, the Page Three Stunna. 'It would be a most interesting challenge to betray a very close friend for a joke,' he says.

The joke had a toe-hold in reality. He had brought Stefs to a restaurant where I was playing the guitar, and I had given her a lift home but it had all ended innocently enough. Willie's central premise, though, seemed to be that not only was I a 'shifty little womaniser' with an 'uninteresting, married man's serial randiness', but that I was also essentially bogus. It is an uncomfortable insight into the way Willie saw me at the time. 'He can deliver a rocket from a standing start – a capability which, as a rule, only civilian women have,' he said of me. 'Had his orientation been different in one regard he'd have made someone an excellent wife.'

Interestingly, Willie was most annoyed, it seemed, by my suggestion that he didn't know enough about me to speculate about what I might or might not do in my marriage. 'Friends,' he wrote in the unpublished version of his memoirs, 'should present themselves as revealingly as characters in a comic novel or what's the point of them?'

What indeed? Looking back now, I realise that it would have been unthinkable to lose my friendship with Willie. Not only did he make the world an incomparably more interesting and unexpected place, but there was something about knowing him which transcended rows and hurt feelings. Beyond the words that he wrote was an honesty of feeling and, behind the playfulness, a seriousness that is difficult to find in life and convey in words. On this point, I have since discovered, those who became close to him from his childhood days to the end of his life are in agreement: friendship with Willie Donaldson was a valuable, intense, important thing.

As far as his idea that friends should reveal themselves to one another goes, I would have liked to have discussed it with him, perhaps making the point that his own self-presentation had not been entirely open down the years, that there are unknowable parts in each of our lives, that reality is in the end more complicated than a comic novel. When we did become friends again, that tricky moment in 1993 was never mentioned. Life was more important than words.

30
shit and damnation

Like many writers of books, Willie saw TV as a promised land where the money is easy and you are surrounded by bright, admiring young people. TV had its eye on Willie too: the comedy cognoscenti had been aware for some time that here was an extraordinary and funny writer. Yet their attempts to bring his work to the screen had come to nothing.

In 1988, a full eight years after he bustled self-importantly on to the scene with a bestselling book under his name, Henry Root began to interest the television world.

Root into Europe, as it would become, is unusual among Willie's projects, most of which ended in litigation, disagreement, and confusion. On this occasion the shambles was there from the start.

As the Eighties wore on, Willie was beginning, financially, to feel the pinch. A combination of the adventures with his Princess and his recent discovery of crack cocaine meant that funds were low and – although a few toilet books were in the offing – so was his income. He was disappointed that there had been no TV series based on his Henry Root character and confided his frustration to an old acquaintance, Anthony Tancred.

Tancred was a childhood friend of Willie's – they had gone fishing together – in Broadstairs, and his name appears, often unexpectedly, through Willie's story. As an actor, he had appeared (with the future Mrs Mouse) in the first play Willie produced, *Meet the Cousin*. He later had connections with Robert Bolt, and was described in Willie's column, under another name, as Bolt's butler.

Tancred, who was on the outer fringes of the production scene, offered to help the TV career of Henry Root and later claimed, in one of several-aggrieved letters, that it was he who came up with the idea of sending the wet-fish merchant into Europe. He had recently sold a business and offered Willie £3,000 for a TV option in all the Root books.

There were discussions, sometimes with Tancred, sometimes without, with various producers: Greg Smith of Elstree Films, Paul Madden of Screen First, Paul Jackson of Noel Gay Television, Mark Chapman of Tiger Aspect. By the autumn Smith was out of the picture, Madden had thought he had secured the project but hadn't and Mark Chapman was speaking to Central TV, which had also heard from Madden and Paul Jackson. At this point Jackson withdrew, explaining in a letter to Willie: 'In view of this continuing complexity, I very much get the feeling that it would be difficult to progress the project cleanly at this stage.' As Tiger Aspect closed on the deal, Willie decided that Tancred was surplus to requirements and tried to edge him out. Willie moved agents from Mark Lucas of Peters Fraser and Dunlop to Cat Ledger of James Sharkey. 'He was a pretty impossible person to work for, always going out to lunch with someone and doing a deal which would completely flummox you,' says Mark Lucas. 'The phrase he would use was "And I heard myself saying ...". It was as if somebody else was doing all this stuff.'

Tancred put the whole matter in the hands of his lawyers. None of this, it seems, was quite muddled enough for Willie, because at this point he added another tier of confusion. Over Sunday lunch with an old friend Ceredig Davies, he expressed his frustration with his inability to decide how best to move the series forward. As Willie explained later in a letter to Cat Ledger: 'At some point during lunch, Davies offered to lend me £5,000 – an offer I quickly took advantage of – immediately producing a blank cheque signed by his wife, which he filled in. I suggested that in return for this he should have some sort of involvement in the Root project, perhaps having a share in what I might make if he helped to get the series produced.'

It is an odd reaction, when hearing a story of artistic frustration, to hand over a cheque for £5,000, and it is one which
Willie's letter does not explain. The fact is that Willie really did
want to get Root on TV. He was also, as a separate matter, rather
broke. Later, in one of several letters that manage to be both
abusive and ingratiating, Tancred would accuse him of being
'mad and totally dishonest'.

Neither charge is entirely true. What is rarely, if ever,
mentioned in the various stories of Willie's financial misdoings, is
the other side of the story. On the whole, those whom he had
helped in the past (with the honourable exception of Spike
Milligan and Miss Picano) preferred to keep quiet about it.

The fact is that when Willie was in funds, he had been happy
to give money to friends who needed it. He parted company with
thousands of pounds, never asking or expecting to be paid back.
His cheerful financial irresponsibility, in other words, cut both
ways. In the letter to Cat Ledger about Ceredig Davies, he wrote:
'I do not even feel guilty about the £5,000 loan since I've
certainly given him much more than that in the past (as he would
be the first to acknowledge).'

Neither Davies nor Tancred is alive to tell their side of the
story, but those who knew and worked with Willie – notably
Cherry Donaldson – have no doubt of his often reckless generosity. He did, however, feel guilt about money. As his finances went
into decline, he would borrow from friends – £200 was the usual
touch – but always offered to pay it back. When, towards the end
of his life, he discovered the joy of credit cards, he would insist
to Roy 'Honest John' Stevens, an expert in creative loan management, that the debt was temporary. 'Willie was different to me,'
Roy says. 'I want to owe more than anyone else – ideally, I'd like
the debt of a small country – but Willie always insisted that he
would pay them back when his royalties came in.'

Willie also had a fondness for people with a defiant, even
fantastic ambition. He had enjoyed working with David Barclay,
who would write those unposted letters to Richard Burton and
Elizabeth Taylor with a view to representing them, and Bruce
Jenkins/Ray Nichol/Ken the Australian Horse-Player, the great

would-be film director. In spite of almost being destroyed by Philip Wiseman, he would write later in a note to himself, 'Wiseman a recurring motif. Why is he all right?' He admired and was fascinated by wild and over-optimistic self-belief.

Tancred's letters suggest that he belonged in this category. He presented himself shamelessly as an 'ideas man, a putting-your-money-where-your-mouth-is man and perhaps eventually … a full-blown producer'. The man who had created Henry Root and written highly successful books about him, had, in his view, 'contributed nothing to this project except shit and damnation'.

After Tiger Aspect sold *Root into Europe* to Central TV, a deal was done with Tancred. He would indeed be part of the team responsible for making the five-part series. He was the stills photographer.

It must have seemed a dream project to Willie. His work was to be on television at last. He would be co-writing with a TV professional, Mark Chapman. There was now a big-name acting star, George Cole, on board (although Willie would have preferred the comic bully John Challis, Boycie in *Only Fools and Horses*). He had become bored, writing on his own, and liked the team at Tiger Aspect. He was to travel around Europe with the producer Justin Judd, the director and co-writer Mark Chapman and assistant producer Jeremy Lovering. They would visit sex shows in Berlin, go out with the riot police in Paris, interview a Mafia-hunting judge and a porn-star MP in Italy. To quote one of Willie's favourite phrases, 'What larks!'.

The five-week reconnaissance trip was not without problems. Willie had a talent for stirring up trouble – 'He would find some-one's Achilles heel and get at them through someone else,' says Jeremy Lovering. The fact that he was also playing games through his *Independent* column was probably not helpful.

It soon became clear that the idea behind the series was flawed. The concept of extemporising comedy in real situations was clever and before its time but, as Chris Morris and Sasha Baron Cohen have shown, the person in the eye of the storm must, for the comedy to work, be its creator. Expecting a profes-

sional actor to come up with improvised funny lines while dealing with real people, sometimes eminences in their field, was
clearly unrealistic.

On paper, Root was at his funniest when he was at his most
outrageous and merciless. Embarrassment works differently on
screen. In the letters, a nobody was dealing with the famous; on
screen, Root was very much a somebody: he was George Cole of
Minder fame. His bigotry – laughing at foreigners and so on – could
seem crass and unfunny. Tiger Aspect had to agree with those partic-
ipating that the joke would always be on Root, never on them.

At first, Willie was intrigued by these challenges, technical
and moral, but by the time the series was to be shot, problems
were beginning to emerge. 'As soon as everything got organised,
the series was more scripted and was relatively straight, Willie
would become bored and subversive,' says Justin Judd. He began
to absent himself from writing the next day's script, disappearing
when a new scene was needed. He discovered that one of the
crew shared his enthusiasm for crack.

The series turned out to be the toughest of Justin Judd's
career. 'We had one blazing row in which I accused Willie of
having no imagination – of being unable to make things up. In
the end, it came down to whether he was able to write for a TV
audience. He said that he had no interest in writing for TV. "I
only want to write for the half-dozen people who really matter."
At that point, Peter Morgan was brought in.'

It is, in fact, a testament to Chapman and Judd that the series
was completed at all. Much as he may have wanted it to be otherwise, Willie's talent was a solitary one. Like any serious writer, he
was essentially arrogant. He could compromise, briefly and skit-
tishly, for a toilet book but the business of filming a
drama-comedy, of doing what he regarded as an essentially unserious thing with complete seriousness, was bound to make him
restless. Henry Root had been created with a hard and dangerous satirical edge; turning him into a crowd-pleaser for
early-evening TV might have worked, but not with Willie
involved. 'He hated it when you closed the door and said, "We've
got to get on with some writing",' Mark Chapman says.

He was not, he discovered yet again, a team player. In the first unpublished draft of his memoir, he wrote that working on *Root into Europe* 'was like being back at school – subjected day and night to a blizzard of movement orders, restricted in our personal arrangements by a morals clause in our contracts and shepherded at every turn by crisp young location women seeking Judd's approval by jogging keenly on the spot and reporting anyone talking after lights out'.

The show won an audience of six or seven million. It was well made and sporadically amusing, but the explosive and outrageous comic energy of the true Henry Root had been fatally toned down. There was briefly talk of a second series but, says Justin Judd, 'no one's heart was really in it'.

As was customary at the time, the television series of *Root into Europe* brought a TV tie-in book in its wake. Geoffrey Strachan of Methuen, having let Willie go just before Henry Root had begun to send out letters, now signed him up once more.

The book of *Root into Europe*, published in 1992, shows distinct signs of authorial weariness, being based on the TV scripts with a few additional flourishes: Geoffrey Wheatcroft was dragged into the action and described rather well as 'the one who writes as if he's combing his hair in the looking-glass'. A few old friends make a return appearance. The joke about wanting eggs in a Spanish supermarket, going 'cluck-cluck' and being given toilet rolls is given its fourth or fifth outing, as is another old favourite from the beach – 'Swedish "models" oiling one another's buttery ballooning thighs'.

By the time he wrote a follow-up volume, *Root Around Britain – Henry Root's Guide to Englishness*, Willie was pretty much running on empty. In the now familiar A-to-Z format, it recycled heavily from *Henry Root's World of Knowledge, Bitov's Britain,* Talbot Church's *Royal Lovebirds* and *1992 and All That*. Although other proposals would be sent out, and he would contribute the occasional journalistic pronouncements, Henry Root had made his last appearance in book form.

Hutchinson's Paul Sidey had paid Willie the first third of an advance to write his memoirs back in 1989. Three years later, there was no sign of it, a combination of the Root revival and the *Independent* column having taken up his time and energy.

Now, while keeping Sidey at bay, Willie began to look for new types of writing projects. He had become increasingly convinced by the argument for the legalisation of drugs and had tried unsuccessfully to interest publishers. Although he would later complain that they refused to consider anything from him was meant seriously, he had researched the project, collecting cuttings, but had not written anything.

He suggested to Justin Judd that the moment for a TV series on the whole idea of intoxication was right and, went so far as to approach his former colleague Jonathan Miller as a possible presenter. When Miller declined, on the grounds that he was busy, Willie sent a follow-up letter, saying that he and Judd would wait for a year, if necessary, for him to become available. He went on to refer a touch tactlessly, given Dr Miller's sensitivity to what had happened in 1961, to the *Beyond The Fringe* cast's works outing to a blue film, writing: 'Meanwhile I have spoken to our friend in New Bond Street, who says she would very much like to entertain us after such a long time.' Dr Miller did not reply.

Then there was the *Karma Chingford,* alternatively known as *Karma Britain,* a series that straddled, rather uncomfortably, the worlds of comedy and erotica. The sex guru, who would be introducing the viewer to the British way of sex, would be none other than Major Ron Ferguson, the gamey old father of the Duchess of York, who would be played by Peter Cook. Briefly, the Playboy Channel was interested. Debbie Mason of the Kudos Production Company, who was to become Willie's friend and fellow adventurer, invited him and Cook to lunch and says the series was almost commissioned. The idea, she says, was before its time.

As he grew older, Willie's attitude to the three writers whose career had been launched by *Beyond The Fringe* varied significantly. He revered Jonathan Miller, whose attitude to him had grown more disdainful over the years, and was polite about Alan Bennett who had never read a word that he had written. Peter Cook, who admired Willie's work and was rather fond of him, he would increasingly describe – in interviews, at least – as an over-rated talent.

Willie had been closest to Cook of all the *Beyond The Fringe* team and had shared an office with him while Cook was setting up the Establishment Club. He had then avoided him during the Seventies and Eighties, seeing him as one of the *Private Eye* gang. They appeared together on a panel at the Cheltenham Literary Festival in 1987, speaking in support of Auberon Waugh and the *Literary Review*. For the next few years, they had what Willie called quite a 'flirty relationship', seeing each other for lunch and talking on the telephone. 'We were a couple of arseholes and we'd get together and talk about drugs and pornographic videos,' he told Harry Thompson in a lengthy taped interview for Thompson's biography of Cook. 'I was then heavily into crack and fuck knows what, and I think I understood him. We were the two sad old addicts, stumbling around, bored in the afternoon.'

In the early 1990s Willie's friend Craig Brown took him out to lunch with Cook and the writer Hugh Massingberd. It went well enough although, according to Massingberd, neither of them were keen to talk about *Beyond The Fringe*. 'I didn't get the impression that Cook thought Willie disliked him,' Craig Brown says. 'He was a generous man, Peter Cook.' The follow-ing day, indeed, Cook rang Willie to suggest that they should work together.

They met up occasionally and compared notes about drugs. It was Cook, Willie would later claim, who suggested that he try ecstasy. 'If you take it, you love everybody,' Cook had promised. 'You'll even like Richard Ingrams.' Willie took some ecstasy while in Ibiza, but didn't get on with it. His view of Ingrams remained unchanged.

Peter Cook was a great admirer of Willie's *Independent* column but, first in the privacy of his memoirs and later in inter-views, Willie became caustic about Cook's reputation. His name attached to any TV project was box office poison, Willie would say. He was lazy and had lost interest in the *Karma Chingford* project as soon as Willie had told him that he would have to appear on set every day during the shoot.

'I have, since his death, become increasingly unpleasant about Peter Cook,' Willie wrote in *From Winchester to This*.

> And this is odd, because at the time of *Beyond The Fringe* we got on rather well – a consequence, I suppose, of recognising in each other (at least by comparison with his colleagues at the time, Jonathan Miller and Alan Bennett) something un-alterably second rate, a silly disposition (much commended by the likes of Malcolm Muggeridge and Richard Ingrams), not to take life too seriously – ever the slogan by which the idle and overmatched proclaim themselves.
>
> Accordingly, and in a small studio at Broadcasting House this afternoon, I hear myself telling the producer of a radio tribute that I never found Cook even slightly funny. He *tried* harder to be funny, I say, than anyone I've ever met (with the exception of Spike Milligan, who, by contrast, always succeeds in this endeavour), but that's rather different. Trapped by 'Cooky on form', deploying the full range of funny voices Oxbridge comedians can muster, and held by the drunk's intimidating challenge not to look away, one shortly found one's encouraging smile setting into a rictus grin.

There is an element of competitiveness here. It must have annoyed Willie that, after his death, Cook acquired the status of a comedy god, particularly since his reputation and loveableness had actually been enhanced by the booziness of his later days: the British love a celebrity alcoholic.

When interviewed by Harry Thompson a year after Cook's death, Willie put much of the adulation down to the guilt of those in the TV and comedy worlds who had spurned Cook over the previous twenty years. He had been 'the perfect undergradu-ate talent – amateurish, clumsy, inspired but very uneasy entertainment'. Once there had been no place for the undergrad-uate sketch. His talent had nowhere to go.

Certainly, as that telling description of 'Cooky on form' suggests, Willie disliked and distrusted relentless humorousness, battering listeners into submission, his own wit being more sly and subversive. Cook's comedy had no basis, he told Thompson. It was funniness for its own sake.

'Willie hated English amateurishness and he decided that Peter Cook represented the English amateur,' says Craig Brown. Certainly in the Thompson interview, he spoke bitterly about 'that *Private Eye* thing about not taking life too seriously'. The last time he had seen Cook, Willie said, he had been making jokes about Jonathan Miller. 'I mean, how tedious.'

A love of alcohol, a need to make jokes, a distrust of seriousness: the wonder is less that Willie was unkind about Cook after his death, more that they were friends in the first place. But perhaps the degree of feeling which lay behind Willie's languidly delivered comments about Cook is explained not by their differences but by their similarities.

They had originally become close, Willie would say, because 'it sort of takes one to know one'. When they became friends once more, he detected in Cook an unbearable boredom, for which intoxication and pornographic sex provided temporary relief. 'Something common to anybody with a terrible addiction, which was what Cook had, is that he is bored,' Willie said in a BBC interview in 2002.

> They want to get away from being alive in the present. You know, it's five o'clock and I'm desperate. How am I going to get through? It's ten past three on a November afternoon. Ghastly business. Terrible, terrible boredom ... But why was Cook so bored? Why was somebody who had this capacity to make people laugh, *why* was he so bored? So bored that he had to read pornography and play funny jokes on people?

The picture, and the note of jokey despair with which it was conveyed, suggest that Willie was not talking exclusively about Peter Cook.

31
That sharp moment

It was not only drugs that could relieve the problem of boredom; sex would play its part. 'A man shaking in search of pornography or some fetish or some ghastly thing in a hotel in the afternoon – one thing he isn't is bored. He's everything else – he's shaking, he's in a terrible state, he's not happy. But he isn't bored,' he once said towards the end of his life. A man in that state, he said, was forever 'living for that sharp moment'.

After Penny had run away with the Fat Man, a succession of escort girls – Abby, Tracey, Isabelle and others – had visited Willie but it was Michelle, described in the memoirs as 'Michelle the common-law wife from hell', whose talents provided an almost perfect fit with his needs. She might even, had she been only slightly different, have been promoted to the highest level in his life to be his baby, his beloved or his princess.

Michelle occupies an odd role in the memoirs – wild, funny, desirable (Willie told a friend that the best sex he had ever had was with Michelle), she was also the woman that the narrator, Willie Donaldson, feared he would be left with; she is his nemesis. Michelle was not damaged, as Melanie and Penny had been – or, if she was, she unsportingly concealed the fact. Nor was she a demure masochist. She was streetwise, a flinty-eyed provider of sex and cocaine. When, in *From Winchester to This*, Michelle first delivers him drugs, telling him, 'You'll be a piece of cake,' Willie writes:

> I'm quite excited. This, if it happens, will be the very oppo-
> site of boring. I'll get quite a kick from this, I think: being

the only respectable old gentleman in the Royal Borough of Kensington and Chelsea who never knows when a passing sociopath in an anklet might put the bite on him. While others of my age and accomplishments snore the night away at a married distance from their wives – and with the radio alarm set for current affairs at 7am – I'll lie awake in appalled anticipation of three rings on the doorbell and the demanding arrival in my front room of Michelle and a posse of street dealers with their hats on back to front.

I thought it would be helpful to meet the real Michelle, rather than the written one. I contacted her through her boyfriend. Michelle had been fond of Willie, he told me, and would be prepared to talk to me but, if there was to be talk of a sexual nature, then she would want to be paid. I was at first reluctant, shelling out £20 notes to a business girl not normally being claimable against an author's expenses, but as a fellow freelance, I appreciated that time is money and that a matter of professional honour was at stake. When I saw Michelle and her boyfriend at their house in the suburbs west of London, I bought with me £100. She was not over-impressed by my generosity but the gesture had been made.

Willie had written that he hated to think of Michelle at home, her hair up, her legs hidden, putting her boyfriend's dinner on the table but that, by a small coincidence, turned out to be precisely what she was doing when I visited. Her boyfriend and I sat at the kitchen table while Michelle talked of crack and sex at Elm Park Mansions.

It was slightly difficult in these circumstances to imagine her as the person Willie had described – 'a really dirty girl who is at once insatiable and contemptuous', who would take him lower than he'd ever imagined possible, to a place from which there was no return. She was thin, dark, pretty, probably in her late thirties. On the face of it, the only indication of another life was a certain coked-up lack of focus in her conversation, which came and went like a faulty radio signal. She said she had been partying for the past couple of days.

Peter Morgan had said that 'you can tell where someone on crack is by the nature of their dealer', and Michelle's account suggested that Willie had slipped some way down the ladder since the days when Gilly would supply him. He was 'absolutely an addict', she says. She would supply crack in the early days but, as time went by, she would arrive, the bottle would be ready and there would be dealers, young usually and black. 'He was being exploited,' she says. 'A lot of stuff was being taken behind his back. What the dealers did was give him a taster. Once he'd had the taster, he'd pay. I'd get away with murder.'

He would be really quiet until he had the crack inside him, Michelle said. 'That's when the perversions started.'

Standing at her cooker in a neat suburban kitchen, Michelle conjured up a vision of hell. Some of the things that she described as happening at Willie's flat were so startlingly perverse and out of character that, thinking about them subsequently, I wondered whether Michelle, like any good professional, was giving value for money and faking it verbally. Some of it, though, filled in details of what he himself had talked about and written.

'He was a game old sod,' she said. 'He loved his mind games. He was really into mind games. Sexually, there was always playtime going on. He was a watcher. Another girl June came over one time with a dark girl from America. The dark girl was with Willie and I was sort of with June and I gave one to June and one to Will. Or Abby would come round with her black boyfriend and they'd do the boyfriend/girlfriend thing for him. It turned him on if someone fucked me.'

Michelle believes that Willie's weakness was for 'bitches, ruthless women. He mentally tortured himself. He liked to play the big king and then he changed and became all submissive. He would be humiliated. I would ignore him and he would get more and more excited by it all.'

Not that he was always the victim. Michelle had been there on the occasion when Willie had played his part in a fantasy set up for one of Abby's clients, a senior banker whom Willie referred to as 'Barclay'. 'The banker wanted to be beaten up by a sleazy guy, a really serious gangster. Willie agreed to play the part and he had to go down to the charity shop to get a trilby and a suit and a striped tie from Oxfam. When the banker was there, Willie pushed him around and slapped him with the back of his hand – bosh, bosh – and then I domineered him a bit too.'

Happy days. Michelle recalled quieter moments – the times when he would get her to wear the Katherine Hamnett skirt ('It was right up to my arse') which seems to have been a relic from the days of Melanie. They would talk about her life. She would tell him stories about drugs. Sometimes after crack, Michelle says, 'he liked to have this intellectual talk. I couldn't understand what he was saying. I knew the words but I couldn't understand the way he put them together.'

It was four years before Willie died that Michelle stopped visiting him. She says, rather startlingly under the circumstances, that he was corrupting her. 'It was either him or me. It was fucking agony, man.'

Across the kitchen table, her boyfriend murmured that the fact that he didn't have any money left might have had something to do with it.

Michelle took this rather uncharitable remark in good part. 'He met his match when he met me,' she said.

One of Willie's more domestic instructions to Michelle had been towards the end of their relationship. 'Don't go to Mr Amin,' he had said. 'Otherwise he'll know I've been spending money.'

Pankaj Amin, who runs a thriving newsagent's on the Fulham Road, played an important part in Willie's life. From the late Eighties onwards, as Willie's finances spiralled downwards, Mr Amin was his banker, receiving cheques and cashing them. Since a money transfer business was part of his impressive portfolio of activities, he had enough cash for it to be possible for cheques from Willie's agent Cat Ledger or from his publishers to be made out to him, so that Willie could withdraw funds without the various difficulties inherent in dealing with the conventional banking system. The fact that here was a banking system available from six in the morning also had its advantages.

Mr Amin was a good friend. When Willie had flu, it was he who brought Lemsip to his door. He could smell the flat, he says, but he was not invited in.

Of all the key locations in the small area of Fulham which was his beat – Finches pub, Macmillans Brasserie, the Pan Bookshop, the Goat in Boots – Mr Amin's newsagent's, a small corner shop packed with stock, is perhaps the most important. Willie took his most honoured guests there, from Sarah Miles to Frankie Fraser. When his new friend Lord Longford came to see him, Willie took him to see Mr Amin, pointing out the magazines on the top shelf of his shop.

There were mentions of Mr Amin in the *Independent* column and now and then Willie would come in with books that he felt the newsagent might enjoy. They would have discussions about football – Mr Amin, in spite of working down the road from the Chelsea ground, is an avid fan of Manchester United and proud to have met Sir Alex Ferguson. Willie would regularly complain that there was no copy of the *Erotic Review* and to the discomfort of other customers, would have mock-rows with Mr Amin. 'Call yourself a newsagent,' he would say.

Pankaj Amin is proud that his business has enabled him to put his three children through private school. With a working day which starts at 4.30am and ends at eight in the evening, he is not an easy man to see but one day he gave me a few minutes of his time at a nearby café.

'I used to say about the models, these people are not good for you, William, and he would say, "You're only jealous, Mr Amin".' He had been honoured to appear in the column, he told me, and pleased to help with his financial affairs. 'I was one of his agents,' he said.

I had heard that, towards the end of his life, Willie had taken to avoiding the newsagent, and had assumed that Mr Amin had joined the long list of creditors, but he denies that Willie ever owed him any significant money. 'William was less humorous towards the end,' he told me. 'He avoided me and I'd say, "Friendship is more important than money".'

One or two of his customers had warned Mr Amin that he should be careful of Willie and of being mentioned in his column, but now his only regret was the way their friendship ended.

Willie confided different things to his various circles of friends. Fellow writers had been involved in the great crisis caused by Philip Wiseman and the case in the High Court. Friends who had seen other aspects of the law, notably Andy Dempsey and Roy Stevens, would hear of types of crisis which were kept secret from those of us whose view of the world had not been broadened by a spell in gaol.

A man came out of his past during the 1990s, a publisher from Oxford, Roy told me. He was demanding money and it had really upset Willie. A figure of £20,000 had been mentioned. It had been to do with something bad Willie had done in the past. Now the man was asking to be paid what he said he was owed.

It seemed an odd story, and a somewhat unlikely one, but then there was a former publisher of Willie's who lived in Oxford. When I had spoken to Mike Franklin, the man who had published Willie's first book *Both the Ladies and the Gentlemen* in 1975, he had been markedly uncomplimentary about Willie's general reliability during the late 1970s when he had been left running the Talmy Franklin office.

I asked him if something had happened which had caused him to talk to Willie about money during the 1990s.

'To be honest, I just don't want to talk about that,' he said. I knew Mike Franklin well – we used to go to football matches together – and I pushed a bit harder.

It's a very difficult one. I don't want to go into it in any detail,' he said. 'What I will tell you is that something had happened to an author to the tune of £10,000. I suddenly got a huge shock when I discovered that a certain amount of money had gone missing some time during the 1980s. Someone had absconded with the money and I thought that someone who had done this was Willie. I rang him up and asked him straight: "Was it you?" And he said, "Yes, Frankle," – which was what he called me – "I don't know what to say".

What had happened, Franklin told me, was that, after the Talmy Franklin office had been closed down and he moved to America, it had been agreed that the mail would be sent on to Willie's home address. 'Willie told me that he had opened a bank account at the NatWest in Sloane Square in the name of Talmy Franklin and somehow had been accepted as a signatory. It crossed my mind to go to the police, and the police would have taken it extremely seriously. He would have been up in court in a trice.'

Four to six cheques had gone missing – maybe more, according to Franklin. 'I was on the one hand annoyed and on the other hand not annoyed because he was a very loveable old friend. He said, "I'll sort this out within two or three days", and he did. He came up with the money.'

Throughout his life, Willie's finances were a muddle and a mystery but I was pretty sure that, at no time in the mid to late 1990s, would he have had capital of £10,000. After all, he was declared bankrupt in August 1994.

I rang his sister Jane. Discussion of any financial matter is difficult with her, not because she is evasive but because she clearly – and probably rightly – regards money-talk as rather vulgar. She does, however, recall that Willie had appeared one day, unannounced, at the drug rehabilitation centre where she worked. 'He was absolutely out of it,' she says. 'He looked terrible – eyes as if they'd been scalded. He said, "I've got to have some money by three this afternoon".'

That event, though, was in the Eighties and the money involved, Jane says, could not have been more than £2,000 because that was the most she was able to withdraw at one time.

There were still things that puzzled me. Although Willie did indeed have Talmy Franklin headed notepaper with his address on it, I found the idea of his setting up a bank account in the firm's name uncharacteristically beady and cool. And where had Roy Steven's figure of £20,000 come from?

I rang Mike Franklin in a final attempt to resolve some of these uncertainties. As amiable as ever, he told me he had said as much as he was going to. He had been very fond of Willie and did not want to get him into further trouble.

'I always assumed that before it had come to this I would have committed a great crime,' Willie wrote later in a note to himself. In his last fifteen years, short of money, desperate, using crack and with nothing much to lose, he was nearer to outright criminality that at any other time in his life. At one point, he considered how best to blackmail a peer of the realm, a well-known racing man, who had had sex with Penny when she was under age. Nothing came of it.

However many cheques went missing, it seems likely that it fell some way short of being a great crime.

A new element of edginess seems to have entered Willie's life by this point. Penny was gone. Cat Ledger was discovering, like other long-suffering agents before her, that for all his wit and amiability, Willie was an impossible client, forever doing deals on his own and sometimes sabotaging his agent's efforts, complaining about them later. Publishers were wary of Willie now, and forays into TV had not worked out. As *Root into Europe* had showed, the cooperative nature of TV, the need to compromise for a mass audience, was antithetical to Willie's talent and personality.

Although Willie had a sound and modern taste when it came to TV comedy, his writing did not suit the medium. The television writer Geoff Atkinson had first worked with Willie in the late 1980s when there had been an idea of using the character of Henry Root in a corporate video. He became friends with Willie and admired his work, even trying to sell the idea of a Root sitcom. Atkinson had been central to the *Karma Britain* project and wanted Willie as a writer of a regular spot for Channel 4's Rory Bremner series, which he produced. The idea, of a man on the top floor of a bus, a voice of the people, discussing the nature of good and evil, never really worked, says Atkinson. It was too verbal.

Television did, however, provide him with some good new friends. Debbie Mason of the production company Kudos remembers a six-hour lunch with Willie and Peter Cook, at which the *Karma Britain* project was discussed, and another marathon with Frankie Fraser – Mad Frankie Fraser, as the press called him – and his girlfriend of the time, Marilyn Wisbey.

Willie had known Fraser for some time and had advised him when he had entered the world of showbusiness with his act 'An Evening with Mad Frankie Fraser' and was looking for an agent to sell his memoirs. Always fond of villains, Willie spent a lot of time with Frankie and Marilyn in the first half of the 1990s, enjoying the whiff of notoriety that attended him.

Later, Willie would become less amused by Fraser's celebrity villainy and would admit that he was afraid of him. There were rumours that he owed Frankie money, having been paid for early work as a ghost-writer on Marilyn's memoirs (eventually written with Patrick Newley), but it seems more likely that Willie, who preferred his violence, like his crack houses, to be written rather than real, had seen rather too much of the real Frankie to be entirely comfortable with it.

'There was a brilliant lunch when Willie introduced me to Frankie Fraser and Marilyn,' Debbie Mason remembers. 'We were in this Italian restaurant on Great Marlborough Street. The lunch went on for so long, with Frankie Fraser telling stories about the past that, by the time we had finished and were about to go, people were already coming in for dinner. Loads of brandies had been drunk but when a waiter came along to give me the bill it was for an astronomical amount. I queried it and the waiter came back with a much smaller one. Frankie looked at him and said, "Did you bring the wrong bill?" The waiter admitted that he had – Frankie laid the waiter's hand on the table and slammed his fist down. The waiter just walked away holding his hand and I said, "I think you've broken his fingers, Frank." He said, "He won't do that again".'

Outside the restaurant, Willie – his glasses, Sellotaped up the middle, now slightly askew – said, 'Shit, I was scared.' They hailed a taxi and went on to a bar owned by a former member of the Richardson gang, where the talk was of coke smuggling and who was going to attend Ronnie Biggs's sixtieth birthday in Rio.

By 1994, the net was closing in. The books published in the previous five years, a European spoof called *1992 and All That*, the two Root books and a collection of *Independent* pieces, *The Big One, The Black One, The Fat One and The Other One* had not been successful. TV projects remained grounded. Attempts to earn some money ghosting the memoirs of Marilyn Wisbey and Michelle had failed. The *Independent* column had lost its daring and comic energy and had become repetitive and tired. It was terminated in 1995.

Willie was as near to the precipice as he had ever been. Cherry Donaldson, in whose name Elm Park Mansions was listed and who had loyally paid the rent, reclaiming it from Willie, now found that the payments were no longer coming through. In desperation, she rang his sister Jane who sent her a cheque. Later, when Willie was put on housing benefit, Cherry was able to repay the debt, but the cheque she sent was never cashed.

Paul Sidey had begun to suggest that, unless Willie delivered the memoirs contracted six years previously, the deal would be cancelled. Now, over a feverish six months, Willie worked on the memoirs.

It was while he was writing that in August 1994 he was declared bankrupt with debts of £75,942. The Official Receiver informed Willie's creditors that a court judgement had been obtained against a third party who owed £24,695 to him, but the funds to pursue this claim were not there.

Bankruptcy provided one of the most memorable scenes in Willie's memoirs, which he delivered in 1995. There were the usual legal worries – Penny, Mrs Mouse and I were deemed to be potential litigants – but Willie worked closely with Paul Sidey and the libel lawyer. Finally, Sidey was convinced that *From*

Sunningdale to This was a confessional memoir of extraordinary originality and was ready for publication.

But a new, hard-eyed approach to publishing was in the air. In meetings, the libel worries and the delays of a book without an obvious commercial niche now caused concern. With the manuscript complete, the legal corrections made and the book scheduled, Random House overruled their editor's impassioned objections and cancelled the contract.

32
Potentially unhelpful publicity

With all his talk of inherited wealth and squandered fortunes, it is easy to forget that, from the moment he returned from Ibiza in 1972 with all his possessions in one small suitcase, Willie lived for the rest of his life almost entirely from his writing. It was a high-wire act without a safety net and, even during the brief, occasional moments of stability, disaster – often self-inflicted – was never far away. But even at those moments when it seemed to be all over for him – no money, no contracts, no prospects – he would soon be back at his desk, writing his way out of trouble. However bad things were, he continued to write with a wild, and somehow optimistic, comic inventiveness. He worked on through hardship, emotional collapse and drugs. It is an extraordinary story of creative resilience and of a sort of heroism.

In 1996, Willie was 61, bankrupt, alone and publisherless. He borrowed small amounts of money from friends and raged, with some justification, against Random House, but never complained generally about his life. He kept going. I was seeing him regularly and was not even aware that he had been declared bankrupt.

It is difficult to sell a manuscript that has been cancelled by a large publisher, allegedly on legal grounds. Willie's relationship with his agent Cat Ledger was semi-detached by this stage and he took it upon himself to approach small, independent publishers (he had given up on the big ones) and agents. He was widely turned down, with the usual expressions of admiration and deep regret for the state of market conditions but at the end the memoirs were taken on by the small literary house Peter Owen. It was 'a very literary piece, full of long asides about the nature of memory and the mortality of art', wrote Owen's enthusiastic reader. It had high sales potential – he mentioned the diaries of Alan Clark and Alan Bennett and even the drug connection in its crack-fuelled narrative was seen as a plus. Owen agreed to pay Willie an advance of £1,000 and scheduled it for the autumn of 1998.

Willie wrote best when he was on the ropes. The new version, substantially rewritten, was shorter than the original, and better. The borrowings from his *Independent* column and from *Is This Allowed?* were excised, as were the sections which had given the libel lawyers such a turn.

Now, the narrative was propelled by the loss of Penny and by Willie's financial collapse. Haunting him, and representing both the shame and the dreariness of past things, was a character called Pratley, a generic name which Willie gave to old acquaintances, who with clumsy cheeriness appears in his life, ringing him and wanting to keep an old friendship alive, usually when Willie was waiting to hear from his dealer.

While he was revising the memoirs, his close friend Jo Drinkwater died of cancer, a loss which added another twist of pain to the narrative. Describing a lunch with Little Jo, as he called her, Willie wrote: 'She reminds me with her radiance, with her received sense of life properly to be led, of how things were supposed to be, but can't be now … without Little Jo, I don't know what I'll do. As long as Little Jo says she loves me I feel I'm safe.'

The book ended with Little Jo's death, and with Willie ringing Penny, who was with her Fat Man down in Cornwall. 'Don't worry,' Penny said in what was presumably an imaginary conversation. 'I'm sure you'll be able to use it to your advantage.'

I had been looking forward to this book but, like many of his friends and admirers of his writing, I was at first disappointed by it. 'With the memoirs, I wanted to know what was true and what wasn't,' says Craig Brown. 'Whereas it didn't matter with Henry Root, it really mattered then.' Mike O'Mara thought it was the work of a talent in decline. In his obituary, Simon Carr used the word 'impenetrable'.

It is, in fact, an extraordinary book about memory and shame, about how the present can shape the past. Re-reading it, I can see that the problem was one of expectation.

Willie had an extraordinary and contradictory life. He had circled around the real events of his past, swooping down for the occasional titbit. His memoirs, we had thought, would see an end to the games-playing. There would be real events, real feeling. He would take us back to Winchester, the navy, Cambridge and onwards, explain what it felt like. Mood, atmosphere, feeling: that was what a memoir of this kind would provide.

Instead, the game of hide-and-seek became, if anything, more hectic and confused. Incidents and characters were flashed before the reader's eyes then whipped away as if the mere act of remembering them was too painful for the writer to bear for long. The story was a puzzle, with several key pieces missing.

But as a self-portrait and a book about the essentially fraudulent business of memoirs, it was an astonishing piece of work – sad, perceptive and slyly constructed, real feelings and revelations emerging between the lines. It was a portrait of the author as pervert and crack user, a narrator whose life was collapsing around him as he wrote. Clear-eyed and impassioned, but with only a hint of self-pity, it deserves to be read today with the best of writers' memoirs. Published in 1998, it was widely ignored by reviewers, and sold badly.

Willie worked hard at his usual form of anti-promotion. Following a pre-publication interview in the *Sunday Times* colour magazine, Simon Smith, his editor at Peter Owen, wrote with saintly patience: 'We've just seen a copy of the *Sunday Times* interview. A large portion seems to be the contents of our book; there is no direct reference to the memoirs, however, apart from when you describe them as crap and say that you don't know when they are coming out. Potentially unhelpful publicity.'

While he was working on the memoirs, another career opportunity opened, and closed. Willie had recorded a personal view from Ibiza for Radio Four, one of whose producers had become convinced that he was a natural performer for radio. Overcoming certain practical problems following his bankruptcy (he was unable to renew his passport or travel to Spain), the BBC commissioned a series of four programmes called *A Retiring Fellow*. A simple and brilliant idea, the series saw Willie visiting Bournemouth, Tuscany, the Cornish town of Fowey and Marbella in search of a suitable place for his retirement. He would interview the locals and attend local events.

In Bournemouth, he looked despairingly at old folks at a tea dance, murmuring to himself, 'It's unforgivable what happens to us.' In Fowey, visited presumably because that was where Penny and the Fat Man were trying to live in peace, he fell out with the harbourmaster. In Marbella, he offended a group of expat thespians, suggesting that, given the reputation of the area for being a resting place for British villains, they should invite his friend Frankie Fraser to put on his one-man show. He gossiped about people behind their back, confiding his thoughts into a microphone as he went. It was superb, subversive radio, and very funny.

Willie in person divided his audience more fundamentally than even the Willie the writer could do. One or two critics thought that 'it could become cult listening' (*Daily Mail*) and was 'very funny … achieving almost Swiftian grandeur' (the *Independent*), while others took a harsher view. For *Time Out*, Willie was variously 'hideous', 'horrible' and 'menopausal'. 'Grizzling about "third-rate people"', its critic wrote, 'this monstrous mediocrity again shows why nowhere this side of the grave can help him.'

Within moments of the programme being broadcast a row broke out. Letters from Bournemouth and Fowey, in particular, rained down on the BBC, and some of them are almost as funny as the programmes themselves. 'I think it was his (the presenter's) reference to one of the people he conversed with as a Maori that first alerted me,' wrote a Hampshire correspondent. 'His reference to living in Bournemouth being "as bad as life can be" tells me more about the person saying it than what he thinks it refers to … Get real!' Visiting Fowey, Willie had been in particularly wicked form, punishing the town and its people for having played host to his former baby, and by a stroke of the ill fortune which somehow Willie seemed to attract, its broadcast was disastrously timed. One of the local dignitaries with whom he had crossed swords during the programme had subsequently died; his funeral had taken place the day before the programme had gone out.

In the local paper, residents angrily refuted Willie's claims that the people of Fowey were 'suspicious little Celts, all 4ft 8ins'. Nor was it true, they said, that 'they all marry their own sisters ... a child could be his own grandfather here'. Willie responded to these remarks by saying that he had warned the people of Fowey that he would be playing a rude character, adding unhelpfully: 'Having said that, I was surprised how chippy they are. I'd have thought they were used to being laughed at.' Willie's radio career was over.

Energised by these excitements in the world of TV, radio and memoir-writing, Willie returned to the medium with which he was most at ease.

The row surrounding *A Retiring Fellow* had revealed that nothing annoys people quite as much as an insult to the area in which they live. Where there is irritation, there is comedy and soon afterwards, Willie and Craig Brown began to work on a book that started life as *Around Britain,* and went on to become *The Naff Atlas of Great Britain* before finally fading out as *The Millennium Atlas.*

The book which emerged from this promising collaboration is as outrageous as the earlier Naff Guides, and rather funnier. Brown managed to keep Willie off his usual hobby horses and brought an essential edge of silliness to the project.

Unfortunately, the authors made two mistakes, one creative, the other practical. At some point, they revived the concept of naffness which had begun to seem distinctly dated. They also accepted a contract with Random House, whose dealing with Willie seemed doomed to non-completion. In 1997, the editor Mark Booth took delivery of the manuscript, writing to Willie that it was 'absolutely hilarious'. There were disagreements about the cover which the authors felt was so bad as to indicate a lack of interest and commitment. Rather bravely (Willie was still emerging from bankruptcy, after all) they made the design a matter of principle and the contract was finally cancelled by mutual consent. Willie attempted to place the manuscript elsewhere but the project now had a secondhand, problematic feel to it and he had lost confidence in it. Willie's instinct about the commercial potential of geographical rudeness was probably correct (a book called *Crap Towns* later became a bestseller) but his collaboration with Craig Brown was never published.

Willie's instinct for hypocrisy, and for being able to get a rise out of the Establishment, had remained intact over the years. *The Henry Root Letters* had tuned into the celebrification of worlds that hitherto had taken themselves seriously and *Henry Root's World of Knowledge* had skewered the idle, snobbish anti-intellectualism of the *Spectator*-reading classes of the early 1980s.

By the late 1990s, particularly after the death of Princess Diana, a tear-soaked emotional exhibitionism and a growing obsession with celebrity had taken hold of the national culture. Willie had always read the tabloid press with delighted disgust. When Alan Bennett referred to how Peter Cook had been 'nurtured by newspapers', which had 'mulched his talents', he might have been writing of Willie. Now tabloid values – prurient, sentimental, vengeful – were everywhere, particularly in television. That, by a stroke good fortune, was a world Willie had been able to see at first hand.

In 1997, a TV production company called Heartfelt Productions was created and began to develop projects from its headquarters at Suites 139–140 Elm Park Mansions. Working under the company motto, 'A Tragedy Aired is a Tragedy Shared', Heartfelt was, as one of their directors put it, a 'bi-media communications outfit, progressing family product across a range of Triumph over Tragedy subjects. If a member of the general public is blown up in an outrage or a grieving mother has a tot with a diaphragmatic hernia we ask them to talk about it in an early evening slot.'

Among the compassion initiatives Heartfelt was progressing were such projects as *Don't Leave it to Boots the Chemist! Get a Loved One into Trouble!*, a celebrity humiliation show called *Back* to *Square One*, *Topless Gladiators* and its sister project *Disabled Gladiators*, and a glittering Christmas tribute *Diana, The People's Princess, Lest We Forget*, which was pitched by Heartfelt's Liz Reed to the Dean of St Paul's, John Moses:

> Here's how the video is shaping up. We'd like the Dean to open the show, either with an original tribute (not too solemn) or with the off-the-cuff remarks he made at the time of the tragedy.
>
> Chris de Burgh will then sing 'There's a New Star in Heaven Tonight', followed by anecdotes (some sad, some humorous) from the Princess's showbiz friends – Lord Deedes, Richard Branson, Billy Connolly, Wayne Sleep, Christopher Biggins and Michael Barrymore (the troubled comedian).
>
> Lest we forget that there were other tragedies during the year, Esther Rantzen and a group of grieving mothers will then recite prayers over footage of catastrophes (pensioners over a cliff, tots force-fed Ecstasy by playground fiends, whatever).
>
> The finale will be more upbeat, with various bands playing Diana's fave music: techno, real, handbag house, garage, hip hop, drum'n'bass etc. A few closing words from the Dean perhaps, and then the credits.

The Dean replied in person, confirming that he was 'agreeable to contributing to the video you are producing', only withdrawing when Heartfelt revealed that the Princess Diana lookalike due to appear in the video had been exposed as a tart and a drug fiend in the *News of the World*.

As with Henry Root, *The Heartfelt Letters* served a satirical purpose, pointing up the eager gullibility of those wanting to make their way in the modern media. But, again like Root, what makes it more than a prank is the letter-writer, on this occasion an increasingly hysterical woman called Liz Reed, who is eventually sent to a clinic suffering from Tourette's Syndrome. The first sign of things not being quite as they should be with Liz follows the rejection of *Disabled Gladiators* by the head of Channel Five, Dawn Airey, to whom she replies:

Dear Dawn,

Well thanks a whole fucking *heap*!

My life's crap at the moment, frankly, I haven't had a holiday for two years, my cat, Mr Boots, died last week, my dealer's shagging my tax adviser, I'm *struggling* to get Heartfelt's act together and then I get your letter saying that the company doesn't come up to the required criteria.

So how do you think that made me feel, Dawn?

I'll tell you. It made me feel like shit. It me feel utterly worthless. It was a real blow to my self-image. It made me want to stick my head down the toilet with the rest of my life.

I mean, what's the fucking *point*, Dawn?

That said, I may have something for you...

The Heartfelt Letters was not published with the straight-faced aplomb of *The Henry Root Letters*, clearly being a spoof, but it was noticed in the right places. David Aaronovitch devoted a think piece to it, in the *Independent*, headlined 'Is there nothing so crass that it won't be embraced by television?' A *Daily Mirror* feature complained, mystifyingly, that 'Donaldson simply seems to get a kick out of making the likes of Richard Branson and Michael Winner look stupid'.

It was a brilliant joke, superbly written and made a telling point but, because of the medium in which it appeared, it was never going to be taken as seriously as, say, a sketch show on TV, or a satirical magazine, or a West End comedy about New Labour. There is no justification for this bias beyond cultural snobbery but Willie, perhaps more than anyone else, must bear responsibility for running down the very form in which he was at his funniest.

'I know at my age it's disgraceful to be playing silly jokes,' Willie said to an interviewer shortly after *The Heartfelt Letters* was published. 'But, I ask you, what are you meant to do if you can't write a sensible book? I was desperate.'

33
Getting the buzz
without leaving the flat

Essentially a romantic, Willie had ideas of loyalty and fidelity which, while unconventional, were nonetheless real and important to him. He was not light-hearted about love and sex, nor was he an opportunist or a ladies' man. Yet, even in the early 1990s, when he was with Penny, he had begun to fantasise about Rachel Garley.

He had first seen her picture in a book of the *Sun*'s greatest Page Three girls. There was, he later told her, an indefinably different quality to her from the other girls. She became an object of distant longing and admiration, rather as Svetlana Beriosova had been almost half a century earlier. While travelling around Europe during the filming of the Root TV series, he would often like to bring the conversation around to Rachel Garley.

With his usual confidence, he worked out a way to get in touch with her. One of his *Independent* columns was to be about the unworldliness of (who else?) Richard Ingrams, a man so out of touch with the modern world, Willie was going to write, that he had never heard of Rachel Garley. In order to write about her, he needed naturally enough to talk to her. He rang her agent, Rachel gave him a quote for the column and he sent her a copy of *Root into Europe*.

Five years later, while being profiled by the *Sunday Times*, he was asked if he would like to be photographed with a couple of friends. Willie nominated Frankie Fraser and Rachel Garley.

During the shoot, they got on well, as he knew they would. He had been able to tell what she was like from her photographs, he later told her, and had sensed that she was everything and more that the photographs had promised.

'I wasn't typical of a girl with her tits out in the *Sun*,' she says now. 'It was a bit dipsy the way I became a model. I went on holiday with my mum and met this photographer. I never had the ambition to be a model. I just ended up doing it.'

After the *Sunday Times* shoot they went for a drink at the club Soho House – 'We really hit it off,' says Rachel – and a few days later, he asked her to accompany him to a charity event at which Frankie Fraser was appearing. Rachel lived with her boyfriend, the photographer Ian McKell, and their daughter Jasmine, and Willie did not wish the date to seem improper. So he paid her £500. That way, he said, she could tell Ian that it was a job.

Rachel.

It seems mildly shocking, this business of paying Rachel to go out with him, just as he had done in the past with Miss Picano – turning a date into a paid event seems a clear indication of a desire to corrupt – but perhaps there is a simpler and more innocent reason for it: handing over money made the occasion serious for Willie, more exciting.

The second time they went out, Willie also paid Rachel £500 at the end of the night, an amount of money which she now realises 'to an old person was a lot'.

An old, recently bankrupt person, Willie might have added. He later confessed to Rachel that finding the second payment had been a struggle. He had in fact resorted to ringing up this High Court judge with whom he had once had an affair when he was at school and telling him he needed some money rather urgently. Rachel thought he might have taken the judge for £1,000.

There had, in fact, been rumours among Willie's friends that, at a low moment, he had resorted to some light blackmail – he even casually mentioned it in an interview a few years later. I had put the story down as the sort of myth which his life seemed to attract.

But Rachel is a reliable witness. She became very fond of Willie, and was the saving of him at a dark time, and it is not difficult to see why she appealed to him. Beyond the Page Three looks and figure she is bright, curious and open. She had an adventurous sex life and liked cocaine. In person, she was the embodiment of his favoured, librarian-with-a-secret-life fantasy.

However he managed to finance it (my suspicion is the judge, who is now dead, was not blackmailed but, like many others, helped Willie out with £200 or so), the friendship with Rachel deepened into what Willie liked to call 'a passionate friendship'.

He had been right about Rachel; in many ways, she was perfect for him. She was happy to take a gram or two of coke, of which he was always the supplier. Sometimes he smoked some crack or occasionally would just talk to her. The subject was almost always what Rachel had been getting up to. 'All we did was sit there and talk about our experiences with other people.

I'd go to an orgy or something and tell him all about it,' she says. 'He would be getting the buzz without leaving the flat.'

Willie's obsession with Rachel was every bit as powerful as the other two great loves of his later years, Melanie and Penny. His files and folders are full of references to her. In a clear-out of his papers shortly before he died, he kept the glamour shots of Rachel Garley. 'Can't bring myself to ditch the magazines,' he wrote in a note to himself. 'What is it about her? Recklessness and innocence. Paradigm of adorable woman.'

Asked to fill out a questionnaire for a BBC documentary in 1998, he made his state of mind very clear:

Who has been the biggest influence in your life? What is your biggest achievement and proudest moment? What has been the worst moment?
Rachel Garley.
Meeting Rachel Garley.
Thinking about not seeing Rachel Garley.

What makes you angry? What makes you happy? What moves you?
People being rude to Rachel Garley.
Seeing Rachel Garley.
Thinking about Rachel Garley.

What events through your life have had most influence and changed the pattern of your life? Have there been any major turning points?
Meeting Rachel Garley.

What concerns you at the moment? What is taking up most of your time?
Rachel Garley.

How do you relax? Hobbies? What are you interested in?
Rachel Garley.

He would talk a lot about Rachel, usually in terms of anguish, jealousy and longing. I would – crassly, I now see – encourage him to be less diffident in his dealings with her. 'Why would she want an old carcass like this?' he would ask.

In fact, Willie knew himself well enough to see that if Rachel went to bed with him, it would be the end of their relationship. With Melanie and Penny, he was, for all the romantic talk, a business proposition. Rachel was different. 'Were she to show any interest in me – even in a fantasy – she would naturally sink in my estimation, and lose all her allure,' he wrote at about this time. 'It delights me just to look at her.'

There are probably few women in the world who could both share wild sexual fantasies or moments of narcotic togetherness, and on the other hand also provide the excursions into domestic normality which Willie secretly enjoyed. He would visit Rachel and Ian at home, sometimes collecting Jasmine from school. He was a regular babysitter for them. Famously allergic to the end-of-the-year climax of family life, he spent three consecutive Christmas Days with Rachel and her family. 'He'd come over on Christmas morning bringing presents, and we'd get some drugs and have a really nice Christmas,' says Rachel.

These cosy moments are not entirely conventional, but they were perhaps as near to contentment as Willie would find in his later years. Rachel recalls her visits to Elm Park Mansions with real warmth. 'He used to sit on the chair and I'd be on the sofa. He'd sit there with his pipe and a brandy and a cigar and sometimes I'd have a Red Bull.' If it were not for the fact that the pipe was crack, it would be a vision of domestic contentment.

Such was his passion for Rachel that he began to involve her in his work. Neither *From Winchester to This* nor *The Heartfelt Letters* had dispelled the idea among publishers that he was a difficult author who tended to bring with him legal problems, whose books invariably lost money and who had contracts all over town for projects that had been signed up, paid for and never delivered.

He was sending out synopses, many of which – *How to Tell if Your Parents Are Not on Drugs, How to be Blonde for Fifteen Minutes, How to Get There Without Intoxicants, The Silly Little Book* – had an air of desperation to them. The ill-fated *Naff Atlas* was re-packaged as *Up Your Way: The Millennium Atlas of Great Britain* but even with Craig Brown's name attached failed to find a publisher. The rejection letters Willie received often revealed the jovial, slightly contemptuous familiarity an editor feels is the appropriate tone of voice when dealing with an old pro, a humour hack. 'I'd be kidding you if I declared it to be anything other than something with REMAINDER stamped all over it!' one of them wrote cheerily. Willie's old friend and former publisher Mike O'Mara, sensing his financial desperation, parted with £3,000 for a project he was convinced he would never see.

The solution to this kind of problem in the past had been to invent a new authorial *persona* for himself: Root, Talbot Church, Jean-Luc Leyris, Dr Kit Bryson, Liz Reed. Now he had a better idea – one that would neatly bring the professional and personal sides to his life. *Canetti et Moi* was a labour of love, which included a central reference to one of his heroes, Elias Canetti, some philosophical games, a few real letters to make fools of publishers, TV production companies and rehabilitation clinics, the teasing out of ideas of identity with particular regard to tabloid celebrities, some jokes about drugs, all of which would be narrated by and under the name of his beloved, Rachel Garley.

It was an ambitious idea – 'Page Three meets philosophy', as the narrator Rachel describes it – and develops several themes which had preoccupied Willie down the years. The real sophisticates are Rachel and Greg and Derek, who are working on her kitchen, while publishers are too stupid to notice that the book proposal *The Many Roads* is a direct lift from Canetti. The fact that Rachel is writing letters to real people gives them the control over her, turning the narrator into the object, illustrating Sartre's comment that 'our everyday selves derive from our experience of others as subjects'.

All this, told in Rachel's cheerfully scatty, sexy prose – or at least Willie's version of it – intrigued some heavyweights in the world of academic philosophy, including Lewis Wolpert, Anthony Quinton and Galen Strawson, all of whom corresponded with Rachel/Willie with varying degrees of learning or flirtatiousness.

When Rachel Garley's *Canetti et Moi* reached the desk of Mal Peachey of the book packaging company Essential Works, he recognised it immediately as the work of Willie Donaldson, of whom he was a great fan. Peachey met Willie and, between them,

With Rachel, 1999.

they came up with the idea of him writing a biography of the writer and comedian Marty Feldman.

The idea was not as dotty as it may seem (and certainly seemed to me at the time): Feldman had written the 1963 show *Wham Bam Thank You Ma'am*, which Willie had produced. Both men shared a love of music hall and slapstick – 'an innocent world of fat bald comedians and nubile dancing girls,' as Willie described it – but their show had been compromised by 'two conflicting needs in Marty: his desire to produce innocent jokes and his need to be serious, to be saying something'. Feldman had been an outsider, distrustful of the various cliques of comedy and showbusiness. He had tried to reinvent himself after the catastrophes of the early Sixties.

There was something familiar about this story which Mal Peachey recognised and welcomed. Willie had discovered a new way of writing about himself. 'New form of biog in which biographer is centre stage' as Willie wrote in a scrawled note. '"Form follows function". Empirical reality exists and novelists have a duty to capture it. BS Johnson... Following this idea, a diary in no chronological order – or, rather, the order is conditioned by the needs of the narrative.'

The book was signed up. Willie made notes and even began some research, ringing up Barry Took, with whom Marty Feldman had written Willie's favourite sitcom of the early 1960s *Bootsie and Snudge*. Took annoyed Willie by claiming that most of the good work on the series had been done by him, indeed that he had in a sense invented Feldman. The biographer called him 'a fucking idiot' and hung up. That seems to have been the full extent of his research, although he continued to brood about the book, and to make notes for it. 'Marty,' he wrote in his notes. 'Maybe if I pitch in, crack on, something will emerge of interest. God knows what.'

It almost goes without saying that a central role in Willie's biography of Marty Feldman was to have been played by Rachel. 'She seems well cast,' Willie wrote. 'I think she'll take direction, play out (fill out) the character I've conceived for her.'

He also had a more immediate plan for Rachel. He suggested to his old friend Nevile Player who had once published his Emma Jane Crampton advice column for *Penthouse* and who had worked for Paul Raymond, that he should set up a series of photographic features called *The Story of P* – an English version of *The Story of O* – in which Rachel would pursue a series of personal fantasies. The first one would involve Sebastian Horsley, the elegant and decadent artist whose startlingly candid column in the *Erotic Review* had made him a highly controversial figure. 'Ever since she read a remark of his in the *Erotic Review* – "the perfect woman should be a cook in the bedroom and a whore in the kitchen" – Rachel has wanted to be a whore in his kitchen,' Willie wrote. 'He will photograph her in his Soho eyrie – the "truth" of the situation bringing a sharp erotic edge to an already dangerous enterprise.'

He was right, at least, about the danger. Horsley had been introduced to Willie in 1998 and had impressed him with the style and daring of his writing and his life. Here was a man who openly wrote about his drugs and his use of prostitutes, who had travelled to the Philippines to have himself crucified as part of a religious ceremony – an interesting masochistic experience, he thought. He became something of a *protégé*, the kind of brilliant, self-destructive younger writer whom Willie found interesting and good company. 'I was expecting a rather demonic character, someone who was very difficult,' Horsley says now. 'He was a frightening character in his books but I immediately liked him and we became friends. I sent him some of my stuff and he became an early champion of my work.' At some point, Rachel saw a photograph of Sebastian at Elm Park Mansions. She thought he was an attractive man, she said.

Willie sent Sebastian some magazine shots of Rachel, suggesting he should ring her when she was feeling depressed, take her out to dinner. Caught up with the real story was the lived fiction which would appear in *Penthouse*. It was a project which mischievously would tease out private feelings – Rachel's, Sebastian's, his own – in a public, staged manner. 'I thought I was being played,' Sebastian says. 'I was part of some sort of game.'

He did indeed take Rachel out to dinner. A few days later, they had lunch at his flat. 'Of course, I fell for her,' says Sebastian.

Willie, usually so good at these games in the past, had overestimated his ability to control the situation – or, rather, to control Rachel. When she and Sebastian became lovers, she did the great unforgivable thing: she cut Willie out. What happened between her and Sebastian was their affair, she decided, not his.

It was several months before the truth was revealed, and in a manner that was somehow appropriate. Sebastian wrote in the *Erotic Review* column how he had given his girlfriend Rachel a treat on her birthday by taking her to a prostitute. There was a photograph of him with, in the background, Rachel, lying on a bed with a black girl.

Willie was devastated, winded by what he saw as a double betrayal. He stopped seeing Rachel but, in contrast to his behaviour towards Melanie and Penny, he did not try to destroy her. His greatest rage was towards Sebastian. 'I felt I had committed an act of patricide,' Sebastian says. 'There was something repellent in setting us up and then hating us for falling in love.'

Willie kept the photographs of Rachel but he never managed entirely to forgive Sebastian.

Willie's private writing changed as the millennium approached. He sporadically began to keep an annotated diary, which may well have been the jottings for that final journey into his own life which he never made, the biography of Marty Feldman.

Although a few of the old anecdotes would doubtless have been there, the tone as well as the approach was different. There was less rage against the various Establishment cliques which had been his enemies down the years. There were fewer forays into the past, less doomed and perverse randiness. In Willie's notes there is no mention of his parents, his family, even of Charlie.

Instead the focus, often rather desperately, was on the present.

Where are we? February 1998. I'm as poor as a church mouse. Income support. I always assumed that before it had come to this I would have committed a great crime... Why let this happen? Could anything be worse than this? And yet something happens to get one going. Craig rings or something. Terror under weight of events. Keep busy. Well at least I was busy. Clean flat. No use. Need Koreans in. Utterly degraded. Who allow in? Michelle and Yardies. People for whom I have no respect. People who have grown dirty with it. At this stage salvation would be entirely fortuitous. Became a cult accidentally. No point in embarrassing oneself by striving.

This anguished, jokeless Willie is difficult to recognise and painful to read. Socially at least, he was still striving. He had begun to show signs of age – his breathing was wheezy, he seemed to have become oddly barrel-chested – and his clothes, which consisted of his neighbour Mike Hanford's cast-offs, were more frayed. There were times when Willie looked like a gentleman tramp.

But if he was miserable, he kept it well hidden. He seemed in good form. He would tease me about the way my fiction was becoming more serious, announcing himself on one occasion when he rang, 'Hullo, Tragedy? Comedy here.'

A certain quiet order was returning to his life. He was more regularly in touch with his sister Jane, overcoming his fear of her husband Christopher, and enjoyed having lunch with his niece Claudia, who lived near him in Fulham. He had, startlingly, left London to stay with Craig and Frances Brown in their house on the Suffolk coast and enjoyed himself.

'Simey's back,' the diary reads at one point. 'Good to have him back. He pitches up with lots of grub. Do I tell Rachel? She thinks I'm made of money.'

139 Elm Park Mansions was now something of a no-go area except for late-night visitors, but in 1998 Willie did receive an unscheduled visit from the police. They had been called by the man who was caretaker at the flats at the time, after a woman who lived across the courtyard had complained that Willie was watching her from his window as she walked around unclothed (one of the sillier accusations levelled at him). Outraged, he looked for help from an unusual source. Lord Longford, the Catholic peer, prison visitor and anti-pornography campaigner in the 1970s, who had earned himself the nickname 'Lord Porn', had met Willie through Roy Stevens. He now wrote on House of Lords notepaper to Sir Paul Condon, the Commissioner of Police, complaining the officers had been 'intimidating and offensive' towards Mr Donaldson. 'I would like to know what the circumstances of the visit by the two officers were; what he is accused of and who by. These do not seem unreasonable questions.'

A few days later, thanks to the intervention of Lord Porn, Willie received an apology from the police.

The diary contains no mention of this humiliation, but there are others, which illustrate the way he was living at this stage in his life. 'Craig rings up and asks me to dinner at Blakes. Doing the Late Show. I bathe and change. Then utilities are cut off. Pitch up in odd shoes. He'll lend me a tenner. Greets me tapping his pocket. "No cash." I pale. "Don't worry. I've got a credit card." No handout though. Grope off in dark. Don't like to tell him that I can't watch him on TV. No utilities.'

Bizarrely, Willie claims in his diary to know the truth about six people – his three wives, Richard Dynevor, Craig Brown and me. It is an odd line-up and is almost a list of those who have not 'revealed themselves' in the way of which he had approved so much in his memoir, but perhaps reflected his more mellow state of mind. Putting down his thoughts on biography, Willie expressed the view that only the work, not the life, should be discussed. 'How truly awful to be written about,' he added.

The Marty Feldman autobiographical project seemed promisingly full of new thoughts, confessions and quotations but the book never advanced beyond these early notes. Another, more immediate and more remunerative project had offered itself.

34
National treasure

In September 1999, Dr William Donaldson, the highly respected author of *The Highland Pipe and Scottish Society 1750–1950*, received an unusual request. As a man well known for his personal interest in drugs, crime and sexual scandal, would he be interested in compiling an encyclopaedia of British rogues, villains and eccentrics?

After this false start had been resolved and Dr Donaldson's namesake in Fulham had been apprised of the idea behind the book, it soon became clear that it was a perfect project for this stage in his career. He was fascinated by sex and gangsters. A lifetime of misbehaviour had provided him with first-hand contacts and experience which would be invaluable, since quite a few of the rogues, villains and eccentrics of the previous fifty years had been friends and associates of his. As for the historical entries, Willie had always been amused and intrigued by society's outsiders.

What would have excited Willie was that it was essentially a serious enterprise. *Brewer's Dictionary of Phrase and Fable* had been an authoritative work compiled with Victorian thoroughness. The same approach, on the surface at least, would be applied to this encyclopaedia of British misbehaviour. It would be a massive 300,000 words long and would have a gravitas befitting its bulk. Libraries would stock it; future historians would refer to it. Jokes, inventions and fictional riffs would need to be kept on a tight rein.

Although he suffered as many publishing setbacks and frustrations as any author, Willie was generally lucky with his publishers. Geoffrey Strachan of Methuen had recognised his peculiar comic genius at an early stage. Simon Dally at Weidenfeld had the vision to publish *The Henry Root Letters* with appropriate mock solemnity. Mike O'Mara had backed a sequence of toilet books. Hutchinson's Paul Sidey had signed up the memoirs, had kept faith with it over five years and had finally chivvied it out of him. The Scottish publishers Mainstream had stuck with him during the late 1990s with *The Heartfelt Letters* and, his last collaboration with me, *The Meaning of Cantona*.

Now the careful and serious-minded approach of Richard Milbank of Weidenfeld & Nicolson was perfect for the author and the occasion. Once Willie had been signed up, with an advance of £22,000, a series of letters discussed the criteria for inclusion in the book and the authorial tone it needed. The style, Willie wrote to Milbank: 'Should be straight-faced and never straining after humour. Entries should be authoritative and true as a primary requirement. Humour would be incidental, a function of the extraordinary facts. Exaggeration would be avoided and the fat, humorous adjectives and adverts so beloved by English comic writers rigorously banned.'

He was slightly pushing it here – several entries may have seemed authoritative and true to the untutored eye, but they were often based on fictions of the past. Responding to an exhaustive libel report, Willie would now and then justify entries by quoting such authoritative sources as *Bitov's Britain* or Talbot Church's *101 Things You Never Knew about the Royal Lovebirds*, omitting to mention that he had written them himself. His instinctive approach, preferring at all times an amusing but unreliable rumour over a more dreary fact, may have been unconventional among encyclopaedists but was perfectly suited to the subject. Entries were frequently eccentric, occasionally roguish and, now and then, frankly villainous.

The format of *Brewer's Rogues, Villains and Eccentrics* provided Willie with a useful constraint: wild running jokes, hysterical voices of a Root and a Liz Reed, the philippics directed at ancient targets and hate figures, had no place in a solid work of reference. The tales from his past were there – *Nights at the Comedy, The Council of Love,* incidents from the days of Emma Jane Crampton, top-notch gossip from gangsters and call girls –

but all were respectably turned out in top hat and tails. The tension between the cool neutrality of the prose and the crazed bedlam of insanity, corruption, perversion and greed that it described was perfectly maintained. Twenty years, perhaps even ten years previously, Willie would have resisted the stylistic straightjacket that would seem to risk squeezing out his favourite jokes and weakening the force of his comic rage. Now it suited his attitude to the world and to writing. Few reference books can have done so much to give respectability to rumours, half-truths and tall stories.

There is evidence, in fact, that some of the inaccuracies were intentional. The entry for Humphry Berkeley, whom Willie had always disliked, described him as 'an ill-mannered politician, broadcaster and occasional writer' and managed in four lines to misspell his Christian name, to get the title of his only famous book wrong, to claim it was published twenty-nine years earlier than it was and to record its author's date of death three years later than it actually happened.

The madder the entries, the more plummily authoritative the tone Willie adopted:

McCartney, Sir Paul (1941–), singer and composer. Bass guitarist with the 1960s pop group, the Beatles, and later with Wings, McCartney announced in October 2001 that he had proposed marriage to ex-model Heather Mills after he received instructions from an owl. Sir Paul understood that the bird was passing on a message from his first wife Linda, who was giving the couple her blessing from 'the other side'. Sir Paul was once a pupil of Maharishi Mahesh Yogi, and has frequently taken mind-expanding drugs. In India three hoots from an owl means that a woman is to be married into a family. Nearer home, Edd Prynn, arch druid of Cornwall, has said, 'The owl is a strong messenger'. On the other hand, it has been said that if you are ever tempted to keep an owl as a pet, think twice. Sir Paul's most successful composition is 'Yesterday', which according to *The Guinness Book of Records* has been covered by more artists than any other song. He gave up cocaine after his first wife, Linda, said: 'Why don't you try reality?' This seemed to beg the question since there is no record of Sir Paul and Lady McCartney having first discussed in what sense 'reality' after taking cocaine might count as less 'real' than 'reality' without cocaine.

For a discussion concerning the nature of reality between the philosopher Galen Strawson and the former glamour model Rachel Garley, *see* STRACHEY, WILLIAM.

A stylistic master-stroke which added to the book's bizarre and largely fraudulent air of scholarship was the comical cross-reference, a joke which Willie had been perfecting in his books since *Henry Root's A–Z of Women.* Few bookshop browsers could fail to be drawn in by entries reading:

Bishop, performing an act of fellatio on a newly consecrated. *See Cleveland, Barbara Villiers, Countess of.*

Or –

Jesus, believing oneself to have carnal relations with. *See Edinburgh, Prince Philip, Duke of.*

Or –

One-legged prostitute has sex with pizza delivery man. *See David Mellor.*

Willie always worked hard at his writing and was utterly professional. His encyclopaedia of roguery was a feat of research, organisation and restraint. When published in the autumn of 2002, it received ecstatic notices:

'Willie Donaldson has never really had the recognition he deserves as a comic genius. Perhaps this magnificent volume will do the trick,' wrote Francis Wheen in the *Mail on Sunday,* warning that 'Anyone foolhardy enough to read more than a few pages at a time might well die of laughing.' *The Times* described it as 'probably the greatest bathroom book ever' while in the *Daily Express,* Roger Lewis went further, describing it as 'the funniest book in the history of the world'. The book sold briskly both in bookshops and to book clubs and had soon earned back its advance.

On the front page of the *Independent on Sunday*, Willie was described as 'crack smoker, retired pimp, serial adulterer, genius, national treasure' and was the subject of a lengthy profile in the newspaper's magazine by Robert Chalmers. One of the most perceptive later portraits of Willie, the interview presented him in his preferred role as irredeemable pervert and immoralist. The only thing that he had tried to get right throughout his life had been bad behaviour, he said. He had, he claimed, 'an unusual capacity for self-forgiveness'. Chalmers asked him if his life had brought him happiness. 'Look at me for fuck's sake,' Willie said. 'Look at my life.'

There were, in fact, signs that his life was settling down. The launch party for *Brewer's Rogues, Villains and Eccentrics*, held at the Pan Bookshop in the Fulham Road, was unusual in that, for the first time, Willie invited members of the various factions in his social life – writers, villains, TV executives, members of the family, reviewers, friends and lovers from the Sixties, Page Three girls – and allowed them to mingle with one another. A glamour model cruises the literary set in search of a ghost-writer, moving from Hugh Massingberd to AN Wilson, whom she grasped by the thigh and asked to be her ghost.

Later, a few of the partygoers crossed the Fulham Road to a local restaurant where, as if some kind of natural evolutionary order was asserting itself, two groups sat at separate tables – the straight, mainly bookish set was on one while the gangsters, models, Rachel and Sebastian, and of course Willie were on the other. Now and then, Willie would pay a visit to the literary table and tell us how he wished he were with us rather than the frightful people he found himself with. Then he would hurry back to the other table. It seemed to me then that he was as happy as I had known him. He had the reviews, he had the work, he had the friends.

The moments in his life when he had been, for a brief, heady moment, the toast of the town occurred roughly at twenty-year intervals. In the early 1960s, there had been *Beyond The Fringe,* the early 1980s had been the boom years of Henry Root. Now, in 2002, Willie was on the front of magazines, national treasure and comic genius, author of the funniest book in the history of the world.

His financial affairs continued to be shambolic and precarious. He was on housing benefit, but had not filed a tax return since 1998. Although he had been de-registered for VAT several years previously, he continued to claim it. On the other hand, he had given up crack and had recently taken to opening credit card accounts. To his delight, one company – with, presumably, a rather inadequate research department – wrote to him offering immediate credit. Helped by Roy Stevens, he shifted his debts from one card to another.

He was now rather in demand. The BBC's Meriel Beale, who had interviewed him for the Peter Cook documentary, had been so amused and impressed by his performance on camera that she was keen to advance his career. 'I couldn't understand why everyone didn't love him more,' she says now. Sensing that he would like to do more TV, even if he felt slightly disgusted with himself as a result, she tried to find a suitable spot for him on a BBC production.

With his wit, knowledge of the world of celebrities and his peculiarly youthful approach to much in life – 'I felt that he was a twenty-year-old in an old man's body,' she says – Meriel Beale came up with the startling and rather brilliant idea that Willie might be a judge on the BBC's latest reality show *Fame Academy.* Willie went as far as doing a screen test but, says Beale, 'they weren't very visionary'.

When he wrote about his past, he was less laceratingly comic, more serious, than he once had been. When commissioned by the London *Evening Standard* to write about crack, which had allegedly become fashionable in middle-class circles, he was the same, funny Willie – 'I've taken the filthy stuff for nearly twenty years,' he wrote. 'As a consequence, coherent prose is even more difficult than it used to be but a few snapshots from the front line might be helpful' – but, having revealed that he had given it up, closed on a note that was unmistakeably sincere and straight-faced.

> I hope I've made it clear that crack is disgusting. At worst, it will kill you or land you in a seaside clinic. At best, like pornography (or masturbation), it's about nothing but itself. It severs you completely from whatever it is that connects us with each other in common decency and honour.
>
> We can be confident, I think, that its appeal to the middle classes – who are honourable, almost by definition – will be slight indeed.

Willie was in demand elsewhere. Even before *Brewers* was published, his publishers had been keen to sign him up with another idea. 'I don't know about you, but when I'm invited to write a book these days, I always go to my shelves to check that I haven't already written it,' he had once joked, but failed to add that now and then, he would still decide to write it again. The idea he now put to Richard Milbank will have seemed distinctly familiar to those who had read *Henry Root's World of Knowledge* two decades previously. It would essentially be a dictionary of received ideas, he explained. 'It should evoke the experience of being stuck in a room with Chris Tarrant and John Motson; alternatively at one of my sister Bobo's Hampshire dinner parties, perhaps with a duff episode of *Inspector Morse* in the background.'

I'm Leaving You Simon, You Disgust Me, as it was to be called, confirmed that the early twenty-first century was as fruitful a source of cliché and lazy thinking as the 1980s had been. A few old favourites, notably Michael Parkinson and Barry Norman, appear in the new book but Willie's eye for cliché drew him to new targets: TV detective shows, celebrity historians, Channel Five, a tired north London marriage. Cleverly, Milbank commissioned a cover illustration from the great cartoonist of middle-class *ennui*, Posy Simmonds.

'Though Donaldson records the empty noise that constitutes our conversation and shapes our dismal personal relationships, he does so with such furious comic genius, that the commonplaces are transformed – made hysterical and blissful,' wrote Roger

Lewis, welcoming *I'm Leaving You Simon, You Disgust Me* as 'a modern moral comedy' in the *Erotic Review*.

It was while he was publicising his new book that Willie was contacted by Hermione Eyre, a young journalist working for the *Independent on Sunday*, who was writing a piece on hangovers. Willie, with his abiding disapproval of drunkenness, was probably less qualified than most to speak on the subject but, when she contacted him on the telephone, he asked Eyre if she knew who wrote a couple of columns in the *Independent on Sunday* called Fancy That and Party On. It was her. Willie had discovered his latest and his last collaborator.

In many ways, Hermione Eyre was an ideal writing partner for Willie. He liked the business and company of collaboration and had not worked with anyone since he and I had written our study of the philosophy of Eric Cantona in 1998. He had become increasingly caught up in the tabloid world of celebrity and, although he wanted to write about it, he was aware that a man in his late sixties was likely to get the details and the language slightly wrong. Besides, there was little future in discussing with any of his usual co-writers the people who now fascinated him – Jade Goody, Posh Beckham, the coughing Major who cheated on *Who Wants to be a Millionaire?* – with any of his usual co-writers. We were all getting too old for him. Hermione was young, intelligent, had a cheerful and sceptical eye for pop culture and, as important as anything, was well bred and nicely spoken. 'You're the right person to do this because you're posh and you don't care what people think,' he told her over lunch at Kettners in January 2004.

Soon the project which Willie had been discussing with Richard Milbank, *A Devil's Dictionary*, was dropped in favour of a dictionary of celebrities. Worried that Hermione Eyre might see herself as a junior partner, he impersonated the role of an old fool tagging along for the ride, assuring her (as he had assured previous co-writers) that hers would be the brilliant material.

I know I said that we shouldn't edit or interfere with each other's stuff but I take that back,' he wrote in an email a month after they had met. 'I think that while it would be absurd to add my starch to your *joie de vivre* it would be a good thing if you spotted here and there opportunities to introduce your language here and there into mine. If I said something like "go girl, go!" or "party on!" it would be embarrassing (like my dancing at a disco) but it would be most refreshing, certainly not embarrassing, to see you doing the tango in an old folks' home.

Hermione had been warned that Willie could be a demonic and corrupting influence (in a profile at around this time, a middle-aged male journalist queasily expressed the worry that Willie might slip some Rohypnol, the date rape drug, into his drink, just for fun). In fact, he behaved perfectly, taking her out to lunch, paying for her taxi home, advising her about her life and her future. He had a natural intuitive sense as to how she was and what she was thinking, and Hermione soon discovered, as Meriel Beale had, that this sensitivity was useful when studying the career and behaviour of a newsreader, footballer or member of a girl band. 'He could see what was going on beneath the surface.'

The older Willie grew, the more he wanted to be with young people. With Rachel Garley, Meriel Beale, Hermione Eyre, and his niece Claudia Downes, he would happily talk about their lives and relationships, or talk about *Pop Idol* and *Big Brother*, or perhaps discuss what exactly was going on between Chris Evans and Billie Piper. 'You're so lucky,' he once sadly said to Hermione. 'You'll be alive to find out what happens to Charlotte Church.'

He may also have found it easier to talk to people who were thirty or forty years younger than him, who knew little about what he had written and done in the past. He told Hermione Eyre, for example, that he now realised that his parents had been good people, that he had loved his father very much. 'It was the way people can suddenly see something that's far away more vividly than ever before,' she says.

With companionship, work and reputation in place, the Willie of old would at this point have done something to undermine and complicate his life. On this occasion though, self-sabotage was unnecessary. His health was failing.

Willie had never been one for physical fitness. Carly Simon had noted in her diary of the summer of 1965 that, at the age of 30, he had the body of an old man. Now that he really was an old man, he was in poor shape.

Before the filming of *Root into Europe* in the early 1990s, he had been obliged to undergo a medical for insurance purposes and that was probably his last visit to a doctor. 'I've never got round to having one – the consequence, I think, of never having quite felt up to it,' he once explained in his *Independent* column. 'You have to be pretty much in the pink, I imagine, to handle a visit to the doctor.'

Throughout the 1990s, his breathing grew more laboured and wheezy. When he was to meet people for lunch, he would invariably be there, waiting, before the appointed time. At the end of the meal, he would say goodbye and tell them that he would make his way home after finishing his drink. His attitude to alcohol had changed during these years. He drank red wine at meals and then, towards the end of the millennium, developed a liking for brandy. He would usually have two large brandies over lunch every day; towards the end of his life, there is evidence that his intake increased and that he drank at home.

He found the three flights of stairs to his flat increasingly difficult, and needed to rest on each landing. Increasingly over his last years, he would succumb to bouts of flu and bronchitis. His voice on the phone was so breathless that he sounded as if he was laughing so much that he was unable to get the words out. As his health declined, he became more reclusive. The older he was, the less he wanted to see people from his past. When the photographer Lewis Morley, whom Willie had first set up in a studio in 1961, visited London in the late 1990s from Australia where he now lived and left messages, Willie went into hiding. Invited by Julian Mitchell to attend his partner's sixtieth birthday, Willie accepted but never turned up. Sarah Miles called by unannounced on one occasion; he declined to let her into the flat, talking to her on the communal balcony which overlooked the courtyard at Elm Park Mansions.

From the late nineties onwards, he had begun to shake off those who sought him out. His publisher Mike O'Mara was startled to be told by Willie that he was now living in the country. Sightings of him doing the shopping on his small territory around Fulham Road suggested that all was not well. When Julian Mitchell ran into him, he seemed confused and out of sorts. Bamber Gascoigne saw him at a bus stop and thought at first that he was a down-and-out. When his nephew Gerard, caught up in a traffic jam on the Fulham Road, saw the familiar figure, and got out to talk to him, Willie recoiled. 'It was as if he had seen a ghost – the look of terror that crossed his face. I'm not even sure he knew who I was.' Some of these surprise encounters may have occurred when he was still using crack, in the aftermath of a session on the pipe ('Your eyes bulge with paranoia, your nerves twang and snap like banjo strings' was the way he described the experience) but health was increasingly the problem.

Gerard's sister Claudia remembers seeing Willie making his way slowly down the Fulham Road, a plastic bag in his hand, now and then holding on to a lamppost while he recovered his breath.

His lungs were giving out, even though he was still in his sixties. Pulmonary damage is one of the most frequently recorded physical effects of crack-smoking and it is fair to assume that he was beginning to pay the price for fifteen years' regular use.

There are signs that the direction his life had taken was bearing down on him in a way which he found increasingly painful. 'The present,' he wrote in a note to himself, 'Never could abide it. The future yes. The past, carefully edited. Not the good bits, not the loss of everything. Unless wanted to feel stab of pain.'

'When aren't we acting?' he asked in his diary. 'When aren't we concealing? Would you like me to have been a fly on your wall yesterday? Did you do nothing shameful? Of course you did. The version of ourselves we present to the world bears no resemblance to the truth. If we knew the truth about each other we could take no one seriously. There isn't one of us who could afford to be caught. That's all life is. Trying not to be found out.'

In 2003, he was given further opportunity to destroy the past and what he called 'the incriminating evidence'. A tap was left running at 139 Elm Park Mansions, causing a minor flood in the flat and seepage into the flat below. When the fire brigade were called round, it was decided that Willie's flat raised certain health and safety issues.

He would clear the place out. All his red writers' notebooks went, and other documents and pictures. The caretaker Andy Edgson, who had become a good and loyal friend to Willie, redecorated the flat over weekends. Willie must have been proud of his makeover because he allowed his niece Claudia to see the place.

Although he was getting out less, he used email to keep in touch with the Sunningdale past. In 2004, Ray Salter, his oldest childhood friend, sent him two limericks, the first about a young fellow called Willie/ Whose behaviour was frequently silly, and the second a scurrilous version of life at their prep school Woodcote House.

'Now look here, Uncle, this simply isn't fair,' Willie replied. 'Your last was brilliant! I can't compete with this. That's what Douglas used to say. "Charles," he'd say, I was still Charles at the age of eight, "You just refuse to compete, even with Smith 2. At the first sign of competition you curl up". Nothing has changed.' He was better at Irish Knock Knock jokes, he said. '"Knock! Knock!" "Who's there?" "Burt" "Burt who?" "Burt Lancaster". I expect you know it. You may not get this.'

He was right about the Irish Knock Knock joke. 'Sorry, Willie,' Ray replied. 'I don't get the Lancaster joke – Probably being slow (again) Plse. Explain. Love Uncle.' It was their last contact.

We used to talk regularly on the telephone but now he became less punctilious in returning calls. At the time, I put it down partly to his absorption in his new project and partly to changes in my own life – I was divorced, and happy in a new relationship. 'Most of the people I know are a little odd,' he had said to Robert Chalmers. 'They're not, in any obvious sense, quite all there.' It seemed to me that as my life became less odd, I interested him less. 'He wants other people to be solid in his shifting world,' Julian Mitchell had once written but, as he grew older, the opposite also became true. He preferred his friends slightly fucked up.

I saw him, a few months before he died, at Finches, a gloomy pub on the Fulham Road. He was there waiting for me, a glass of brandy in front of him. He had bangers and mash for lunch as usual and, as usual, only ate half of it. Something fundamental had changed in him or maybe had changed between us. It was not simply that there were no jokes, but there was not much curiosity or conversation either. Even the mention of David Beckham and Posh Spice, a couple I much admired to his great rage, failed to quicken much interest. He seemed bored, boring. Conversation was hard work. I was going to walk with him back to the flat but he preferred to finish his brandy, and I left him in Finches.

Others had similar experiences, notably his great and admired friend Craig Brown and his once-adored Miss Picano. After a disastrous encounter at the Goat in Boots, Peter Morgan told his wife that he might have 'to let Willie go' as a friend. 'He became really vicious to me,' he says. 'The kindness had gone. He sneered at me for what he thought was my success. He was effectively a tramp, sitting in the Goat in Boots, spitting hatred. Even his face had changed. It wasn't Willie's face any more.'

People have an animal-like tendency to close in on themselves as they sense the end approaching. Willie's company over those last few months was his friend Andy Edgson in the caretaker's office, his collaborator Hermione Eyre and his neighbour of many years Mike Hanford who, on occasions when Willie was too ill, would do his shopping for him.

The work, though, continued. Now seventy and dying, Willie was kept going by writing about Paris Hilton ('Looks like a shivering whippet dipped in bleach'), Carol Smillie ('nose like a trigonometry problem'), Richie Benaud ('prim old cowpat') and, of course, his *bête noire* of thirty years standing:

Parkinson, Michael (b. 1935). It has been noted by Salter, Horrocks-Taylor and De Santos (*The Celebrity Syndrome:*

Notes Towards a Diagnosis, Sussex University Press, 2004) that not all celebrities are exhibitionists; some are natural voyeurs and have the capacity to take on the protective colouring and mannerisms of their celebrity environment. Chat-show legend Michael Parkinson, for instance, can moderate his appearance, voice and manner according to his interviewee: vacuously mid-Atlantic for an American, grittily provincial for his mates from Barnsley. When interviewing the late David Rappaport, an actor of restricted growth, he shrank to the size of a dwarf.

'Writing was what really mattered to Willie,' Hermione Eyre says. Even while he was physically becoming feebler, his prose was as full of mad comic energy as ever.

Perhaps aware that time was running out for him, Willie became uncharacteristically impatient when his co-writer, who had a full-time job, failed to ring him back or respond to messages on her answering machine; on another occasion he called her one evening, drunk and abusive. His publisher Richard Milbank was similarly startled by a tone of uncharacteristic rage in some of his calls.

The Dictionary of National Celebrity was all but complete when, on the evening of Monday, June 20, 2005, Willie rang Hermione to discuss the few remaining entries. He was unusually wheezy and breathless, she remembers.

It was a heatwave and Willie was feeling ill. The next day he rang Andy Edgson. 'I'm finished,' he said. He asked Andy to get some pills – a packet of Zantac and some congestion tablets called Do-Dos. When Andy passed them through the door, Willie told him, 'You're a lifesaver, Andy.'

There had been scares before – 'I thought I was a goner there, Andy,' Willie would sometimes say – but the caretaker was sufficiently concerned now to call Willie's neighbour Mike Hanford and tell him that Willie sounded terrible. Mike rang. They agreed that he would take Willie to his doctor later in the week. 'Perhaps you should see him now,' Mike said. Willie refused. Then Hanford went out to buy him some food, leaving the plastic bag hanging on Willie's door-handle and knocking on the door, as was his habit.

The next day, the bag was still there, and calls to his number were not returned. Andy called the police and let them into the flat.

Willie was dead, his lungs having finally given out in the early hours of the morning of June 22. He was lying in the literary room.

35
The last laugh

It is a strange business, writing the life of a dead friend. Researched, discussed, considered and written, the person you once knew changes on the page. In the early days while working on this biography, I found myself slipping into old habits. 'I must talk about that with Willie,' I would think, before remembering that it was Willie who was the project. When people told me that he was a wonderful subject, I felt a stab of guilt and remembered the words of his diary: 'How awful to be written about'.

I was worried that the Willie Donaldson I discovered while investigating the parts of his life that he had kept hidden or had presented – mispresented, often – in comic shorthand, would be different from the man I knew, that I would have found a subject but lost a friend.

It has been startling to be reminded of the extent to which some people didn't get Willie, and never would. He was a sort of addict, they thought, a monstrous mediocrity, an idiotic flâneur. 'The best place for him would be an otherwise uninhabited island,' an enraged listener told the BBC after hearing his radio series. A number of other people reached similar conclusions throughout his adult life. There were the actors whose professionalism was insulted during the 1960s, the recipients of letters from Henry Root, Clive James, the victims of some of his later jokes, Michael Winner, the residents of Fowey, Richard Ingrams, and many more. At different times, two senior suits in the publishing business declared, as if it were a basic tenet of their professional faith: 'We are not going to publish any book by Willie Donaldson.' As if to confirm this view, the publishers of *Brewer's Rogues, Villains and Eccentrics* were sued by Judge

King-Hamilton, who at the age of 101 is probably the oldest litigant in history. For these people, he stood for something dangerous, slippery, unreliable. 'How would you describe your job?' he was asked in a publicity questionnaire during the 1990s. 'Dodgy,' he wrote.

But the vast majority of those I have contacted – friends, from childhood to his later years, wives, lovers, former colleagues – have not only wanted to talk about Willie but have done so with unusual warmth. 'I smile when I think of him, and I miss his style,' Michael Palin wrote in a letter to *The Times* shortly after Willie's obituary had been published. Few people who have felt themselves to be unlovable, who have believed that they have said and done terrible things, can have been remembered with such love.

Another oddity: a theme of shame and guilt runs through Willie's life and work, and has coloured the way he has been seen since his death. Yet my conversations with those who knew him have again and again returned to ideas of morality. As he moved restlessly through the worlds of theatre and books, becoming caught up in matters of sex, class, fame and villainy, he may have behaved badly but his legacy has been curiously moral. To himself, but to no one else, he once wrote the words: 'We must live the truth, otherwise we learn nothing.'

Here was the true surprise which emerged while I was researching the life of Willie Donaldson. Through the tangle of heartbreak, disappointment, bankruptcy and addiction, beyond what often seemed to be a perverse refusal to allow himself ordinary happiness, a real and extraordinary story of courage and integrity is played out. I knew that he was the funniest writer of his generation and wonderful company; now he seems to me to be a considerable figure not only in his writing but in the way he lived. The life which he worked so hard to present as an uncertain stagger, full of wrong turnings, dead ends and pratfalls, was, in fact, extraordinarily consistent. Past the seductions of money and fashion, ignoring the repeated temptation to take up a cosy niche within an established world, he remained true to his ideas and to himself – on the outside, laughing.

Re-reading Willie's books has been one of the joys of writing about him. Whenever the project has faltered, it has been Willie's prose that has cheered me up, and I have often found myself sitting at my desk, laughing helplessly. If for nothing else, he deserves to be read and remembered for the fizzing, innocent joy that he took in comic description, in a phrase or story. The best of his books offer readers a rare pleasure. 'His humour outlives him,' as Craig Brown has written. 'It will outlive us all.' Or, as Willie himself put it, in a letter to his schoolgirl pal Claudia Fitzherbert: 'It's a marvellous world, I think, which contains a man who writes as beautifully as this.'

Seven months after his death, on February 11, 2006, there was a reading of some of Willie's works at the National Theatre. Among those on stage were Julian Mitchell, his fellow sailor and *Gemini* editor from the 1950s, Terry Jones and Michael Palin, the two men whom he gave their first paid work in 1965, his good friends Craig Brown and Christopher Matthew, and his last co-writer Hermione Eyre.

There were several layers of irony to this celebration of Willie Donaldson. He had always claimed to hate the theatre. The performance took place where Sir Laurence Olivier, who had cuckolded him back in the 1960s, once reigned supreme. There were queues for the celebrity members of the cast to sign copies of Willie's books. The royalties could not be paid to his estate because there was no estate. None of it mattered. The evening was a sell-out. The place rocked with laughter.

What was said about Willie's life on that occasion will have had its share of his famous lived fictions, and no doubt these pages have too, but, as he put it in his very first book: 'I've always taken it as axiomatic that the truth should never be allowed to stand in the way of a huge, life-enhancing joke.'

Willie, 2003.

Willie Donaldson
1935–2005

'Willie was a great and unbelievable friend. Nothing has detracted
from him – it was all part of the same magnificent picture.'
***Richard Dynevor** divides his time between Wales and Chiswick*

'He used to say what a useless life he'd had and I'd tell him
that he had written these amazing books – that he had a lot
because he had those wonderful books.'
***Jane Downes** is living in Hampshire*

'He was the most graceful of writers and in a way one of the
most thoughtful, certainly comparable to Evelyn Waugh. He
was never taken as seriously as he should have been.'
***Allan Scott** has recently produced and co-written a musical
version of* The Adventures of Priscilla, Queen of the Desert

'For young people he was inspirational because he didn't talk to
you as a child, but with real interest.'
***Claudia Downes** has just completed her first novel,* See Inside
For Details

'He was a very, very good man. He had all the strokes.'
***Sarah Miles** is writing a diary of her house's ghosts*

'There was not a nasty bone in his body but he just had to
ruffle a few feathers now and then.'
***Frankie Fraser** conducts regular gangland tours of London*

'He had a poet's eye for things. He sensed things. He was a sensory man.'
Eleanor Fazan *lives in London*

'I'll never have a friend like that because I had been through viciousness with him and also great kindness. I've not met many more brilliant people.'
Peter Morgan *is writing a film about Brian Clough*

'Willie was passionate for truth in a totally philosophical sense.'
Geoffrey Strachan *has just completed his translation of Andreï Makine's novel* L'Amour Humain

'My overall message is that he was terrific. I was extremely fond of Willie but he was terribly, terribly naughty.'
Ray Salter *lives near Winchester*

'The more waves he could make, the more energy he felt. He could never turn his enormous energy into something simple.'
Carly Simon's *new album is called* Into White

'It was quite innocent, apart from the talk of blow jobs and the drugs. He was a really good friend, really loyal.'
Rachel Garley *stars in Sebastian Horsley's 2007 memoir,* Dandy in the Underworld

'For me, he would always have the enthusiasm, charm, mischief and occasional treachery of an extraordinary child.'
Donald Langdon *is living in America*

'He was so funny, so sharp, so generous, so foolish, so spoiled, so wrecked, so totally unreliable, so entirely his own man.'
Julian Mitchell *is writing for the theatre, cinema and TV*

'He was fucking unique.'
Andy Edgson *is caretaker at Elm Park Mansions*

Acknowledgements

Willie Donaldson had excellent taste in friends, colleagues, wives and lovers, and remembering him with them while researching this book has been a delight and a privilege. Talking to those who knew Willie, sometimes years ago, but whose memories have remained sharp and affectionate has reminded me that no book could ever quite convey the personal wit, warmth and spirit of a very unusual man.

Several people have been extraordinarily generous with their time and their personal archives. I would particularly like to thank Willie's sister Jane Downes and Cherry Donaldson for their help and friendship, and Julian Mitchell for giving me access to his extraordinary diary and to his correspondence with Willie. Without Richard Dynevor's ever-helpful guidance, Eleanor Fazan's unpublished essays, Craig Brown's encouragement, Claudia Fitzherbert's letters and Carly Simon's kindness, writing this book would have been incomparably less enjoyable.

Others to whom I owe varying debts of gratitude are: John Adams; Pankaj Amin; Geoff Atkinson; Michael Barber; John Bassett; Meriel Beale; Anthony Beerbohm; Alan Bennett; Oliver Bernard; John Bird; Angela Bodell; Gaye Brown; Mark Chapman; Jonathan Clowes; Michael Codron; Tim Connery; Wendy Cook; Professor James Cornford; Andy Dempsey; JP Donleavy; Claudia Downes; Gerard Downes; Andrew Edgson; Hermione Eyre; John Farmer; Fenella Fielding; John Fowler; Mike Franklin; Frankie Fraser; Winston Fletcher; Rachel Garley; Bamber Gascoigne; Claire Gordon; Jinx Grafftey-Smith; Tony Gray; Alexander Games; Paul Halloran; Michael Hanford; Billy Hart; Ian Hislop; Sonia Hobbs; Phillip Hodson; Sebastian Horsley; Lord Howell; Richard Ingrams; Brian Innes; Virginia Ironside; Amy Jenkins; Terry Jones; Justin Judd; Kim

Kindersley; Sonia Lamb; Donald Langdon; Cat Ledger; Amber Leighton; Jean Legris; Nigel Lilley; Jeremy Lovering; Elisabeth Luard; Mark Lucas; David Mallet; Debby Mason; Hugh Massingberd; Christopher Matthew; Roddy Maude-Roxby; Michelle; Richard Milbank; Sarah Miles; Sir Jonathan Miller; Lewis Morley; Peter Morgan; Professor Anthony O'Hear, Mike O'Mara; Anthony Page; Michael Palin; Mal Peachey; Rowan Pelling; Anthony Perry; Nevile Player; John Powell; Jane Pullee; Frank Pulley; Tom Rosenthal; Jonathan Sale; Ray Salter; Philip Saville; Allan Scott; Geoffrey Scott; Will Self; Ned Sherrin; Paul Sidey; Jane Skinner; Carl Snitcher; Andrew Sinclair; Rebecca Sparkes; Roy Stevens; Geoffrey Strachan; Simon Tyszko; Bill Wallis; Miranda Walker; Richard Walton; Tony Walton; Simone Washington; Michael White; Philip Wiseman.

I have been greatly assisted by the research of Jenny Prior, and by Joe Moser of the University of Texas, Austin. I would also like to thank Hilary Lowinger of *Private Eye*, Malcolm Edwards and Rosie Anderson at Weidenfeld & Nicolson, Simon Smith at Peter Owen Publishers, the Kenneth Tynan Archive at the British Library, the Harry Ransom Center at the University of Texas, the Peter Cook Appreciation Society, Brett Croft at *Tatler*, and the *Independent*.

Lydia Alexander accomplished the titanic task of typing out interviews, notes and then the whole text with efficiency and good humour, and kept me going with her cheerfulness and encouragement.

On the publishing side, I am grateful to Ebury's crack team of Andrew Goodfellow, Verity Willcocks, Bernice Davison and Ian Allen. My agent Gill Coleridge has, as ever, been a tower of strength.

Several friends have helped me with invaluable advice on subjects ranging from the writing of biography to existentialism by way of co-dependency, as well as providing much-needed moral support, and I would particularly like to thank Will Buckley, Tania Kindersley, Roger Lewis, Andy Martin, Deborah Moggach and Sue Roe. My good friend Roger Deakin, who died during the writing of this book, was characteristically generous with his time and wise with his advice.

No author could have a better reader, editor, critic, counsellor and cheerleader than I have with Angela Sykes. This book is dedicated to her, with love and gratitude.

References

I don't see... Letter to Julian Mitchell, July 23, 1955.
Emma Jane seems... *Both the Ladies and the Gentlemen* (Talmy Franklin, London, 1975).
She's driving me... *Independent*, March 13, 1995.
The wicked acts... Note to himself, c 2000.

1. A LIFE OF SORTS
6. **Donaldson lived by...** *Guardian*, June 25, 2005.
   A womanising satirist... *The Times*, June 27, 2005.
   In the absence... *Independent*, June 25, 2005.

2. FAMILY FANTASY
11. **I'm in a mood...** *Independent*, September 1, 1990.
23. **Wouldn't you drink...** Pilot for *Other People's Lives* (Kudos Television, 1996), never shown.

3. VAGUELY WICKED
28. **I was enthralled...** *From Winchester to This* (Peter Owen, London, 1998).
    An illicit drug... ibid.
29. **Small wonder that...** ibid.

4. OUR TROUBLE, BASICALLY, IS THAT WE'RE NORMAL
31. **Charles says he...** War diary, volume one.
32. **We gasped...** *The Times*, June 29, 2005.

5. WHAT'S THE LITTLE MAN UP TO NOW?
44. **A factor not to be...** *Something Like Fire – Peter Cook Remembered*, edited by Lin Cook (Arrow Books, London, 2003).
45. **It hurts to be...** *Cambridge Opinion 6*, January 1958.
48. **I knew that...** *Sunday Times*, September 20, 1998.
49. **Regarded Cambridge as...** Julian Mitchell, *The Undiscovered Country* (Constable, London, 1968).
50. **He never knew...** *Other People's Lives*, op. cit.
    We both thought... *The Undiscovered Country*, op. cit.
52. **And Plath wrote to Willie...** Willie's letter to Julian Mitchell, 1955.

As much an impresario... Dom Moraes, *My Son's Father* (Secker and Warburg, London, 1968).

6. WILLIE DONALDSON AS EMPLOYEE: A BRIEF CHAPTER

58. **Uncontrollable blubbing.** Letter to Winston Fletcher, August 24, 1990.

8. THE ANGRIEST REACTION FROM AN AUDIENCE SHE EVER HAD

65. **Around £3 million now...** All conversions are based on the National Archive Currency Converter.

69. **It was time...** Interview in Humphrey Carpenter's *That Was The Satire That Was* (Orion, London, 2000).

72. **The angriest reaction...** Sheila Hancock, *Ramblings of an Actress* (Hutchinson, London, 1987).

73. **Revue had more...** Michael Frayn, introduction to *The Complete Beyond The Fringe*, edited by Roger Wilmut (Souvenir Press, London, 1963).

9. AN INNOCENT ABROAD

75. **To him it's as foreign...** 'Relative Values', *Sunday Times*, July 9, 2006.

80. **On looking back...** Interview, not broadcast, for the BBC documentary *Peter Cook – At a Slight Angle to the Universe*, December 18, 2002.
A deceptively gentle and kindly figure... Alan Bennett, *London Review of Books*, January 5, 2006.

81. **Unable to raise...** Source: Ronald Bergan, *Beyond The Fringe... and Beyond* (Virgin, London, 1989).

82. **I could well understand...** Eleanor Fazan, 'Beyond The Fringe', an unpublished essay.
There was still... ibid.
He did have a short... ibid.

83. **Should I ask...** Eleanor Fazan, 'William Donaldson', an unpublished essay.

84. **Slumped and mucked...** Fazan, 'Beyond The Fringe', op. cit.

87. **I still fiercely...** Bergan, op. cit.
I look back on those years... Bergan, op. cit.

88. **I don't think...** Bergan, op. cit.
I look back on the show... Bergan, op. cit.
It was a miracle... *Queen*, November 1962.
Interviewed forty years... Interview, *Peter Cook – At a Slight Angle to the Universe*, op. cit.

11. FREEWHEELIN' WITH BOB

89. **One day I returned...** *From Winchester to This*, op. cit.

12. NUDES AND PEACOCKS

99. **Perhaps the most interesting...** *Queen*, November 1962.

103. **A 'comic' group...** Dan Farson, *Never a Normal Man* (HarperCollins, London, 1997).

104. **Your letter is...** Letter, November 18, 1963.

105. **Zounds!...** *Private Eye*, April 23, 1971.

13. THE LOVE SHOW
108. **If one woman...** *From Winchester to This*, op. cit.
111. **Willie would rise...** Sarah Miles, *Serves Me Right* (Macmillan, London, 1994).
112. **Though his appetite...** ibid.
117. **'You?' I was so...** *From Winchester to This*, op. cit.
     Carly quite embarrassed me... ibid.
118. **The tragedy for...** ibid.

14. A BITTER INSULT TO PROFESSIONALS
119. **Powell, through a mutual...** Source: Michael Barber, *Anthony Powell: A Life* (Duckworth, London, 2004).
     A pale, fair-haired young man... Anthony Powell, *The Strangers All Are Gone* (Heinemann, London, 1982).
     No one seemed... ibid.
121. **I know what...** Letter, January 20, 1966.

15. MR BEAR AND MRS MOUSE DO THE SIXTIES
123. **I had big breasts...** *News of the World*, June 14, 1992.
     Everyone thought Claire... ibid.
124. **Found Scott very sexy...** ibid.
127. **Neither of us...** ibid.
     I'd do the Sixties... *From Winchester to This*, op. cit.
128. **Sexy antics proved...** *News of the World*, June 14, 1992.
129. **It turned out...** *From Winchester to This*, op. cit.
     Looking back on it... *News of the World*, June 14, 1992.

16. BLASPHEMY AT THE CRITERION
133. **Really did seem...** *The Oldie*, July 12, 2005.
135. **Dearest Eleanor...** Letter, August 20, 1970.
138. **Whenever I've tried...** *Independent* column, 1990.

17. THROUGH THE BOTTOM OF A GLASS-BOTTOMED BOAT
139. **Had a moment...** Diary, May 6, 1971.
140. **Ibiza was discovered...** *Nth Position*, online magazine.

18. HOW MANY PUPILS OF FR LEAVIS HAVE EVER BECOME PONCES?
143. **A collection of Cambridge...** *Light Blue Dark Blue*, edited by John Fuller, Julian Mitchell, William Donaldson and Robin McLaren (Macdonald, London, 1960).
144. **In many ways...** *Both the Ladies and the Gentlemen*, op. cit.
     Living in a brothel... ibid.
150. **My book's been out...** *The Balloons in the Black Bag* (Eyre Methuen, London, 1978).
151. **Clive James has called ...** *The Diaries of Kenneth Tynan*, edited by John Lahr (Bloomsbury, London, 2001).
152. **Bull artist...** Clive James, *North Face of Soho* (Picador, London, 2006).

153. **Fuck it...** *The Balloons in the Black Bag*, op. cit.
154. **Savoy Sell-Out...** Preface to *Letters to Emma Jane* (Eyre Methuen, 1977).
     He hates to... ibid.

19. JUST A PENSÉE
156. **Dear Mr Donaldson...** *The Balloons in the Black Bag*, op. cit.

20. CHARLIE DONALDSON
161. **In the hope that...** *The Diaries of Kenneth Tynan*, op. cit.
162. **I could do without...** *Birmingham Post*, May 9, 1981.
163. **Most people have...** Adam Bellow, 'Missing my father', *New York Times*, June 10, 2006.

21. THE CRY OF A BULL MOOSE CAUGHT BY THE KNACKERS IN A TRAP
168. **Dear Mr Wintour...** Letter, April 4, 1978.
169. **OLIVIER, Sir Lawrence of...** *Emma Jane's Reference Book*, unpublished.
171. **I'm not mad...** Don Novello's letter to Victor Lownes, May 3, 1980.
     One of the funniest... Auberon Waugh, *Books and Bookmen*, April 1980.
     Another brilliant columnist... Source: *Daily Telegraph*, April 7, 1980.
172. **Born January 4...** *Henry Root Letters* (Weidenfeld & Nicolson, London, 1980).
180. **In a funny...** *Daily Telegraph*, July 9, 2005.

23. YOU KNOW WHERE YOU ARE WITH PLAICE
189. **I will tell...** *Birmingham Post*, May 9, 1981.
     I enjoy being... *The Bulletin*, 1981.
190. **Willie Donaldson seems...** *Evening Standard*, October 9, 1981.

24. WHERE NOT TO GO, HOW NOT TO SPEAK, WHO NOT TO BE
197. **You would find...** Letter quoted in Geoffrey Wall's *Flaubert: A Life* (Faber and Faber, London, 2001).
198. **Almost everyone is here...** *Henry Root's World of Knowledge* (Weidenfeld & Nicolson, London, 1982).
199. **Sartre wrote somewhere...** *Common Reading*, spring 1996.
200. **The letters of...** ibid.
     A mask that eats... John Updike, *Self-Consciousness* (André Deutsch, London, 1989).
     The satisfaction... *Is This Allowed?* (Macdonald, London, 1987).
204. **Naff lines of poetry...** Dr Kit Bryson, Selina Fitzherbert and Jean-Luc Leyris, *The Complete Naff Guide* (Arrow Books, London, 1983).
206. **Once, he looked...** *Independent*, June 25, 2005.
     In 1984, a book... *Great Disasters of the Stage* (Arthur Barker, London, 1984).
     There was a collaboration... Oleg Bitov, *Bitov's Britain* (Viking, London, 1985).
207. **What is there...** *Henry Root's A–Z of Women* (Weidenfeld & Nicolson, London, 1985).

25. BUST-UP AT THE SHEFFIELD CLUB
214. **He provided the...** *Independent*, June 25, 2005.

26. IBIZA'S JUST THE PLACE FOR WOMEN WITH HURT EYES
216. **I once thought...** *Is This Allowed?*, op. cit.
219. **Homes are so sad...** ibid.
223. **I keep thinking...** ibid.
224. **One night...** ibid.
225. **Using cocaine was...** *Daily Express*, May 27, 1986.
You are meant... London *Daily News*, 1987.
226. **Older man is...** *Independent*, November 21, 1992.
David Sexton, literary editor... *Sunday Correspondent*, December 3, 1989.
228. **You want the...** Dr Kit Bryson and Jean-Luc Leyris, *You Want, You'd Settle For, You Get* (Michael O'Mara Books, London, 1986).
Since I never... Unpublished questionnaire with *Story of P* proposal, c. 2000.

27. SITTING ON THE WRONG END OF A SHOOTING STICK
232. **In November 1984...** Talbot Church, *101 Things You Didn't Know About the Royal Lovebirds* (Michael O'Mara Books and Pan, London, 1986).
233. **Henceforth talk to women...** *The Soap Letters* (Michael O'Mara Books, London, 1988).

28. A PROFOUND INSTINCT TO CORRUPT AND DESTROY
240. **On crack, you know...** *Evening Standard*, August 8, 2003.
It was the strongest hit... Will Self, 'The Rock of Crack as Big as the Ritz' from *Tough, Tough Toys for Tough, Tough Boys* (Penguin Books, London, 1999).
242. **You cannot value...** Undated letter.
243. **The most perverse drug...** *Evening Standard*, August 8, 2003.
244. **I'm more at ease...** *Evening Standard*, October 9, 1980.
245. **Meyer, a game old...** Source: Obituary by Andrew Roth, *Guardian*, January 8, 2005.
248. **Britain's most talented scriptwriter...** *Evening Standard*, October 27, 2006.

29. I AM THE FAT MAN
254. **A writer's autobiography...** Jeremy Adler, introduction to Elias Canetti's *Party in the Blitz* (Harvill, London, 2005).
256. **I am easily disturbed...** *Story of P* questionnaire, op. cit.

30. SHIT AND DAMNATION
267. **In view of...** Letter, February 8, 1989.
At some point... Written statement to Cat Ledger, December 23, 1991.
268. **Mad and totally dishonest...** Letter, January 11, 1989.
I do not even... Letter, December 23, 1991.
269. **Ideas man....** Letter, January 19, 1989
270. **By the time...** *Root Around Britain* (Methuen, London, 1993), *1992 and All That* (Angus and Robertson, London, 1990).
273. **We were a couple...** Taped interview with Harry Thompson, 1996.
275. **They want to...** Interview, *Peter Cook – At a Slight Angle to the Universe*, op. cit.

31. THAT SHARP MOMENT

276. **A man shaking...** Interview, *Peter Cook – At a Slight Angle to the Universe*, op. cit.
277. **A really dirty girl...** *From Winchester to This*, op. cit.

32. POTENTIALLY UNHELPFUL PUBLICITY

290. **The BBC commissioned...** *A Retiring Fellow*, BBC Radio Four, April–May 1996.
292. **Nurtured by newspapers...** *Something Like Fire – Peter Cook Remembered*, op. cit.
293. **Here's how the video...** Liz Reed, *The Heartfelt Letters* (Mainstream Publishing, Edinburgh, 1998).
294. **I know at my age...** *Sunday Times*, September 20, 1998.

33. GETTING THE BUZZ WITHOUT LEAVING THE FLAT

298. **Who has been...** Questionnaire for *Real Lives*, BBC Radio Leeds.
299. **Were she to show...** *Story of P* questionnaire, op. cit.
302. **Ever since she read...** Proposal for 'Art, exhibitionism and abuse – *The Story of P*'.

34. NATIONAL TREASURE

309. **McCartney, Sir Paul...** *Brewer's Rogues, Villains and Eccentrics* (Weidenfeld & Nicolson, London, 2002).
310. **Willie Donaldson has never...** *Mail on Sunday*, December 15, 2002.
     Probably the greatest... *The Times*, November 2, 2002.
     The funniest book... *Daily Express*, December 28, 2002.
311. **Crack smoker, retired pimp...** *Independent on Sunday*, October 27, 2002.
312. **I've taken the filthy...** *Evening Standard*, August 8, 2003.
313. **I don't know about you...** *Independent* column.
     It should evoke... Letter, March 21, 2002.
     A few old favourites... *I'm Leaving You Simon, You Disgust Me* (Weidenfeld & Nicolson, London, 2003).
     Though Donaldson records... *Erotic Review*, December 2003.
314. **I know I said...** Email, February 16, 2004.
318. **Most of the people...** *Independent on Sunday*, October 27, 2002.
     He wants other people... Diary.
319. **Parkinson, Michael...** *The Dictionary of National Celebrity*, with Hermione Eyre (Weidenfeld & Nicolson, London, 2005).

35. THE LAST LAUGH

323. **How would you describe...** Questionnaire for *Real Lives*, BBC Radio Leeds.
     I smile when... Letter to *The Times*, June 30, 2005.
324. **His humour outlives ...** *Daily Telegraph*, July 9, 2005.
     I've always taken... *Both the Ladies and the Gentlemen*, op. cit.

WILLIE DONALDSON 1935–2005

327. **He was so funny...** *Daily Telegraph*, July 16, 2005.

Index

homosexuality 29, 30; interest in his friends' inclinations 260–2; loses virginity 41–2; love of prostitutes 39–41, 48, 83–4, 108, 188, 200, 216, 219, 220–7, 228–9, 242, 261–2, 276; self-confessed pervert 48, 260, 278–9, 289, 311; as staged/observed 28–9, 108, 200, 255
teenager
   education 25–8, 29–30, 165; West End trips 28–9, 37
and Terence Blacker 204–5, 206, 230, 246, 261, 263–4, 285, 305, 308, 318–19
as theatrical impresario 65–6, 69–74, 75–7, 78–88, 93–105, **98**, 106, 108–11, 119, 130–8; and *A Fairy Tale of New York* 95–6; and *Beyond The Fringe* 3, 73, 75–6, 78–88, 94, 97, 99, 104, 105, 126, 148, 272–3, 274, 312; conned in business ventures 94–5; end of his career 119–22; erotic work 101, 108–10, 133–8; and *Here Is The News* 70–3, 81; runs 'papering the house' scheme 95–6; sets up William Donaldson Associates 97–9; and *The Last Laugh* 69–70
TV appearances 152
wealth 11–12, 47–8
opens Westminster Artists 130–1
as writer 126, 143–4, 146–7
101 Things You Didn't Know About the Royal Love Birds (under pseudonym Talbot Church) 231–3, 271, 308; *1992 and All That* 271, 285; *Bitov's Britain* (under pseudonym Oleg Bitov with O'Hear and Blacker) 206, 271, 308; *Both the Ladies and the Gentlemen* 146–53, 155, 156, 165, 181, 188, 198, 199, 208, 210, 281 (film rights 152–3); *Brewer's Rogues, Villains and Eccentrics* 307–12, 313, 322–3; *Canetti et Moi* 300; *Emma Jane's Reference Book* 169–70, **169**; uncommissioned

synopses 299–300; *From Winchester to This* (memoirs) 2, 3–4, 6–7, 30, 240, 248, 256, 264, 274, 276–7, 285–6, 287–9, 299; *Further Letters of Henry Root* (under pseudonym Root) 178, 188; *Great Disasters of the Stage* 70, 102, 206; *Henry Root – Robert Maxwell Letters* (never written) 237–8, **237**; *Henry Root and the House of Windsor* (never written) 238; *Henry Root Letters* 3, 5–6, 171–80, 181–3, 187, 188, 189–90, 199–200, 204, 292, 308; *Henry Root's A–Z of Women* 207, 218–19, 310; *Henry Root's World of Knowledge* 197–8, 201–3, 271, 292, 313; HFB project (never written) 237; *I'm Leaving You Simon, You Disgust Me* 313–14; on inauthenticity 199–200; *Independent* 'William Donaldson's Week' column 159, 251–8, 260, 262–4, 269, 272, 273–4, 280, 288, 295, 316; *Is this Allowed?* (autobiographical novel) 3, 5, 9, 200, 220–2, 223, 225–7, 228–9, 230, 236, 239, 241, 242, 251, 256, 288; *Karma Chingford/Britain* 272, 274, 283, 284; *Letters to Emma Jane* (under pseudonym Emma Jane Crampton) 165–9, 170, 199; *Mail on Sunday* column (under pseudonym Henry Root) 192–6; Marty Feldman biography project 301–2, 304, 306; *Meaning of Cantona* (with Blacker) 308; *Mrs Root's Diary* (never written) 206; pseudonyms 3, 190–1, 192, 204, 207, 226, 293–4, 300, 308; *Root Around Britain – Henry Root's Guide to Englishness* 271–2; *Root into Europe* 66, 271, 295 (TV series 266–8, 269–71, 283, 316); success 188–90; Talbot Church character 231–3, 234, 271, 300; *Tatler* foodie column (under pseudonym Henry Root) 191–2, 197; *The Balloons*

in the Black Bag 163, 166, 170, 197, 217 (re-titled *Nicknames Only* 188); *The Big One, The Black One, The Fat One and The Other One* 285; *The Complete Naff Guide* (with Carr) 204–7; *The Diary of Emma Jane Crampton* 169, 170; *The Dictionary of National Celebrity* (with Eyre) 199, 314–15, 320–1; *The English Way of Doing Things (One Good Apple/The Name of the Game)* (play written with Wiseman) play: 210–13, 214, 215, 223, novel: 208, 212–3, 215, sitcom pilot (with Blacker) 231; *The Heartfelt Letters* 293–4, 299, 308; *The Millennium Atlas of Great Britain* (with Brown) 291–2, 299; *The Soap Letters* (under pseudonym Henry Root) 233, 234–7, **235**; 'toilet books' 203–7, 227–8, 230, 243; and the Wiseman legal case 209–14, 241; *You Want, You'd Settle For, You Get* (with Carr) 228, 263
Donaldson, Charles William (Willie's grandfather) 11
Donaldson, Charlie (Willie's son) 5, 9, 62, 63, 106, 111, 113, 157–8, 159–63, 207, 241, 246, 304
Donaldson (née Hatrick), Cherry (Willie's wife) 116, 130–1, 154, 157–62, 170–1, 175, 179, 183, 187, 188, **189**, 199, 216, 239, 268
   decline of her relationship with Willie 218–20, 223–5, 227, 285
   and Willie's death 4–5, 9
Donaldson (née Gordon), Claire (Mrs Mouse) (Willie's second wife) 66, 121, 123–9, **125**, 132, 139–41, 216, 285
Donaldson (née Stockley) Elizabeth (Betty) (Willie's mother) 12–20, **13**, 21, 23, 24, 28, 31, 42, 47, 62, 253–5
Donaldson, Fred (Willie's uncle) 11, 12, 120
Donaldson, Grace (Willie's grandmother) 112, 121, 124, 127, 130, 139